D0081154

HELLENISM

HELLENISM

THE HISTORY OF A CIVILIZATION

ARNOLD J. TOYNBEE

GREENWOOD PRESS, PUBLISHERS
WESTPORT, CONNECTICUT

Library of Congress Cataloging in Publication Data

Toynbee, Arnold Joseph, 1889-1975.
Hellenism, the history of a civilization.

Reprint of the ed. published by Oxford University Press, New York.
Bibliography: p.
Includes index.
1. Hellenism--History. I. Title.
[DE71.T6 1981] 938 80-27772
ISBN 0-313-22742-X (lib. bdg.)

This is a reprint of the original 1959 Oxford University Press edition.

Reprinted by arrangement with Oxford University Press.

Reprinted in 1981 by Greenwood Press
A division of Congressional Information Service, Inc.
88 Post Road West, Westport, Connecticut 06881

Printed in the United States of America

10 9 8 7 6 5 4 3 2 1

πολλὰ τὰ δεινὰ κοὐδὲν ἀν/θρώπου δεινότερον πέλει

— Sophocles: *Antigonê,* ll. 332–3

Wonders are many, but none there be
So strange, so fell, as the Child of Man.

— Gilbert Murray's translation

Thou shalt worship the Lord thy God, and Him only shalt thou serve.

— Matt. iv. 10 and Luke iv. 8, quoting Deut. vi. 13

PREFACE

THIS book was commissioned in 1914 for the Home University Library by one of the editors, Professor Gilbert Murray. At the beginning of the Oxford long vacation of that year I made notes for a plan of the work and submitted these to Professor Murray for his criticisms. I have before me, as I write, a letter of his, dated 20 July 1914, which opens with the words: 'I am ashamed not to have written before. I was merely absorbed in finishing *Alcestis* and forgot the rest of the world.' From the beginning of the following month until the end of his life, nearly forty-three years later, Murray devoted himself to the cause of world peace. But this sentence, written at this date, shows how completely unforeseen, in England, the outbreak of the First World War was, even to a scholar who, since his schooldays, had always felt an unusually keen interest in politics.

By the day when the war began, I had digested Murray's illuminating comments on my notes and had written a draft of the first four chapters. Since then I have not re-read either this draft or the notes.

In 1951, during a holiday in Switzerland, I made a new set of notes and submitted these to Professor Murray in their turn; and, this time, I have not been prevented by a public catastrophe from writing the whole of a new draft — though unhappily I did not complete this in time to be able to show it to Murray before his death.

The present version of the book has been written, between April 1956 and October 1957, in a number of different parts of the World: the Pacific Ocean, Tasmania, Westmorland, Iceland, Hampstead, Sussex. While I was writing it, I did not revisit the heart of the Hellenic World in the basin of the Aegean Sea, but I did see something of the vast areas that were added to it by the overland conquests of Alexander of Macedon and Demetrius of Bactria and by the pacific maritime radiation of the economic and cultural influence of the city of Alexandria-on-Nile into countries east of the Arabian Sea.

When one is trying to write the history of a civilization, it is a great help to have seen something, however little, of the theatre in which the drama was performed. One instant's glimpse of a landscape with one's own eyes can tell one more than years spent on studying maps and texts.

In 1911–12, before making my first set of notes for the book, I had travelled on foot (the best way) over the country round Rome as far as Tarquinii (Corneto), Hispellum (Spello), and Caieta (Gaeta), and over Continental European Greece as far north as Pharsalus and the Ambracian Gulf; and I had also walked over the eastern two-thirds of the island of Crete and over the Athos peninsula. In 1921 I saw Constantinople, the Asiatic shores of the Sea of Marmara, the western seaboard of Anatolia as far south as the River Maeander, and also northern Thessaly and western Macedon, including Lyncestis, Eordaea, and Elimiotis. In 1923 I visited Ankara (Ancyra); and in 1929 I travelled, via Ankara and the Cilician Gates, to the two northern cities of the Seleucis, Antioch-on-Orontes and Seleucia Pieria, *en route,* through Aleppo and Damascus, for Basra and Japan. In 1948 my wife and I did a week's travelling by road, as guests of the Turkish Government, in East Central Anatolia. We visited Boghazqal'eh, Amasia, Tokat, Sivas (Sebastia), Cappadocian Caesarea, the Cilician Gates again (this time by road, not by rail), Tarsus, and Adana. In a journey round the world from east to west in 1956–7 — the journey during which the first half of this book was written — we first struck the post-Alexandrine

Hellenic World in February 1957 at Arikamedu, the Hellenic 'factory' on the south-east coast of India, just south of Pondichéry. Between that date and the beginning of August 1957, we visited Takshasila (Taxila) and Purushapura (Peshawar) in Gandhara, the capitals of the Kushan Empire; I travelled from Babylon to within sight of the Caspian Gates, up the great north-east road which was the Seleucid monarchy's spinal cord, as it had been the Persian Empire's; and, from a base of operations in Beirut (the Phoenician city and Roman colony Berytus), I also visited Hatra and Arbela, and we both visited Petra and Palmyra; the two southern cities of the Seleucis: Laodicea (Lattaqieh) and Apamea-over-Orontes; the Phoenician cities Aradus (Ruad) and Antaradus (Tartus); and a number of places in Coele Syria: Baalbek and the springs of Orontes and of Jordan; the cities of the imperial age of Hellenic history in the Jabal Druz and the Hauran; Philadelphia ('Amman), Gerasa, and Gadara in the Decapolis; Byblos, Sidon, and Tyre on the Phoenician coast; Gaza and Raphia on the Philistine coast; and finally the walled city of Jerusalem, whose street-plan reveals that of Hadrian's Aelia Capitolina.

The gaps in my first-hand knowledge of the Hellenic World are large and serious. I have not yet seen Magna Graecia, Sicily, or Tunisia; Epirus or Paeonia (the present Jugoslav Macedonia); Amphipolis or Philippi or Mount Pangaeus; Rhodes, Caria, or Lycia; the Ukraine or Egypt (the two main sources of the Hellenic World's grain supply); or Bactria or the Paropanisadae (both now in Afghanistan). To venture to write about such important regions without having set eyes on them is hazardous; but the alternative would be to put off writing till the Greek Kalends. So the best that I can do is to put my cards on the table for the reader to inspect.

ARNOLD TOYNBEE

16 October 1957

CONTENTS

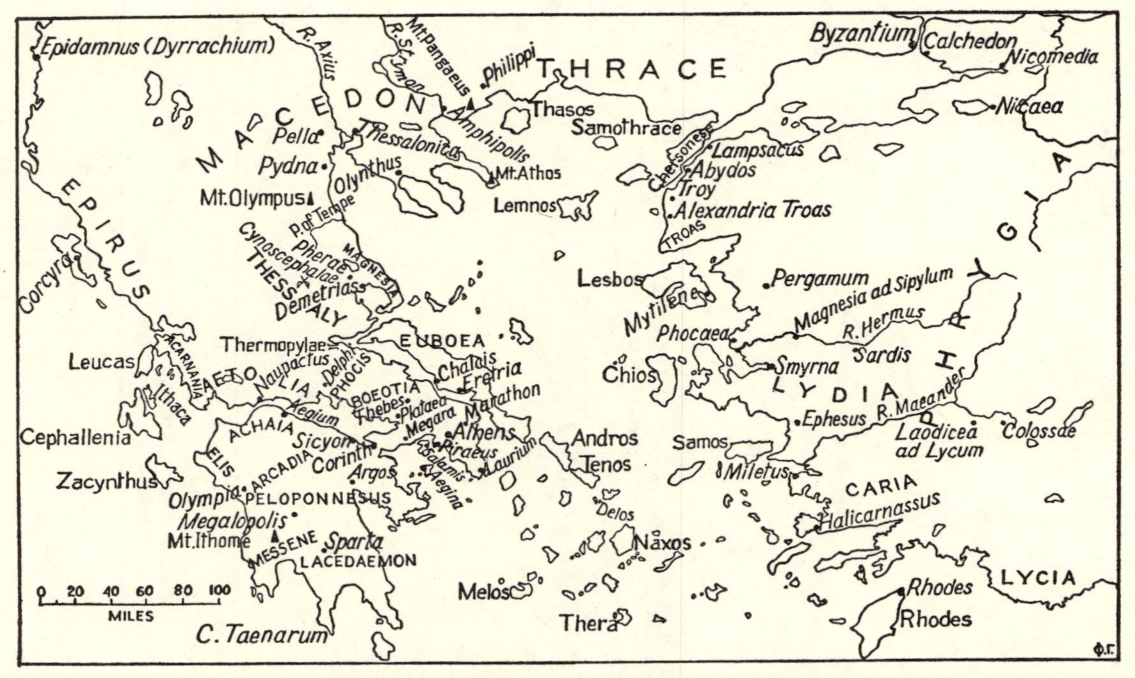

SOME OF THE PLACES SHOWN WERE NOT CONTEMPORARY WITH EACH OTHER

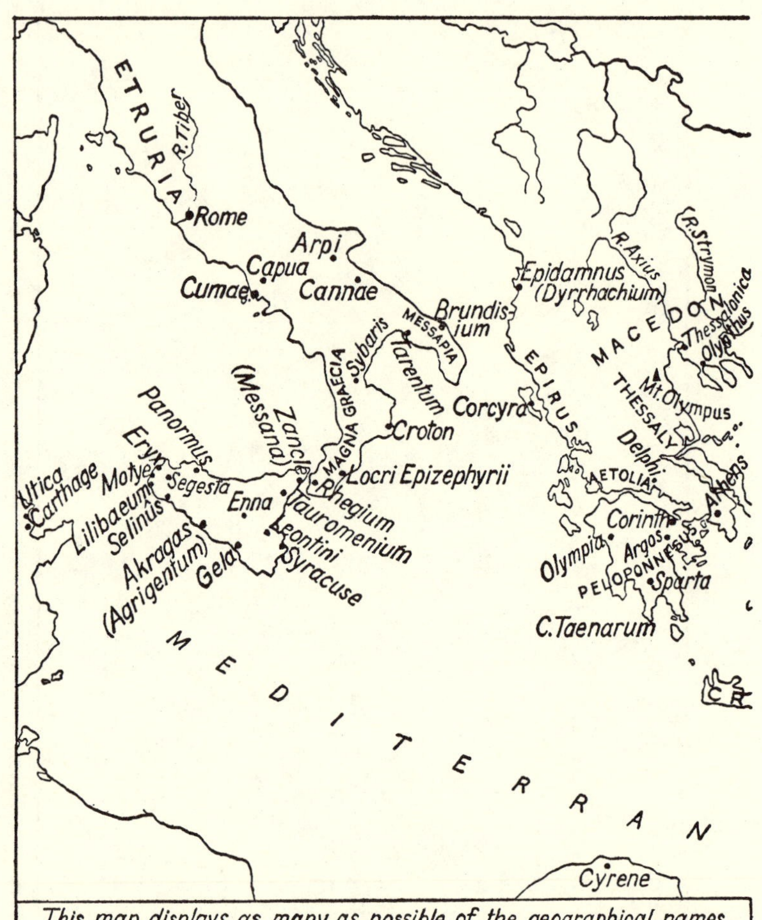

This map displays as many as possible of the geographical names mentioned in the text. It does not present only places that were in existence contemporaneously at some particular date. Some of the places marked were not contemporary with each other.

100 0 100 200 Miles
100 0 100 200 300 Km.
BLACK SEA
THRACE
Sinope
Amisûs
Trebizond
Byzantium
Calchedon
Heraclea Pontica
Thasos
Abydos
Alexandria Troas
Boghazqal'eh
R. Halys
Lesbos
Mytilene
Pergamum
PHRYGIA
R. Hermus
Sardis
Chios
Smyrna
LYDIA
Laodicea-ad-Lycum
Andros
Samos
R. Maeander
Colossae
R. Eurymedon
CARIA
Naxos
Halicarnassus
PAMPHYLIA
LYCIA
Cilician Gates
CILICIA
Tarsus
Doliche
Carchemish
Seleucia-in-Pieria
Antioch
R. Orontes
Apamea
Rhodes
Rhodes
Thera
Cnossus
Phaestus
CYPRUS
Laodicea
Aradus
Tripolis
Berytus
PHOENICIA
SYRIA
Sidon
Damascus
Tyre
COELE
Gadara
Gerasa
Philadelphia
Samaria
PHILISTIA
R. Jordan
Jerusalem
Gaza
Raphia
EAN SEA
Alexandria
Naucratis
Pelusium
Φ.Γ.

HELLENISM

I

THE PLOT OF THE PLAY

HELLENISM was a civilization which came into existence towards the end of the second millennium B.C. and preserved its identity from then onwards until the seventh century of the Christian Era. It made its first appearance astride the Aegean Sea, spread from there round the shores of the Black Sea and the Mediterranean, and eventually expanded overland eastwards into Central Asia and India and westwards as far as the Atlantic coast of North Africa and Europe, including part of the island of Britain.

'Hellenism' is not a word that is in everyday use in the vocabulary of the English language. The words 'Greek' and 'Greece' are used more frequently; but neither of these words exactly describes the subject of this book, and to have called it 'a history of Greek civilization' or 'a history of Greece' would have been misleading.

Greece is the name of a country, at the tip of the south-easternmost peninsula of Europe, that has been on the physical map of the surface of our planet ever since the lands and seas took their present shape. Thus Greece was in existence ages before the Hellenic civilization arose, and it is still on the map today, giving its name to a kingdom that is one of the states of the present-day world, thirteen hundred years after the date at which the Hellenic civilization became extinct. Greece has also seen other civilizations, besides the Hellenic, come and go. The Minoan-Mycenaean civilization occupied Greece before the Hellenic civilization's day, and the Byzantine civilization after it, while, between the Byzantine and the modern age, Greece was annexed successively by the Crusaders to Medieval Western Christendom and by the Ottoman Turks to the World of Islam. Even during the period of about eighteen hundred years during which the Hellenic Civilization was in existence, the area that it covered never more than partially coincided with the area of Greece in the common usage of the term. From beginning to end, one of the principal seats of the Hellenic civilization was the west coast of Asia Minor, which lies, not in Greece, but in Turkey. On the other hand, the northern part of Continental European Greece was not fully incorporated in the Hellenic World till the fourth century B.C.

As for the word 'Greek', it is indissolubly associated in English usage, as it is in Latin, with the Greek language; and the Greek language and the Hellenic civilization have not been either coeval or coextensive. Today, when the Hellenic civilization has been dead for about thirteen hundred years, Greek is still a living language, and it was already a living language for an unknown number of centuries before the Hellenic civilization came to birth. Since the Second World War, an English scholar, the late Michael Ventris, has successfully deciphered documents written in Greek which date from the fifteenth to the thirteenth century B.C. They were found at Cnossos in Crete and at Mycenae and Pylos in the Morea, three of the Minoan-Mycenaean World's capitals. They are inscribed on clay tablets, and the script is not the Phoenician alphabet, in which the Greek language has been written since the eighth century B.C. It is the Minoan 'Linear Script B', which is not alphabetic but syllabic. The Greek language may have been brought into Continental European Greece as early as the twentieth century B.C., and we do not know how long before that date Greek may have taken to extricate itself from the matrix of the Indo-European languages, somewhere in the heartland of the Old World, and to travel from the North-Eastern Steppe into the Mediterranean Basin. In any case the Greek language has had a longer history than the Hellenic civilization. It has both antedated it and outlasted it; and, even during the period when the language and the civilization were in existence contemporaneously, the areas that they occupied never coincided.

During the greater part of the course of Hellenic history, there were Greek-speaking peoples who were not members of the Hellenic society. Those who occupied the north of Continental Greece, north and west of a line drawn across Central Greece from south to north, a little to the west of Delphi and Thermopylae, were not converted to Hellenism till the fourth century B.C.; and, in the opposite direction, the Greek-speaking populations in Cyprus and along the south coast of Asia Minor, on the coastal plains of Cilicia and Pamphylia (the home country and the first mission-field of the Greek-speaking Jewish Roman citizen Saint Paul), were not fully Hellenized till about the same date. There were even some backward Greek-speaking tribes in the north-west corner of Thrace, round the headwaters of the Rivers Strymon (Struma) and Oescus (Isker), who remained outside the pale of Hellenism till the first century of the Christian Era, when they were Hellenized, more or less compulsorily, by the Latin-speaking Romans.

The Romans were, of course, the most important of all the converts, Greek-speaking or non-Greek-speaking, that Hellenism ever made. But the Romans were late converts. Other non-Greek-speaking peoples — for instance, the Messapians, Apulians, and Etruscans in Italy and the Lydians in Asia Minor — were Hellenized before the Romans were; and at the southern end of the west coast of Asia Minor there were other non-Greek-speaking peoples, the Carians and the Lycians, who were original members of the Hellenic society, like their Greek-speaking neighbours on both sides of the Aegean. Their role in Hellenic history was never so prominent as the Romans' role came to be; but they enjoyed the distinction of being Hellenic in their way of life from the first to the last chapter of the story of Hellenism.

In the last chapter the Romans not only gave political unity and internal peace to all Hellenes round the shores of the Mediterranean by bringing them under a single government; they also gave the Hellenic civilization a second linguistic vehicle, to supplement the Greek language. The official parity of the Greek and Latin languages in the Roman Empire was justified by the achievement of Cicero, Virgil, Horace, and other great Roman men of letters who produced, in Latin, Hellenic works of art that could bear comparison with the best of those written in Greek. In this imperial age of Hellenic history, the leading spirits of the Hellenic World were bilingual. The Emperor Marcus Aurelius Antoninus, whose family came from Spain and whose mother-tongue was Latin, wrote his journal in Greek. The historian Ammianus Marcellinus came from Antioch and the poet Claudian from Alexandria, and their mother-tongue was Greek, but they both wrote their works in Latin.

These are some of the reasons why it would be incorrect to call the Hellenic civilization either 'the Greek civilization' or 'the civilization of Greece'. Though the words 'Hellenism', 'Hellenic', 'Hellenes', 'Hellas' are less familiar than the words 'Greece' and 'Greek' to the English-speaking public, they have two advantages. They are not misleading; and they are the words which, in the Greek language, the Hellenes themselves used to designate their civilization, their world, and themselves. 'Hellas' seems originally to have been the name of the region round the head of the Maliac Gulf, on the border between Central and Northern Greece, which contained the shrine of Earth and Apollo at Delphi and the shrine of Artemis at Anthela near Thermopylae (the narrow passage between sea and mountain that has been the highway from Central Greece to Northern Greece and thence to the great Eurasian Continent into which Northern Greece merges). 'Hellenes', signifying 'inhabitants of Hellas', presumably acquired its broader meaning, signifying 'members of the Hellenic society', through being used as a corporate name for the association of local peoples, the Amphictyones ('neighbours'), which administered the shrines at Delphi and Thermopylae and organized the Pythian Festival that was connected with them. This was one of four festivals in the Hellenic World that came to be recognized as 'Panhellenic' ('international'), and not merely parochial, events. The other three were the Isthmian Festival held in the territory of Corinth; the Nemean, held in the territory of Phlius, in the Peloponnese (Morea) slightly south-west of the Isthmus of Corinth; and the Olympian, held in the territory of Elis in the west of the Peloponnese, to the north of Pylos. At a festival that had acquired Panhellenic status, the prizes awarded to winners of the artistic and athletic competitions were tokens that had no economic value. Parochial festivals had to attract competitors by offering valuable prizes; but the honour of being a victor at one of the Panhellenic festivals was so great that a material gratuity was unnecessary.

Though it was the Pythian Panhellenic Festival that gave the Hellenes their common name, the Olympian was the earliest of the four to acquire Panhellenic status. Public events were dated by Hellenic historians as having occurred in such and such an Olympiad (the Olympian Festival was held at intervals of four years); and admission to compete at Olympia came to be the test of recognition as being a Hellene. For instance, King Alexander I of Macedon, an unwilling subject of the Persian Emperor Xerxes who had given useful intelligence to the high command of the Hellenic coalition during the Persian invasion of Continental European Greece in 480–479 B.C., was rewarded by being admitted to compete at Olympia, not in virtue of the Macedonians' speaking Greek as their mother-tongue, but on the strength of a legendary genealogy which derived the Macedonian royal family from Argos, a city in the north-east of the Peloponnese which was one of the most venerable of all the cities of Hellas. The Romans were admitted to compete at the Isthmian Festival as a token of gratitude for the service which they had rendered to the Hellenic World in 229 B.C. in suppressing the Illyrian pirates who had been ravaging the west coast of Continental European Greece.

If Hellenism cannot be identified with any particular country or particular language, how are we to define it? Its essence was not geographical or linguistic but social and cultural. Hellenism was a distinctive way of life which was embodied in a master-institution, city-states; and anyone who acclimatized himself to life as it was lived in an Hellenic city-state would be accepted as a Hellene, no matter what his orgin and background might have been. King Alexander I of Macedon and the Eurasian Nomad khan Scyles the Scythian in the fifth century B.C. and the Roman general Titus Quinctius Flamininus and the Jewish high priest Joshua-Jason in the second century B.C. are conspicuous examples of such Hellenes by adoption.

Our definition of Hellenism is, however, still imperfect; for its distinctive institution was not peculiar to it. Though it is the Greek word for 'city-state', 'polis', that has passed into the language of the modern Western World in the derivative words 'politics', 'policy', and 'police', city-states were not an Hellenic invention. They were in existence in Sumer (the lower basin of the Rivers Tigris and Euphrates) by the year 3000 B.C., about two thousand years before the date of the Hellenic civilization's birth. City-states were also characteristic of a civilization in the Land of Canaan that was the Hellenic civilization's contemporary and sister. Famous examples of Canaanite city-states are the Phoenician cities Sidon, Tyre, and Aradus (Arvad) along the coast of Syria, and Gades (Cadiz), Carthage, and the other Phoenician colonies in Southern Spain and North-West Africa; and in the Old Testament we have a record of the transformation of the canton of Judah into the city-state of Jerusalem by King Josiah in the seventh century B.C. There was also a renaissance of this institution in Western Christendom, a society, affiliated to the Hellenic, which came to birth after the Hellenic society had gone into dissolution. Famous examples of medieval Western city-states are Venice, Milan, Florence, and Siena in Northern and Central Italy; Marseilles in Provence; Barcelona in Catalonia; Ghent, Bruges, and Ypres in Flanders; the Hansa Towns in Northern Germany. In the Middle Ages, Western Christendom narrowly missed becoming a society of city-states, such as Hellas had been; and even today, nearly 500 years after the date when the nation state became the characteristic institution of our Western World, the abortive medieval city-state dispensation is still represented by such notable survivals as Hamburg, Bremen, Basel, Geneva, Bern, Zurich, and San Marino. The last-named, though the smallest, is remarkable for being still fully sovereign and independent.

Thus the mere institution of city-states is not, in itself, the distinctive mark of the Hellenic way of life. What is distinctive of Hellenism is the use that it made of this institution as a means of giving practical expression to a particular outlook on the Universe. In the fifth century

B.C. the Hellenic philosopher Protagoras of Abdera expressed this in his celebrated dictum that 'man is the measure of all things'. In traditional Jewish-Christian-Muslim language we should say that the Hellenes saw in Man 'the Lord of Creation' and worshipped him as an idol in the place of God.

Man-worship or Humanism is not an exclusively Hellenic form of idolatry. There is a sense in which it has been the characteristic religion of man in process of civilization at all times and places. It is, for instance, manifestly the dominant religion, in fact though not avowedly, in the Western World today. Westerners are enthusiastic worshippers of man's collective power, particularly of his power over non-human Nature through the practical application of the discoveries made by modern Western physical scientists. The eighteenth-century Western rationalists and the fifteenth-century Western humanists were also man-worshippers in their own ways. What distinguishes the Hellenic experiment in Humanism is that it was the most whole-hearted and uncompromising practice of man-worship that is on record up to date. This is the distinctive mark of Hellenic history, and it raises an interesting question: What was the connexion between the Hellenes' worship of man and Hellenism's rise, achievements, breakdown, and eventual fall?

That is the subject of this book. But, before embarking on the story and trying to read its meaning, we have to ask ourselves why Hellenism should have been the first of the civilizations to put its treasure in Humanism unreservedly and also have been the only one to do this up to date — for no later civilization, not even our own, has ever again committed itself to Humanism so completely. Here are some considerations that may help us to find an answer to this preliminary question.

Humanism is the religion that appeals to man during

the stage of his history when he has already become conscious of having won a mastery over non-human Nature but has not yet been forced, by bitter experience, to face the truth that he is still not master of himself.

Man's mastery over non-human Nature was achieved by the civilizations of the first generation: the Sumerian civilization in the lower basin of the Rivers Tigris and Euphrates, the Indus civilization in Western Pakistan, the Shang civilization in the lower valley of the Yellow River, the Egyptian civilization in the lower valley of the Nile, the Minoan-Mycenaean civilization in the Aegean Archipelago. Before the rise of the Hellenic civilization and of its contemporary and sister in Canaan, the older civilizations had already made or inherited technical inventions — agriculture, the domestication of animals, the wheel, the boat — which, in point of creative genius, imaginativeness, and daring, surpass all previous inventions except primitive man's mastery of the use of fire, as well as all subsequent inventions, for which these have provided the basis. Yet, though these primary civilizations asserted man's victory over non-human Nature so triumphantly in their achievements, they were not tempted to worship man's power. Springing, as they did, out of primitive life, after a relatively short transitional stage that is known as the Neolithic Age, the primary civilizations were still living under the spell of previous aeons during which primitive man — in spite of his command of fire and his gift of speech — had not been master of Nature and had therefore worshipped her because he was conscious that she was his mistress. In particular, the primary civilizations had not mastered one element in Nature which concerns man more intimately than any other because it is the root, in Nature, to which individual human personalities are attached. They had not mastered the family: human beings were left still in bondage to it.

Primitive Nature-worship was the stuff out of which the primary civilizations made the higher religions that were their response to the experience of social breakdown and disintegration. Primitive man's worship of Nature embodied in the family and Nature embodied in the crops gave a means of expression to primary civilizations that were the first of their kind to taste the bitterness of failure. It gave them a symbol both for the tragic vein in human life and for life's miraculous victory that springs, so unexpectedly, out of life's defeat. These experiences were expressed in the image of the seed that dies and is buried in the womb of Mother Earth and then rises again in next year's crop or in the next generation of a human family. The image went into action in the worship of the sorrowing mother or wife and her suffering son or husband who has met a violent death and achieved a glorious resurrection. This religion radiated out of the Land of Sumer to the ends of the Earth. The Sumerian goddess Inanna (better known under her Akkadian name Ishtar) and her consort Tammuz reappear in Egypt as Isis and Osiris, in Canaan as Astarte and Adonis, in the Hittite World as Cybele and Attis, and in distant Scandinavia as Nana and Balder — the goddess here still bearing her original Sumerian name, while the god, in Scandinavia as in Canaan, becomes an anonymous 'Our Lord'.

The most famous Hellenic seat of this almost world-wide cult of the sorrowing goddess and her male associate who dies and rises again was Eleusis, the shrine of Demeter ('Mother Earth'), her daughter Persephone, and the grain god Triptolemus. We may guess that the Eleusinian mysteries were a legacy to the Hellenic civilization from the Minoan-Mycenaean civilization that had preceded it. But, in the Hellenic World, it was exceptional for the worship of Nature to be the paramount religion, as it had continued to be at Eleusis. Nature-worship had not been eradicated. It was still the religion of the women and the peasantry; and these, together, constituted a large majority of the population. But they were a depressed majority, and their religion had gone underground with them.

This had happened because, in contrast to the relative continuity of civilization in the valleys of the Nile and of the Tigris and Euphrates, there had been a sharp and violent break, in the basin of the Aegean Sea, between the fall of the Minoan-Mycenaean civilization there and the rise of its Hellenic successor. The debris of the fallen society had been submerged under a flood of barbarian invasion; and the traces of the past had been effaced so thoroughly that, in Hellenic folk-memory, hardly any recollection of the antecedent civilization had survived. The Hellenic civilization had had to start life by living on two legacies from the barbarians: the epic poems ascribed to the poet Homer, which became for the Hellenes the equivalent of what the Bible is for Christians and the Qur'an for Muslims, and a pantheon of gods who were not symbols of the mysterious vicissitudes of Nature, but were made in the image of man, and of barbarian man, of all men.

These Olympian gods were life-like reproductions of their human prototype; and this was unfortunate, because barbarian human nature is peculiarly unedifying. The barbarian is a primitive man who has had the ill-luck to be drawn into an encounter with the last representatives of a decadent civilization. This historical accident has suddenly shattered the framework of the barbarian's traditional manners and customs and has thus released him from restraint before he has become ripe for freedom. The barbarian is, in fact, an adolescent who has lost the innocence of a child without having acquired the self-control of an adult. The upstart gods who had imposed their paramountcy upon the ancient Nature gods during the social interregnum in which the Minoan-Mycenaean civilization had foundered and the Hellenic civilization had emerged were a war-band of superhumanly potent but characteristically disreputable barbarians. They had established themselves on Mount Olympus and were domineering over the Universe from this magnificent brigands' eyrie.

The barbarian human nature that was reflected in the Olympian pantheon with painful realism was such an unworthy object of worship for a society in process of civilization that it quickly fell into disrepute in the Hellenic World. Even in the Homeric poems, in the final recension in which these became canonical, the Olympians are beginning to be discredited and derided. By the sixth century B.C. they were being indignantly denounced by the philosopher Xenophanes of Colophon. The Hellenes were driven to look for some alternative object of worship, and this quest went on until Hellenism itself passed out of existence; but the Hellenes, who achieved such prodigies in the fields of art and thought, never succeeded in breaking away, unaided, from the man-worship that they had inherited from their barbarian sires. They merely oscillated between two forms of man-worship that were less repugnant than the worship of deified barbarian warriors and viragos. One of these two alternatives was the worship of collective human power as manifested, first, in local city-states and finally in a single empire which seemed to its subjects to embrace the whole World and which did, in fact, embrace all the Hellenic city-states round the shores of the Mediterranean Sea. The second alternative was the worship of an individual human being who was deified because he appeared to be a saviour. There was the Sicilian despot or Macedonian king or Roman emperor who presented himself as a saviour of society; and there was the Stoic or Epicurean sage who seemed able to save other individuals by his chilly example because he had apparently saved himself by his own austere exertions.

The Hellenes never felt at ease in the practice of man-worship, even in its less ignoble forms. The measure of their uneasiness was their dread of becoming guilty of 'hybris', the overweening pride that draws down upon a human being who gives way to it the resentment and retribution of the gods. The Hellenes recognized that man cannot deify himself with impunity.

In the end, the Hellenes came to find the penalties of hybris so crushing, and the practice of man-worship in any form so unsatisfying, that they surrendered to two eastern religions that had arisen, under the impact of Hellenism, in Asian societies that the Hellenes had conquered by force of arms. In India and Central Asia the Hellenes became converts to Buddhism in the younger form of it that is known among its followers as 'the Great Career' (Mahayana); in the Mediterranean basin they became converts to Christianity.

These two religions eventually converted the Hellenes from Humanism because they both offered an object of worship that was not man. The God of Israel, who became also the God of Christianity, was, like the Hellenic gods Apollo and Epicurus and Augustus, a person with whom human beings could have encounters and hold intercourse; but the common ground between God and man did not have the same basis in the two religions. The Hellenic gods were accessible to man because they had been created by man in man's image; the God of Israel was accessible to man because he had created man in his own image. As for the bodhisattvas (potential buddhas), whom the Mahayanian Buddhists venerated with a devotion that was tantamount to worship, they were presences that, in their quest of Buddhism's goal of self-annihilation, had sloughed off every vestige of human nature. They had come so near to their goal that they had it in their power at any moment to slough off existence itself; and nothing now restrained them from making their exit into Nirvana except a compassion for other sentient beings who needed help in extricating themselves from the toils of desire. The Mahayana was even farther removed from man-worship than Judaism was. Yet, in surrendering to these two non-man-worshipping eastern religions, Hellenism impressed something of its own Humanism upon both of them.

The Christianity that eventually captivated half the Hellenic World was a transformation of Judaism; and this metamorphosis had been brought about by the injection into Judaism of an Hellenic idea that, in Jewish eyes, was the very antithesis of what Judaism stood for. According to Christian belief, the God of Israel who has created man in his own image has also provided a means of salvation for his human creatures by himself becoming incarnate in a human being. For the Jews, this revolutionary Christian doctrine of God's incarnation was a blasphemous importation into Judaism of a myth that was one of the most damnable of all the errors in Hellenic paganism. This was a betrayal of everything that Judaism had achieved in a long and arduous struggle to purify and elevate man's vision of God's nature, and no orthodox Jew would have been capable of it. The enormity could have been perpetrated only by Galilaeans who had been under Hellenic influence for a quarter of a millennium before the forcible conversion of Galilee to Judaism in the early years of the last century B.C. The influence of Hellenism on the doctrine and outlook of Christianity was, indeed, profound; for, in becoming a human being, God exposes himself to the suffering that is a human being's inescapable lot. It is true that the vision of a suffering god, which is latent in man-worship, was rejected by Hellenic man-worshippers. Saint Paul was aware that Christ crucified, besides being a stumbling-block to the Jews, was a folly in the sight of the Hellenes. Hellenic logic here gave way to an Hellenic educated man's contempt for the underground religion of women and peasants. But the injection into Judaism of the Hellenic idea of incarnation had the effect of bringing up again to the surface, this time in Christianity, the worship of the god whose tragic death and triumphant resurrection had never lost their hold over human hearts in the great underworld of the Hellenic society.

Compared to this, Hellenism's other effects on the victorious eastern religions may seem trivial; yet these too have been important nevertheless. In Hellenic art, both Christianity and the Mahayana found a visual medium for presenting their ideas and ideals to the illiterate majority of their converts. In Hellenic philosophy, Christianity found an intellectual medium for the statement of Christian beliefs in terms acceptable to an Hellenically educated minority of society. In the administrative structure of the Roman Empire — an oecumenical body politic built up out of cells constituted by city-states — the Christian Church found a working model for its own organization.

The Hellenic experiment in civilization would have been a fascinating episode in the history of mankind, even if it had had no after-effects. But, in retrospect, we can now see that there is a significance and a value for posterity in the contribution that Hellenism has made to the ideas and ideals of Christianity, the Mahayana, and the other higher religions, especially Islam and post-Buddhaic Hinduism, which have arisen out of the encounter between Hellenism and the two civilizations that were Hellenism's contemporaries in Canaan and in India. These higher religions are the greatest spiritual forces in human life today, and Hellenism is still alive in the influence that it has had upon them. Hellenism's contributions to the higher religions have been both negative and positive.

Its greatest negative contribution has been its tragic demonstration of the inadequacy of man-worship; its greatest positive contribution has been the evocation of Christianity through the injection into Judaism of the counter-Jewish idea of incarnation.

II

THE PHYSICAL ENVIRONMENT OF THE HELLENIC WAY OF LIFE

THE centre and main thoroughfare of the Hellenic World was always a waterway. After Alexander the Great had extended the domain of Hellenism far inland eastwards and southwards by overthrowing the Persian Empire, the Hellenic successors of the Persian emperors in South-West Asia and Egypt found themselves irresistibly re-attracted towards the waterside, and would sacrifice a whole province in the continental hinterland of Hellas for the sake of winning a single island in the Aegean Archipelago. In a later chapter of Hellenic history, after the Romans had united the western half of the enlarged Hellenic World under a single government, the capital of this Hellenic 'world-state' was eventually transferred from Rome to Byzantium on the shore of the Bosphorus.

In being centred on a waterway the Hellenic World was not unique. It shared this geographical structure with the contemporary civilizations bestriding the Nile, the Tigris and Euphrates, the Indus, and the Yellow River. But the Hellenic World shared with its own predecessor the Minoan-Mycenaean civilization alone the peculiarity that its central waterway was not a river but was the sea. It was not till after the beginning of the Christian Era, at a date when Hellenism was in its last agonies, that other sea-centred civilizations came to birth in Indonesia and Japan.

The cradle of Hellenism was the basin of the Aegean Sea. The eastern shore was just as much a part of Hellas as the western shore or as the islands in between. Indeed, the Hellenic city-states along the west coast of Asia Minor played the leading role in Hellenic life until the sixth century B.C., when they fell under the dominion of foreign powers in their hinterland and had to resign the leadership of Hellas to Hellas-in-Europe, which included the Peloponnese (Morea) and Central Greece as far west as Delphi and Thermopylae.

The landscape of the Aegean basin is intricate. Chains of mountains break up the lowlands, and strings of islands intersect the sea. This structure is the result of the folding, faulting, and foundering of the Earth's surface. The Aegean basin is, in fact, one small section of an immense zone, running three-quarters of the way round the globe, in which these physical disturbances have occurred. This zone extends from the southern tip of South America, where it emerges out of the Antarctic Ocean, to Morocco and Spain, where it dips below the surface of the Atlantic. An arc of folded mountains sweeps, in gigantic curves, round three sides of the Pacific Ocean, from the western slope of the Americas to the southernmost of the festoons of islands that skirt the east coast of Asia. In Celebes this arc ties into another one that writhes its way from New Zealand through Indonesia and the Himalayas to the Pamir Plateau; and from there the folds continue westwards, in parallel lines, across the western half of the Old World. The Aegean basin is not the only section of the zone in which the folds have collapsed and subsided below sea level. The same thing has happened in the Caribbean, at the Behring Straits, in Japan, in the Philippines, and in Indonesia, as well as in the basins of the Black Sea and the Western Mediterranean, between which the Aegean basin is the connecting link. But it is the Aegean specimen of this broken landscape that concerns us here, because this was the Hellenic civilization's original habitat and permanent focus.

The structure and location of the Aegean basin have given it three salient physical features that have had important effects on the life of its inhabitants.

In the first place the Aegean basin provides excellent maritime communications. While it is laborious to travel across country from one little plain to another over the steep and rugged mountains that separate them, many of the plains have a window on the wide world in consequence of their dipping below the sea's surface. At points on the coast where plain and mountain meet, there are, in many cases, convenient natural harbours, and an apprenticeship in navigation is offered by the strings of islands — peaks of submerged sections of the mountain ranges — that run diagonally across the sea, from shore to shore, in parallel lines. The local navigator who has learnt his seamanship in the Aegean, where land is never far out of sight and ports are seldom out of reach, can then find channels that will lead him out into broader waters. Sailing north-eastwards out of the Aegean through the Dardanelles (Hellespont), the Sea of Marmara (Propontis), and the Bosphorus, the Aegean mariner debouches into the Black Sea. Sailing south-eastwards through a bridge of islands, of which the largest and best placed is Rhodes, between the east end of Crete and the south-west corner of Asia Minor, he debouches into the Eastern Mediterranean, and, if he hugs its eastern coast till he reaches the delta of the Nile, and then sails up-stream, he will find first a portage and in a later age a ship canal to convey him from the head of the delta to the head of the Gulf of Suez, where he will be on the threshold of the Indian Ocean. Sailing out of the Aegean south-westwards between the west end of Crete and the south-easternmost prong of the Peloponnese

— the perilous Cape Malea — the mariner has the central and western basins of the Mediterranean ahead of him. He can thread his way through the Straits of Messina to the mouths of the Tiber, Arno, Rhône, and Ebro; or, taking the wider passage between Sicily and Tunisia, he can venture out, between the Pillars of Hercules, through the Straits of Gibraltar into the Atlantic.

A second effect of the structure of the Aegean basin is that it provides its inhabitants with arable land that is excellent in quality but is rigidly limited in area. The steepness of the mountains causes the soil to collect in the hollows like porridge in a bowl. The depth of soil here is great, and the surface is level; but, at the line where this level surface meets the mountainside, cultivation ceases. The mountains themselves are so bare that, even if the cultivator performs the hard labour of terracing their lower slopes, the amount of soil that he can conserve above the level of the plain will be so small that it will be good for little beyond maintaining a few olive trees. In a precipitous country with an abundant rainfall, such as the Atlantic slope of the highlands of Peru, it pays to terrace the mountainside almost up to the summit; but in the Aegean basin the climate is too dry and the mountainside too bare to make this enormous labour worth while. It is true that the Aegean basin, like the highlands of Peru, can depend on the rain to provide the water for its crops. Yet in the Aegean the dividing line between the desert and the sown is almost as sharp as, in Peru, it is along the rainless coast, where cultivation is wholly dependent on irrigation and the vegetation stops dead at the point beyond which the life-giving waters cannot be made to flow.

The effect of the location of the Aegean basin is to produce extreme seasonal variations in the climate. Situated, as it is, on the borderline between Europe and Africa, the Aegean has European winters and African summers; and the severity of both seasons is startling to visitors from regions such as the Atlantic seaboard of Europe or the Pacific seaboard of Peru, where the oscillations of the climate are kept within a much narrower range by the moderating influence of an oceanic current whose temperature is more or less constant.

The seasonal extremes to which the unregulated climate of the Aegean basin runs have repeatedly taken the writer of this book by surprise. For instance, on 27–30 December 1911, he walked over the highlands of Northern Arcadia, in the Peloponnese, from Argos to the monastery of Meghaspíleon. He found the highlands covered with a blanket of snow that in places was several feet deep, and it was impossible to move except where mules and men had trodden a single-file track along which one could edge one's way between two snow-walls. Again, in the second week of January 1912, he went to Thessaly with the intention of walking about in the countryside, but he was defeated by the bitterness of the cold. A north wind was blowing from the western bay of the Great Eurasian Steppe, which runs along the north coast of the Black Sea to the eastern foot of the Carpathians, and the ground was in the grip of a numbing black frost. He had a third experience of what the Aegean winter can do on a late November day in 1948, when he and his wife drove by car from Athens to Corinth and back. On that winter day the colours of the landscape were those of El Greco's picture of Toledo in a thunderstorm. The sky was leaden, the sea was steely. He had to flounder through snowdrifts in making his way up to the peak of the Acrocorinthus, and, on the drive back to Athens along the Kakì Skála ('Nasty Landing') over the brow of the Scironian Rocks, the wind, beating down in gusts, lashed the waters of the Saronic Gulf into foam and almost swept the onlooker off his feet. As one peered across at the storm-swept mountains of the

Argolid, one might have fancied, if one had not known where one was, that one was gazing at the coast of Iceland. At the opposite extreme of the seasonal gamut the summer heat is quite as formidable in its own way. On 17 July 1912 the writer landed at Itéa at 5 o'clock in the morning and set out on foot for Delphi. It was a long climb uphill, and the traveller soon realized that he was running a race with the Sun. He was overtaken by the scorching rays before reaching his journey's end, though he staggered into Delphi long before the Sun was near his zenith. Seventeen years later he found himself at Baghdad in September, with the temperature at 117 degrees Fahrenheit in the shade and without the benefit of the north wind from the Steppes which, in Aegean summers, becomes man's friend. Yet he has not felt the heat in 'Iraq or in Sa'udi Arabia more severely than he has felt it in Greece.

These physical features of the Aegean basin were potent forces in Hellenic history. The dearth of agricultural land at home, and the impossibility of appreciably extending the cultivable area there, drove the Hellenic peoples first to expand at the expense of weaker neighbours, and afterwards to supplement agriculture by taking to commerce and manufacturing industry when their expansion was being brought to a halt by the resistance of their victims and their competitors. The Hellenes' mastery of the sea at their doorstep opened the way for them into a larger and more complex world. And their familiarity with the extreme seasonal variations of the Aegean climate trained them to make themselves at home over a wide range of different physical environments.

The lines of least resistance for the Hellenic peoples' expansion overseas were westward along the Mediterranean and north-eastward through the Straits into the Black Sea; for in both these directions the native peoples were more backward in civilization than the Hellenes and therefore were no match for them, so that the Hellenes' only serious opponents here were the rival pioneers of other Levantine societies. Hellenic colonists planted a 'Great Hellas' (in the sense of a 'Great Central Greece') on the 'instep' and 'toe' of Italy; a second and more fertile Peloponnese in Sicily; a second Crete in Cyrenaica; a miniature Ionia on the distant coast of the French riviera. This maritime expansion was carried beyond the limits of the Hellenic emigrants' native climate. The north coast of the Aegean, where the Chalcidians founded a new Chalcidicê, was far more inclement than the French riviera, though it lay so near to the colonists' homeland. The north coast of the Black Sea, where the Milesians established trading-posts at the mouths of the great Russian rivers, was more inclement still. In the opposite direction the Panhellenic settlement at Naucratis, on a north-westerly arm of the Nile delta, lay in a decidedly hotter zone than the Aegean; and Naucratis was the forerunner of Alexandria, the metropolis of the Hellenic World during an age that began with the overthrow of the Persian Empire by Alexander the Great and that was brought to a close by the Romans' conquest of the Mediterranean basin.

The expansion of the Hellenic World, which had followed the sea routes in its first bout, till this maritime movement had been checked towards the end of the sixth century B.C., was set in motion again before the end of the fourth century B.C. by Alexander the Great and before the end of the third century B.C. by the Romans; and this time the movement travelled overland. In the second century B.C. the successors of Alexander carried Hellenism into the basin of the Rivers Jumna and Ganges, in the realm of the monsoons; in the last century B.C. the Romans carried it to the Atlantic seaboard of Europe, in the realm of the Gulf Stream.

In this overland expansion south-eastward and north-westward, Hellenic city-states struck root in even more exotic environments than that of icy Borysthenes on the Dniepr or that of scorching Naucratis on the Nile. Dura-Europus maintained itself on the bank of the Euphrates in a section of the river's course where it runs through the North Arabian steppe. Seleucia-on-Tigris and Antioch-on-Eulaeus and Bucephala-on-Hydaspes maintained themselves on the torrid plains of 'Iraq and Khuzistan and the Panjab. Other Hellenic settlements maintained themselves on the Anatolian and Iranian plateaux and in the basin of the Rivers Oxus and Jaxartes, where the country is under snow for half the year. In the opposite direction, the names of the modern cities Köln (Colonia Agrippina) in the Rhineland and Lincoln (Lindum Colonia) among the wolds of Eastern England bear witness to the hardihood of Roman colonists who sowed North-Western Europe with Hellenic city-states in Latin dress.

The pioneers of Hellenism overland schooled themselves to hold their own in uncongenial environments, but naturally they took most kindly to those spots — few and far between in the tiny Aegean basin's vast encompassing continental hinterlands — where climate or flora or waters reminded them of home. The Hellenic settlers — discharged veterans or enterprising civilians — who flooded into South-West Asia and Egypt in the track of Alexander's army, pounced, for example, upon the hill-country of Transjordan, with its rain-fed streams and its woods; and, when they reached the remote land of the Paropanisadae — those cool highlands round the head-waters of the rivers of Afghanistan where roads converge from all four quarters of Asia — they hailed this vine-clad paradise as the god Dionysus's own country. Hellenic colonists occupied the Paropanisadae in force, and they were still holding out there in the last century B.C., when all the rest of the Hellenic World east of the River Euphrates had been overrun by Eurasian Nomad invaders. The Crimean and the Pontic riviera — two veritable Ionias on the shores of the Black Sea that had been occupied by Hellenic colonists during the maritime bout of Hellenic expansion — were the last refuges of Hellenic city-states. On the fringe of the Crimean riviera, Chersonesus Taurica (on the site of the modern Sevastopol) maintained itself as an autonomous city-state till the ninth century of the Christian Era; and on the Pontic riviera the city of Trebizond recovered its independence, and preserved it for a quarter of a millennium, after the overthrow of the East Roman Empire by the Western Crusaders in A.D. 1204.

In fact the expatriated Hellenes' endurance of uncongenial environments was a *tour de force*, and, in their exile, they never ceased to feel the magnetic attraction of their native Hellas. Towards the end of the sixth century B.C. a Hellene from 'Great Hellas', the physician Dêmocêdês of Croton in the 'toe' of Italy, found himself unexpectedly deported into the interior of the Persian Empire. He had been employed as public health officer in the Hellenic island of Samos, off the west coast of Asia Minor, and had shared the fate of his employers when Samos was occupied by a Persian expeditionary force. By a stroke of luck he was called in to treat the Persian emperor Darius I for injuries that the emperor had received in a fall from his horse; and, as a reward for his success in healing his august patient, he was appointed to be the emperor's personal medical adviser. Yet this brilliant situation did not console Dêmocêdês for being marooned in Khuzistan; and, since Darius was unwilling to release him, he cajoled the emperor into letting him serve as intelligence officer on a Persian naval reconnaissance into the Western Mediterranean basin and succeeded, as he had intended, in deserting when the Persian flotilla touched at his home town, Croton.

This homesickness for Hellas was an hereditary weakness of the Seleucidae, who, of all post-Alexandrine Hellenic dynasties, pushed their frontiers the farthest afield into the interior of the Continent. Seleucus the Victor had founded the fortunes of his house, after the death of his master Alexander, by seizing Babylonia ('Iraq), which was the key province of South-West Asia both as a source of supply and as a node of communications. Yet he could not rest till he had also provided himself with a Mediterranean seaboard, and he had no sooner conquered Northern Syria than he transferred the administrative and military headquarters of his empire to this eccentric maritime corner of it. Seleucia-on-Tigris had to yield precedence to Antioch-on-Orontes, planted at the point where the Syrian river ran through a Syrian replica of the Vale of Tempe to a Syrian Picria on its way to the Hellenic sea. A new Cyrrhesticê, Anthemusias, Mygdonia, and Odomantis were called into existence, along the northern edge of 'the Fertile Crescent'. Yet this evocation of the names of the provinces of Macedon in Syria and Mesopotamia did not assuage Seleucus's longing for his native land; and, when, in the last of the wars of succession, he had added Asia Minor and Thrace to his vast Asian realm, his one thought was to revisit the Macedon from which he had been absent by then for fifty-three years. This nostalgia for the Aegean cost Seleucus the Victor his life: he was assassinated on his way. It cost his descendant Antiochus III the Great his empire by bringing him into collision with the Romans. Yet these sharp lessons did not deter Antiochus IV Epiphanes from spending the Seleucid Monarchy's dwindling revenues in the seductive Aegean on the embellishment of Athens. He sought to immortalize his name in this 'Hellas of Hellas' by re-starting work there on the building of the giant temple of Olympian Zeus, which the Athenian despot Peisistratus had begun, and which the Roman Emperor Hadrian was to finish. The conduct of the Seleucidae is evidence that, however far from the Aegean a Hellene might roam, his human heart would remain attached to the geographical heart of Hellas.

III

RESPONSES TO THE CHALLENGES OF ANARCHY AND STRINGENCY

THE historical background to the first chapter of the history of Hellenism was the decline and fall of the Minoan-Mycenaean civilization that had preceded Hellenism in the Aegean basin. The downfall of the non-Greek Minoans, who had been the founders of this older civilization, may have been either a consequence or a cause of the rise of the Greek-speaking Continental European Mycenaeans, who occupied Cnossos, the metropolis of Minoan Crete, before it was sacked at the close of the fifteenth century B.C. By comparison with the Minoans, the Mycenaeans were barbarians, but they were heirs and guardians of the Minoan tradition by comparison with the outer barbarians who came in at their heels. The Mycenaeans did create something that partly replaced what they had destroyed. For instance, they created the Achaean sea-power which, in a rough-handed way, carried on 'King Minos's' work of policing the seas. The whole period running from the close of the fifteenth century to the close of the twelfth was, no doubt, an age of disintegration; but the great break in social and cultural continuity came, not at the beginning, but towards the end. The supreme catastrophe was not the fifteenth-century sack of Cnossos: it was the mass-migration (Völkerwanderung) set in motion by the following wave of barbarians at the beginning of the twelfth century B.C. This not only devastated Mycenae and the other seats of the

Mycenaean civilization in the Aegean basin but swept like a tidal wave over Asia Minor and overwhelmed Hattusas (now known by its Turkish name Boghazqal'eh), the capital of the Hittite Empire. If one stands today among the ruins of Hattusas, and tries to conjure up the scene of the sack by recalling the Roman poet Virgil's imaginary description of the sack of Troy in the Second Book of the Aeneid, one begins to realize how great the twelfth-century catastrophe was. The flood of militant migrants rolled on, with still unspent force, round the east coast of the Mediterranean till it was brought to a halt at the north-eastern corner of the Nile delta by the desperate resistance of the Egyptian sea and land forces. The survivors of the discomfited Philistines settled on the seaboard of Palestine and gave their name to the country.

Our information about the age of violent change which began with the sack of Cnossos and ended at the Battle of the Nile in 1188 B.C. comes partly from fragments of the public records of the Egyptian, Hittite, and Assyrian governments that have been recovered by modern archaeologists; partly from a retrospective interpretation of the linguistic map of the Aegean basin, Asia Minor, Syria, and Canaan as we find it in the last millennium B.C., after the dust has settled; and partly from the two Hellenic epics, the *Iliad* and the *Odyssey,* the authorship of which is traditionally ascribed to Homer.

The Egyptian records inform us that the disturbance was wide-spread. The great irruption of invading peoples from the north in the early years of the twelfth century B.C., which was the climax and culmination of the whole upheaval, had been anticipated in the fourteenth century by the first wave of an invasion of Canaan and Syria from the east, out of the North Arabian Desert, and in the fourteenth and thirteenth centuries by repeated invasions of the Nile delta, out of the Western Desert, by barbarians who seem to have come from as far afield as Tunisia, Sicily, and perhaps even Sardinia. The wideness of the area of disturbance is explained by the fact that, in the second half of the second millennium B.C., the Minoan society was not the only Levantine civilization that was in decline. The Egyptians and Hittites had exhausted themselves by fighting a hundred-years' war for the possession of Syria and Canaan which had ended about the year 1278 B.C. in an agreement to divide the disputed territory between them. The Hittites had still further sapped their strength by a series of wars with the Empire of Arzawa, in western Asia Minor — a contest which had ended, some time in the latter part of the fourteenth century, in a Hittite victory that subsequently proved to have been too costly. In fact the social vacuum into which the barbarians were being drawn from all quarters of the compass extended not over the Aegean basin only but over the whole of the Levant.

The subsequent linguistic map of this region tells us something more about who the migrants were and what routes the migrations followed. A broad arrow of intrusive Phrygian-speaking peoples now runs diagonally across Asia Minor south-eastwards from the Dardanelles; and a detachment of the invaders has pushed the Carians down the Maeander valley to the country at the mouth of the river, from which the Carians, in their turn, have pushed the Lycians out into the 'ball' of the 'toe' of the peninsula. We know from the records of King Tiglath-Pileser I of Assyria that the vanguard of the Phrygian migration from South-Eastern Europe had reached the upper basin of the River Tigris before the Assyrian army brought it to a halt towards the close of the twelfth century B.C. Another arrow of intrusive peoples runs diagonally across Continental European Greece and the Aegean basin from Epirus ('the Mainland'), on the east side of the Straits of Otranto, opposite the 'heel' of Italy, to Rhodes and the adjacent smaller islands off the south-west corner of Asia Minor.

The language spoken by these Continental European intruders into the Aegean basin was a dialect of Greek — the dialect known, in Hellenic terminology, as Doric, perhaps because it was spoken in Doris, the cluster of islands which was the farthest point, south-eastward, that these intruders reached. The arrow of Doric-speaking invaders had cleft through the older stratum of Greek-speaking peoples in the area who had maintained the Mycenaean civilization and had wielded the Achaean sea-power. The new invaders had either submerged them or else pushed them out. The older stratum in the Peloponnese now survives only in the central highlands (Arcadia) and far away overseas in Cyprus, which had been occupied by Achaean adventurers in the fourteenth century B.C. The older stratum of Greek-speaking peoples in Central Greece now retains no foothold on the European Continent except in Attica and in Euboea (technically an island, but virtually part of the European mainland). The majority of these Ionian-speaking Greeks have been pushed across the water on to the Aegean islands and beyond into a new Ionia on the west coast of Anatolia, where the collapse of the Hittite Empire has at last left the coast clear (a bridgehead at Miletus had been the only foothold on the Asian mainland that the Achaean sea-power had managed to win). The older stratum of Greek-speaking peoples in Northern Greece has likewise been pushed overseas into Aeolis, on the west coast of Asia Minor to the north of Ionia. In Europe, the Aeolic-speaking Greeks are now represented only by one enclave in Thessaly and by another in Boeotia, where, under pressure from the Doric-speaking invaders in their rear, they have supplanted the previous Ionic-speaking inhabitants. The name 'Boeotians' testifies that this Aeolic-speaking people has come from

Northern Greece, since the name means 'inhabitants of Boion', which is a synonym for Mount Pindus.

In Syria and Canaan, the new linguistic map tells a similar tale. In Syria the old Amorite Semitic-speaking peoples have been submerged under a wave of Hittite refugees from Asia Minor who have been carried up the Orontes valley nearly as far as the river's headwaters, and by a counter-wave of Aramaean Semitic-speaking invaders from North Arabia, who have pushed their way into the foothills of the Antitaurus and the Amanus. In Canaan the older stratum of Semitic-speaking peoples now survives only in isolated enclaves, like the Aeolic-speaking and Arcadian-speaking peoples in European Greece. Except for Phoenicia, the coast has been occupied by Philistine refugees from the Aegean, and the interior by Hebrew peoples: Moab, Judah, Ammon, Israel.

Of our three sources of information about the age of violence, the *Iliad* and the *Odyssey* are the most circumstantial and the most attractive, but they are also the most elusive and the least trustworthy. It is true that the city of Ilion (alias Troy), standing at the point where the waterway between the Aegean and the Black Sea is crossed by the ferry between South-Eastern Europe and Asia Minor, must have played a prominent part in this episode of history. In fact, the discovery and archaeological exploration of the site in modern times has made it certain that Troy was an important place from the third millennium down to the thirteenth century B.C. The Homeric picture of a ten-years' siege of this strategic position by the Achaeans, and of their subsequent wanderings in search of their way home, fits in well with the picture of the age that the Egyptian and the Hittite public records give us. In these too, as well as in the Homeric poems, the Achaeans figure as aggressive sea-rovers. Moreover, the traditional date of the fall of Troy — 1194–3 B.C. on one reckoning,

1183 B.C. on another — is remarkably close to the date assigned by modern Egyptologists to the Battle of the Nile, in which the Sea Peoples were defeated by the Egyptians. Yet any attempt to use the *Iliad* and the *Odyssey* as historical sources would be beset with pitfalls. For example, the villain of the *Iliad,* Paris, alias 'Alexandros of Ilion', makes his appearance in the Hittite public records as 'Aleksandus of Wilusa'; but in this context, which is his authentic historical context, he turns up, not in the twelfth century B.C., but before the end of the fourteenth. Either Paris and Alexandros were not really the same person, or, if they were, this person had nothing to do with a siege of Troy at the time of the great twelfth-century upheaval. The truth is that epic poets are too good artists to make conscientious historians. Though their themes are authentic historical events, their first concern is to hold the attention of their listeners; and they will therefore mould their story into a work of art at the expense of historical accuracy — sometimes even at the cost of changing it out of all recognition.

Two incompatible pictures of the turbulent social interregnum in the Aegean basin are presented, side by side, by the Hellenic poet Hesiod, writing four or five hundred years after the event, in the darkness before the dawn of a new civilization. In one picture the barbarians are realistically portrayed as the baleful race of bronze; in the other picture they are idealized, as they are in the Homeric epics, as the noble race of heros. In the second picture we are seeing the barbarians through their own eyes; in the first we are seeing them as they appeared to their victims. In the Hellenic literary tradition the idealistic picture prevailed — partly thanks to the genius of Hellenism, which fashioned such consummate works of art as the *Iliad* and the *Odyssey* out of barbarian epic poetry, and partly, perhaps, also because the Hellenic society had not inherited from its Minoan predecessor any counterpart of the Bible, which superseded the Teutonic epics in Western Christendom, or of the Qur'an, which pushed the surviving poetry of the pagan Arabs into the background in the Islamic World. The Hellenic founders of the city-state dispensation in the first chapter of the history of Hellenism succumbed to the barbarian heroes' charm; but, while they were idealizing the age of barbarism in the Homeric poems, they were getting rid of it in real life.

The legacy of the age of barbarism in the Aegean basin was anarchy; and the first chapter of Hellenic history was a dark age which must have lasted for about four hundred years before the darkness was finally dispelled in the eighth century B.C. This dark age was an unhappy time to live in, as the poet Hesiod bears witness. Yet, unlike the social interregnum that preceded it, it was an age of constructive achievement. It saw the re-establishment of order in the Aegean basin through a victory of lowland farmers over highland shepherds.

In the Aegean basin, as in the Japanese archipelago, about 90 per cent. of the land is occupied by uncultivable mountains, and only about 10 per cent. is level and arable. Yet, in a struggle between highlanders and lowlanders, the lowlanders had three advantages. The population of the lowlands was more numerous, more closely concentrated, and less poor, and this gave them possibilities of organization and equipment that were not within the reach of their scattered and poverty-stricken highland adversaries.

The military equipment at the lowlanders' disposal must have been invented at some time during the latter half of the second millennium B.C. In the last millennium B.C. this equipment was in use throughout an area extending from Assyria on the south-east through Urartu (Armenia) and Asia Minor to the western outposts of Hellenism, including peoples then in process of Hellenization in the western basin of the Mediterranean. Its distinctive elements were a round metal shield and a metal helmet with a horsehair crest. The inventors must have held horses in high esteem and have had an aptitude for metallurgy and an ample supply of ore; and these three considerations point to the Hittites, who are known to have had a passion for horses and to have been pioneers in the working of iron. In the fourteenth and thirteenth centuries B.C. the Hittite land-empire in Asia Minor was in immediate contact with the Achaean sea-power that had supplanted the Minoan sea-power in the Aegean, and the Achaeans were then learning from their Hittite neighbours how to use war-chariots; so this may also have been the time when metal armour began to be adopted by the Aegean peoples. Alternatively, it may have been brought into the Aegean area during the Völkerwanderung of the twelfth century B.C. by the Carians, to whom the fifth-century Carian historian Herodotus attributes the invention of the horsehair crest. It is assumed in the *Iliad* that this equipment was already in use among the champions on both sides at the siege of Troy; and, as we have already seen, this siege, if it was indeed an historical event, must have been one of the incidents in the Völkerwanderung. In the age of the Völkerwanderung and throughout the dark age that followed it, metal armour and chariots were the monopoly of an hereditary aristocracy whose warriors operated as a mounted infantry, manoeuvring on wheels but fighting on foot in single combat. This heavy-armed chariotry had an advantage, on its own ground in the plains, over light-armed highlanders on foot; but this advantage was not decisive, as was demonstrated in Canaan, where, in the course of the dark age, the lowland charioteers were overwhelmed by the highlanders everywhere except along the coast. The victory of the lowlanders in Hellas may have been due not so much to their equipment with armour and chariots as to their organization in city-states.

In the Hellenic World in the dark age, city-states were brought into existence by the political unification of communities that, in isolation, would each have been too small to be able to constitute an effective body politic. The Greek word for this process of political consolidation is 'synoecism', and its literal meaning is 'housing together'; but this technical term must not be taken quite *au pied de la lettre.* It does not mean just 'conurbation'. No doubt in every case the operation did have a topographical aspect. The Greek word for the city-state that was the product of a synoecism is 'polis'; and the original meaning of 'polis' is 'citadel'. The communities 'housing together' in a city-state will at least have established a common citadel, if only as a city of refuge in which the people of the plain, with their flocks and herds and their portable property, could take refuge from hostile raiders. But, since synoecism also implies the establishment of a common government, the citadel will usually have contained within its walls a permanent civic centre, with temples for public worship and meeting places, some out in the open and others under cover, for the transaction of secular public business. In March 1912, in the neighbourhood of Sitía, towards the east end of the island of Crete, the writer visited the site of a fortified civic centre of the kind. Here the foundations of the public buildings were conspicuous, but there was no evidence of there ever having been private dwelling houses within the circuit of the walls. Usually again, no doubt, the permanent civic centre did eventually gather a permanent urban settlement round it; and this embryonic town, in its turn, might eventually be enclosed within a ring-wall of its own. But it was probably unusual to see the whole population of a city-state take up its abode inside the town walls, even where the territory was so small that all the land under cultivation was within easy reach; and this would obviously have been impossible where the territory was extensive.

The city-state of Sparta, for example, was a union of five villages in the broad plain of Lacedaemon, which the River Eurotas traverses in the middle part of its course. Four of these villages do seem to have coalesced into a town, but the fifth village, Amyclae, was tied, by the sanctity of the local shrine of Apollo, to its original site three miles away down the valley. Yet, in law, the Amyclaeans were citizens of Sparta on the same footing, and with the same rights and duties, as their fellow-citizens whose homes were in Sparta town. Again, every native inhabitant of Attica, the territory of the city-state of Athens, was an Athenian citizen; but Attica, too, was a large territory. From Cape Sunium, at the tip of the Attic peninsula, to the city of Athens it is a long day's walk — a distance of about forty miles. It is probable that a majority of the citizens of Athens had their homes in some country town or village outside the city until, at the outbreak of the great Atheno-Peloponnesian War in 431 B.C., the rural population camped between the Long Walls, by which, at that date, the city was connected with its ports, in order to take shelter from the invading Peloponnesian army. It is true that the territories of Athens and Sparta were exceptionally large. The two Siceliot city-states Syracuse and Akragas (Agrigentum) were the only others of comparable size in the whole Hellenic World until Rome began to enlarge her territory by conquest in the fourth century B.C. All the same, the incompleteness of the topographical synoecism of Athens and Sparta was not abnormal. The essence of synoecism was a union, not of houses, but of hearts; and this psychological unification could not be produced artificially. In 369 B.C. the Theban statesman Epameinondas synoecized the village communities of South-Western Arcadia into a city-state, Megalopolis ('megale polis' means 'great city'). The new state was to be a buffer against Sparta, and the new city was to be a barrier-fortress. To provide Megalopolis with sufficient urban man-power to ensure its effective defence, the founder put pressure on the Arcadian villagers to leave their ancestral homes in the countryside and settle within the new ring-wall; but this move was so unpopular that, to save the new state from falling apart again into its constituent elements, it was found politic to permit the people of a number of the transplanted villages to return to their old homes while retaining their new Megalopolitan citizenship. In this instance the political synoecism of a city-state was salvaged at the price of allowing its topographical synoecism to be partially disbanded.

We do not know where in the Hellenic World the process of synoecism started; but we may guess that the place was the west coast of Asia Minor, where the Ionic-speaking and Aeolic-speaking refugees, pushed out of European Greece by Doric-speaking invaders, had to maintain their footing against a hostile hinterland. If the new arrivals were to survive, they must club together to fortify common citadels and set up common governments inside them. We are informed that the founders of these city-states on Asian ground were of very diverse origin (the Asian Greek geographical name Aiolis means 'variegated'). Ship's companies from many different parts of European Greece would coalesce to form a new body politic on Asian soil. In Hellenic constitutional terminology the name for the main sub-divisions of a city-state is 'phylae'. The literal meaning of the word is 'nations' or 'races', and this term would be a natural one to apply to the ship's companies, of different nationalities, that united to found a Phocaea or a Colophon; but it would be an incongruous name for the people of a group of several village communities — living as neighbours on the same little plain somewhere in European Greece since, perhaps, time immemorial — to think of applying to one another when they united to establish a city-state, if, by then, the term had not already become current as part of the established technical vocabulary of the institution. These considerations suggest that, in the Hellenic World, city-states may have made their first appearance on the Asian coast of the Aegean and have spread to European Greece from there.

In any case, the lowlanders' adoption of this political institution helped them to get the better of the highlanders almost everywhere in Hellas. The establishment of a city-state brought to its citizens the boon of public security. The practice of wearing swords fell into disuse, and even the carrying of a walking-stick came to be felt offensive. A classic illustration of this result is provided by Sparta. The Greek word 'sparta' means 'sown land'. In the basin of the River Eurotas, the lowlanders had defeated and cowed the highlanders so thoroughly that they were able to lay out their city in the open fields. Sparta had no city-wall and no citadel. Its safety was ensured by the military ascendency of the united forces of the five synoecized villages of the vale. At the same time the contemporary history of Canaan shows that the outcome of the struggle in Lacedaemon (Laconia) between the Spartans and the surrounding highlanders was not a foregone conclusion. Canaan had been a world of city-states already before the Völkerwanderung; and, after it, the city-state dispensation held its own along the coast. In the interior, on the other hand, the struggle between lowlanders and highlanders in the dark age resulted, as we have seen, in the lowlanders being overwhelmed; and the synoecism of the victorious highland communities Israel and Judah was a later chapter in the story, which had its counterpart in Hellenic history in the eventual synoecism of the highland communities in Arcadia.

The victory of the lowlanders over the highlanders in most parts of Hellas brought in its train the re-establishment, in the Aegean basin, of the ancient law and order that had been first shaken when the Mycenaeans had wrested the command of the sea from the Minoans, and had been finally shattered when the Achaean sea-power had been swept away in its turn. This victory was the first step towards the building-up of a new civilization. It was a difficult step, and the way had been opened for it by the invention of city-states. The institution that had performed this social service naturally won prestige and gratitude. 'The city-state came into existence to make life possible', as Aristotle said. But everything that is of value has to be purchased at a price.

Part of the price of the restoration of order in the Aegean was the creation of social injustice. Most Hellenic city-states — Athens was a signal exception to the rule — started life handicapped by a division of the people into a body of first-class citizens, living in the city and on the arable land adjoining it, and an outer circle of second-class citizens descended from the subjugated highlanders; and this schism in the community was a fruitful cause of subsequent social conflict. The Spartan city-state treated its girdle of subjugated highland communities in Lacedaemon more generously and wisely than was usual. It allowed these perioeci ('satellites') to retain their autonomy in miniature city-states of their own. Their principal obligation to their suzerain was to serve in the united Lacedaemonian forces in wartime. Here they were brigaded with their Spartan overlords; and, from beginning to end of the history of the Lacedaemonian army, there was never any suggestion that the non-Spartiate Lacedaemonian soldier was any less steady or less valiant than his

Spartiate comrade in arms. On the other hand, when Sparta conquered the coastal plain of the Eurotas basin, she treated the conquered population here with a harshness that was exceptional in this stage of Hellenic history. These helots (in Greek, 'heilôtes', signifying either 'prisoners of war' or 'fenmen') were deemed to have forfeited their human rights and were degraded to a status of permanent serfdom.

Another part of the price of the restoration of order is indicated in a saying of the early-fifth-century (B.C.) philosopher, Heracleitus of Ephesus. 'War', said Heracleitus, 'is the father of all things.' He was thinking not in political but in cosmic terms and was using the word 'war' metaphorically in this context. Yet his saying was literally true of the method by which order had been restored in the Hellenic Dark Age. The victory of the lowlands over the highlands had been won by military force; and war — the operation by which this first step in the rise of the Hellenic civilization had been achieved — became, like city-states, a basic institution of Hellenic life. This early marriage of war with civilization in Hellenic history was the more ominous because the new order, unlike the old order, was based on a large number of local centres that were politically independent of one another and that might therefore easily fall into conflict. The sea-power of Minos had imposed peace on all the coasts and islands of the Aegean basin, and its successor, the sea-power of the Achaeans, had performed the same international public service in some degree. There was no such paramount keeper of the peace in the new world of Hellenic city-states that the warfare between highlanders and lowlanders had called into existence.

The institution of war, which had been employed to solve the earliest of the Hellenic society's problems, was likewise employed to solve the next problem, by which the Hellenes found themselves beset as a result of the solution of the first. The restoration of law and order in the Aegean basin, thanks to the establishment of city-states, allowed the population to increase in numbers up to the limits of the regional means of subsistence. We have seen that these limits were fixed with unusual rigidity by the region's geological structure. The Hellenes were therefore now penalized for their success in taking the first step towards civilization. They were confronted in the eighth century B.C. by the choice of starving or else exporting their surplus population overseas to take possession of new cultivable land by military force. The organized expeditions of 'embattled farmers' which the city-states of Hellas were able to send over the water proved more than a match for the relatively backward natives of the coasts of North-West Greece, the 'instep' and 'toe' of Italy, the island of Sicily, the green belt of Cyrenaica, and the shores of the Hellespont, Propontis, Bosphorus, and Black Sea; and, in the course of rather more than two hundred years (running from about the third quarter of the eighth century B.C. to the last quarter of the sixth), the Hellenic World achieved the vast maritime expansion that has been briefly sketched in the preceding chapter.

The Hellenic peoples that played the leading parts in organizing this massive migration overseas were the Achaeans and Locrians, who were the principal colonists of the 'instep' and 'toe' of Italy; the Corinthians, who colonized the coast of North-West Greece, including the strategically important island of Corcyra (Corfù), and founded Syracuse in Sicily; the Corinthians' neighbours on their isthmus, the Megarians, who took advantage of their possession of two seaboards to found colonies both in Sicily and on the shores of the Bosphorus and the Black Sea; the Chalcidians, whose city's position on the Euripus (the narrow channel between the island of Euboea and the mainland of Central Greece) enabled them to send out colonies to Sicily in one direction and in the other to plant a whole Chalcidicê on the northern shore of the Aegean; the Milesians in Ionia, who played, in the Black Sea and in the narrow seas leading into it, the dominant role that the Corinthians played in the west; and the Phocaeans, the adventurous Ionian founders of Massilia (Marseilles) on the French riviera. The cluster of Hellenic colonies in Cyrenaica was planted there by bold explorers from the tiny Aegean island of Thera (Santorin) — a fragment of the ruin of a foundered and flooded volcano.

There was one colonial Hellenic city-state, and this an important one, that traced its origin to Sparta. Taras (Tarentum) — well placed on a natural harbour under the 'heel' of Italy — commemorated as its founders the Spartan Partheniae ('sons of unmarried mothers'). The story was that all male Spartan citizens of military age were kept in the field for so many years on end during the war in which the Spartans conquered Messene that the rising generation of Spartan girls at last lost patience and got themselves children by irregular unions. These children born out of wedlock were not recognized as citizens of Sparta by the Lacedaemonian Government; and, when, in disgust, they decided to emigrate in a body, the Government was not sorry to see the last of them. The tale of the Partheniae may be a fable, but it was true that Taras was the only colony that Sparta ever founded, and also true that her alternative solution for the common Hellenic problem of over-population was one that was peculiar to her. She conquered her new agricultural land, not overseas, but from her next-door neighbours in the Peloponnese; and she cultivated the conquered fields, not by the hands of her own citizens, but by reducing the occupants and former owners to the status of serfdom to which she had already reduced the inhabitants of the lower Eurotas valley.

This Spartan solution for a common problem may not have been more immoral than the normal recourse of seizing land overseas; but it proved to be far more difficult to carry through. There were colonial Hellenic city-states — Taras, Syracuse, Akragas, Heraclea Pontica — with subject populations that were comparable in numbers to Sparta's in Messene; and their subjects, too, were restive. The conquered Messapians revolted against Taras successfully, and the conquered Sicels gave Syracuse serious trouble. But these overseas subjects of colonial Hellenic city-states derived at least some cultural benefit from the loss of their political and economic liberty. They had been forcibly inducted into a civilization that they recognized to be superior to their own, and this opened the way for their eventual assimilation to their conquerors. The Messenians had no such benefit to gain from being conquered by Sparta. They never reconciled themselves to their fate; and they became the Poles of the Hellenic World — seizing every opportunity to revolt and never letting their spirit be broken by repression. After having conquered Messene in the eighth century in a long and exhausting war, the Spartans had to wage a more fearful war in the seventh century to stamp out the first in the long series of Messenian revolts. When the Messenians had been re-subdued, the Spartans still had on their hands the unending task of holding them down.

The nemesis of Sparta's conquest of Messene was ironical. In order to keep the conquered Messenians enslaved as agricultural serfs, the Spartans themselves had to submit to the slavery of serving, from the age of seven to the age of sixty, as full-time military conscripts. They had liberated themselves from the *corvée* of working with their own hands on the land, only to have to spend their days on the drill-ground and in the barrackroom. Sparta was the first Hellenic city-state to become a democracy. The former nobles were merged in the commons. All male Spartiates became one another's 'peers'. Every citizen-soldier was assigned an allotment of Messenian land, with serfs attached to it, to provide for him his obligatory contribution in kind to his mess; and the mess became the unit out of which the cadres of the Spartan military organization were built up.

This peculiar way of life ('agôgê'), in which the Spartan conquerors of Messene could not call their souls their own — not to speak of their time, their property, and their families — was said to have been devised by 'Lycurgus'. But Lycurgus was not an historical character. He was a god; and he figured in Greek mythology as a king in Thrace who once fell foul of the god Dionysus. The so-called 'Lycurgean' system was not a social reformer's blue print. It was the outcome of a reluctant adaptation of Spartan life to the inexorable requirements of Sparta's ascendancy over Messene. The seventh-century Spartan lyric poet Alcman was the equal of his contemporaries in other Hellenic city-states, but at Sparta he had no successors. The same story can be read in dumb show in present-day Sparta if one walks round the local museum. In the seventh-century and sixth-century exhibits, one sees the Spartans holding their own among their contemporaries in Hellas in the arts of vase-painting and ivory-carving. But towards the close of the sixth century these arts wither away, and the next exhibits are undistinguished bas-reliefs dating from the second century B.C. The barren intervening three and a half centuries coincide with the age during which the Lycurgean system was in force at

Sparta and the arts were in their heyday in the rest of Hellas. Such was the fate that Sparta brought on herself by going her own peculiar way.

The Lacedaemonian Government deliberately put an end to Sparta's participation in the common life of Hellas by forbidding Spartan 'peers' to compete at the Panhellenic festivals. They were afraid that the soldier's discipline would be undermined if he were allowed to win personal fame as an international athlete. This restriction did not apply to Spartan ladies. A Spartan heiress was free to spend her fortune on entering a team for the four-horse chariot race. Spartan women served the régime by helping, with their merciless tongues, to keep their unnaturally repressed menfolk up to the mark. From the sixth to the fourth century B.C. they were the only uninhibited women in Hellas.

IV

THE EMANCIPATION OF INDIVIDUALS BY CITY-STATES

THE unhappy change of spirit that came over Sparta before the end of the sixth century B.C. was an omen of the future of the Hellenic city-states and, with them, of Hellenism itself. The Hellenes took to worshipping their city-states as gods, instead of treating them simply as public utilities; the demands that the deified city-states made on their citizens eventually became as sacrificial as those made on Juggernaut-worshippers by Juggernaut; and this spelled the doom of the institution. Like the venerable god Kronos when he had taken to devouring his children, the Hellenic city-states finally provoked their long-suffering devotees into a reaction and revolt against them.

However, Sparta's development was precocious, and it was not the eventual militarization of Spartan life, but the previous flowering of Spartan art, that was characteristic of the course of Hellenic civilization during the age of its overseas expansion — though, in this age too, the Hellenic city-states, like all institutions that produce effective results, made demands that were exacting. They required obedience to the local laws, submission to military training and discipline, and a readiness to risk one's life in battle on behalf of one's own state against its adversaries.

This might mean fighting in a very bad cause. The Athenian poet Sophocles served as one of the commanders of the Athenian expeditionary force that re-subdued Samos in 439 B.C.; the Athenian philosopher Socrates served in the force that re-subdued Potidaea in the overture to the great Atheno-Peloponnesian war of 431–404 B.C. The Samians and the Potidaeans had been unjustly subjugated by the Athenians, and were 'rightly struggling to be free'. It reflects badly on the master-institution of Hellenism that the ordinary course of a citizen's duties should have involved two noble-minded men of genius in fighting for their country when she was in the wrong; and such experiences portended a conflict between country and conscience. This was, indeed, the theme of Sophocles' tragedy *Antigonê,* which was produced shortly before the year in which its author served his country against Samos. The heroine deliberately incurs the death-penalty by disobeying the Government's orders to leave unburied the corpse of her brother, who has been guilty of heinous high treason against his country. Antigonê chooses to die rather than be false to her conviction that her duty to give her brother's corpse decent burial overrides her duty to obey the public authorities. Forty-two years later, in 399 B.C., the stand taken at Athens by Sophocles in the person of his heroine was taken in his own person by Socrates. Yet, on the whole, down to the fateful year 431 B.C., Hellenic city-states, other than Sparta, gave to their citizens, individually as well as collectively, much more than they took from them. After enabling the Hellenes to solve the two successive problems of anarchy and stringency, their city-states made it possible for them, not only 'to have life', but 'to have it more abundantly'. The passage quoted in the preceding chapter from Aristotle's *Politics,* which says that 'the city-state came into existence to make life possible', goes on to say that 'the institution's *raison d'être* is to make life worth living'. And this second dictum of Aristotle's would have been justified by the facts if he had been writing about a hundred years earlier than he actually was. For at least three centuries, ending in the year 431 B.C., Hellenic city-states did give individual human beings both scope and stimulus.

They gave scope to individuals by freeing them from the bonds of Nature-worship — above all, from the particularly cramping bonds of the worship of Nature in the form of the family. Family life holds mankind in bondage to non-human Nature. In the bosom of the family, human beings are not independent personalities, with minds and wills of their own; they are twigs of a family tree, which, in turn, is a branch of the evolutionary tree of life whose roots reach down into the abyss of the subconscious psyche.

In the Athenian tragic poet Aeschylus's 'trilogy' of plays dealing with the story of the House of Atreus, which was first performed in 458 B.C., we have a dramatic representation of an individual's desperate struggle to break out of a psychological impasse into which he has been led by his family obligations, and of his liberation from his undeserved agony by the humane intervention of a city-state. It is the story of a family whose members have taken to killing their own kin, with the consequence that the survivors are confronted with irreconcilable imperative demands upon them. The god Apollo tells Orestes to avenge his father Agamemnon's death by slaying his father's murderess Clytaemnestra, Agamemnon's wife and Orestes' mother — whereupon the Erinyes mercilessly persecute Orestes for having taken the life of the closest kinswoman that a man can have. The Erinyes are mythical personifications of our human feelings of guilt. Within the vicious circle of conflicting family duties, there is no way for Orestes to escape from his fearful plight, though common sense declares that he is not a villain but a victim. He is rescued by the goddess Athênê, who is a mythical personification of the Athenian city-state. She persuades the Erinyes to accept the jurisdiction of an Athenian jury court; and, when the jurymen's votes are equally divided between the litigants, Athênê, as the president of the court, gives her casting vote in favour of mercy and sanity.

City-state law, and even city-state military service, did liberate individuals, at the price of a new servitude to a city-state, from their old servitude to a family. At Athens, by Aeschylus's day, the issue had been decided by the city-state in the individual's favour already, but this not so long ago to make the theme of the *Oresteia* a stale or meaningless one for a fifth-century Athenian audience. In Latium, on the western fringe of an expanding Hellenic World, the family fought a more stubborn rearguard action in defence of its primeval claims. In the long history of Roman law, the father of a family retained many of his ancient despotic rights over his wife and his adult children even in the final codification made, by the orders of the Emperor Justinian, in the sixth century of the Christian Era, at a date when Roman law had been exposed for seven hundred years to the humane influence of Hellenic philosophy, and for two hundred years to the gentle influence of Christianity. During the greater part of the course of Roman history, an adult male Roman citizen had been virtually his father's slave till his father's dying day; but there had been one place where, since the foundation of the Roman state, this slave-son had been a freeman, and that was in the camp. When father and son were mobilized, the son was his father's peer as his fellow soldier in the service of the republic.

Besides giving individuals this scope, the city-states gave them stimulus. In liberating them from their age-old bondage to their families, they did not impoverish their lives by depriving them of the intimacy that is the charm of life within the family circle. The city-states themselves were communities of a small enough size for it to be possible, to a large extent, to make them work — as a family works — through direct dealings between individuals. Of course, however small the scale of political life may be, law is an impersonal affair by comparison with family custom, and war by comparison with blood feuds. On the other hand, by comparison with the impersonalness of human relations in the Roman Empire or in a modern Western nation-state, an Hellenic city-state of the pre-imperial age had the stimulating immediacy of a family writ rather larger. Aristotle prescribes that the citizen-body ought not to be too large for 'an announcer without a loud-speaker' ('kêryx mè stentóreios') to be able to be heard by the whole assembly; and, as a matter of historical fact, few Hellenic city-states — perhaps only Athens, Syracuse, Akragas (Agrigentum), and eventually Rome, had citizen-bodies that did not fall within Aristotle's limit. Sparta was not one of the exceptions; for, although, after her conquest of Messene, her territory occupied about two-fifths of the area of the Peloponnese, all but a fraction of its population consisted of perioeci and helots. The dominant minority of adult male Spartiates of military age are said to have been five thousand strong at the time of the Persian Emperor Xerxes' invasion of Continental European Greece (480–479 B.C.), but this looks like an exaggeration; for the figure appears to have been less than 3500 when Sparta went to war with Athens in 431 B.C.

The degree of the new scope and stimulus that were given to individuals by city-states in the Hellenic World in the age of its overseas expansion (eighth to sixth centuries B.C.) is indicated by the achievements, in this age, of individuals who made a name for themselves in various fields of activity. In the field of literature there were poets such as Mimnermus of Colophon, Archilochus of Paros, and Alcaeus and Sappho of Lesbos. Their themes were the experiences of the individual when he has become conscious of himself: the pleasures and penalties of sex and alcohol, the loyalties and rancours of politics, but, above all, 'the grandeur and misery' of mortal man's lot. Archilochus had emancipated himself so completely that he had the nerve to flaunt his failure to perform his civic duty on the field of battle. In an unjust war of conquest that Paros was waging against the Thracian natives of the island of Thasos in the Northern Aegean, Archilochus once saved his skin by throwing away his shield. Instead of hiding his head in shame, he boasted of his unsoldierlike conduct in a poem; and the fact that this poem is extant today tells us that the poet must have found sympathizers among his contemporaries. In the field of thought, there were physicists who speculated about the nature of the material universe. Was the primary substance water or indeterminate stuff or mind? This was the question in debate between Thales of Miletus and his fellow-countryman Anaximander and Anaxagoras of Clazomenae. Was the Universe an undifferentiated and motionless unity? Or was there multiplicity in it and diversity and movement and rhythm? And was its rhythm an alternation of the intermingling and segregation of qualitatively different elements? Or were the apparent qualities as well as shapes of all things visible the product of an everlasting rain of myriads of uniform atoms? This was the question in debate between Zeno of Elea and Empedocles of Akragas and Leucippus of Miletus (?).

There were also famous names in the field of technology: for instance, Ameinias of Corinth, the first Hellene to design ships propelled by triple oar-power, and Theodorus of Samos, the first Hellene to make casts in bronze. In technology, however, the Hellenes were never pioneers. It was a pursuit that they despised, and their contempt for it extended to most other kinds of manual work except agriculture. For instance, they set little store by vase-painting, which, in our eyes, is one of the finest products of their artistic genius. Even the great masters of the fine arts did not enjoy high social esteem, and there was no counterpart, in Hellenic history, of that fruitful partnership between technology and science that has been the making of both these pursuits in the modern Western World since the seventeenth century of the Christian Era. The bent of Hellenic science was speculative, not experimental, from first to last. Mathematics and philosophy and poetry were the fields in which the Hellenes felt at home.

In these fields the Hellenes' achievements in the age of Hellenism's overseas expansion were already so great that it is no wonder that they idolized the political institution that had given free play to individual genius. By this time the worship of collective human power incorporated in city-states had replaced the worship of the Olympian pantheon in fact, though not avowedly or officially, as the paramount religion of the Hellenic World. The city-states were worshipped by their citizens in the guise of older divinities — some of them Olympian and others far older than that — who were conscripted to play this new role. Here and there the conscript divinity was a male god. The sea-faring Corinthians, for example, took Poseidon, the Olympian god of the sea, to serve as the tutelary deity of their city. Most city-states, however, were represented by tutelary goddesses: for example, Athens by Athênê Poliûchus ('the Keeper of the City'), Sparta by Athânâ Chalcioecus ('Our Lady of the Brazen House'), Aegina by Athânâ Aphaiâ, Argos by Hera, Ephesus by Artemis, and so on. The tutelary goddess stood for the collective power of a city-state's male citizens. In the language of modern Western psychologists, one might say that, in worshipping her, they were worshipping their own collective anima. The Corinthians' projected anima was Aphrodite.

A city-state was a worthier object of devotion than Olympian gods made in the image of human barbarians; and the emancipated human personality comes to grief if it does not find some more or less worthy object of devotion outside itself. City-states deserved to receive devotion from their citizens in so far as they provided them with a social environment that stimulated them to turn their talents to account. But did a local political community whose hand was against its neighbours, and whose neighbours' hand was against it, fully deserve the amount of devotion that it demanded and exacted? Was it capable of giving scope to the individual's highest capacities, and of stimulating him to be his best self? These were the issues on which the future of Hellenism depended. Unlike the Hellenes themselves in the age of overseas expansion, we know what that future was to be, and, with the insight that comes after the event, we can discern at least two grave defects in the institution in which the Hellenes had put their treasure.

The fundamental defect of the city-states of the Hellenic World was that there were a number of them, and not just one. If the number of human beings in the world had been no more than the maximum number of citizens that a city-state ought to have according to Aristotle's prescription, there could have been such a thing as '*the* city-state', and this might have been the optimum political dispensation for mankind. In reality, of course, the total population of the Hellenic World alone, without taking account of its neighbours, was vastly larger than this, even from the start. So there never was any such thing as 'the city-state' in real life. In the singular, it was an imaginary abstraction. In reality there were always city-states in the plural until the last chapter of Hellenic history, when Rome made herself *the* city-state of the western half of an enlarged Hellenic World by wiping some of her sisters off the map and reducing the rest of them to the status of municipalities. Till then — and by then it was too late to save the situation — there had been sovereign city-states and perennial inter-state warfare. In the first chapter of Hellenic history every nascent city-state had acquired the habit of making war against the surrounding highlanders; and, after the highlanders had been subjugated, each city-state continued to cultivate the war-making habit by going to war with other city-states within its range. Hence the institution of city-states in the plural carried with it the institution of war — unless and until effective steps were taken to impose peace.

A second defect of the city-states was that the scope and stimulus which they gave to their citizens were fully enjoyed by one element only in the community: that is, by male citizens who had time to spend in the market-place where public business was transacted, as well as in the fields and workshops where the community's livelihood was gained. This penalized *de facto,* though not *de jure,* those peasant citizens whose land lay at some distance from the state's civic centre. But the principal losers from the rise of the city-states were the women (of all social classes) and the slaves. In the barbaric life of the post-Minoan and pre-Hellenic age of anarchy, as recollected in the *Odyssey,* women and slaves had been members of society, such as it was. Life as lived in an Hellenic city-state in and after the eighth century B.C. represented a great advance towards civilization, but in this advance the women and slaves had been left behind.

The social setting of a city-state had given so much new interest and zest to life for the men that their mothers and wives and daughters were now no longer their mental equals. It is significant that the polite name for a prostitute in this age was 'companion' (hetaira). A prostitute in an Hellenic city-state, like her sister in modern Japan, must have mental accomplishments as well as physical attractiveness. She must be able to enter into her male clients' intellectual interests. It is also significant that the typical romantic love affair was one, not with a woman, but with a boy, and that homosexual liaisons were condemned only mildly by Hellenic public opinion. When, now and again, a woman broke into the men's world, not as an hetaira, but in her own right, by excelling in some male accomplishment — for instance, in poetry — she was apt to enter into homosexual relations too; and this indicates that even the most highly accomplished woman could not find happiness in the natural satisfaction for her sexual impulses because she could not become a wife, or even a mistress, on terms of genuine equality with a man. The Athenian statesman Pericles, in his funeral speech in honour of the Athenians killed in action in the first year of the great Atheno-Peloponnesian war of 431–404 B.C., is represented by the Athenian historian Thucydides son of Olorus as curtly advising the women of Athens that their first and last duty is to make themselves inconspicuous and to bear some more children to replace the community's war casualties. At Sparta alone — and Sparta was always both peculiar and precocious — the women recovered, in the course of the Hellenic age of overseas expansion, something like the status that they had enjoyed everywhere in the pre-Hellenic age of anarchy and barbarism. This gain of theirs was a windfall from the descent of the heavy weight of the 'Lycurgean' system upon the backs of the Spartan men. Spartan girls were regimented too, but the grown-up women got off more lightly. In this connexion, Aristotle acutely observes that militaristic peoples are prone to fall under 'the monstrous regiment of women' (as it was called by John Knox).

The defects exhibited by Hellenic city-states made them inadequate for serving as frameworks for the whole of life or as objects of exclusive devotion. Their inadequacy can be gauged by the importance of the institutions, outside the city-state framework, that existed, or came into existence, in the Hellenic World in the eight, seventh, and sixth centuries B.C., and by the number of those, among them, that were importations into the Hellenic World from abroad. A survey of these complementary institutions reveals three needs for which the city-states did not provide — or, at least, not satisfactorily. Classes in society, particularly the slaves and the women, that did not benefit by the amenities of city-state life needed psychological compensation in some other sphere. All classes in society needed a wider framework for life than a petty state with its narrow horizon. They needed to live part of life in a larger world — in a social framework that would be Panhellenic instead of parochial. All classes, again, needed religious experience and satisfaction that they could not obtain either from the worship of city-states or from the worship of the Olympians. More than one of these three needs were met by most of the non-city-state institutions that had a hold on the Hellenes' feelings and imaginations in this age.

The slaves' and women's need for psychological compensation can be measured by the tenacity with which they maintained the celebration of rites of Nature-worship that, in the liturgical calendars of the city-states, had been driven into the background, first by the worship of the Olympian pantheon, and then by the worship of the city-states' tutelary goddesses. But these depreciated cults of Nature did not provide satisfaction enough, and the still unsatisfied need made the fortune of the indigenous Eleusinian mysteries and of the imported cult of the Thracian Nature-god Dionysus (alias Bacchus). The mysteries celebrated at Eleusis, in Attica, were a local Nature-cult which had preserved its status as the paramount religion of the place, and which had been kept open to women and slaves and thrown open to foreigners. The little that we know about the Eleusinian ritual and its significance suggests that the annual death and resurrection of the grain may have been interpreted to the initiates as an assurance of a personal after-life, as distinct from the impersonal immortality of a family or a state. The worship of Dionysus made itself at home in the Hellenic World in spite of an unsuccessful resistance to it that was commemorated in the myths of the invading god's temporary discomfiture by his opponents Lycurgus and Pentheus. The features of the cult of Dionysus that repelled some Hellenic souls were, we may guess, just those that captivated others. This religion gave a dominant role to women, and it provided a vent for the irrational passions of the subconscious depths of the psyche.

The Orphic rites and doctrines and the Pythagorean system of philosophy seem to have been the 'low-brow' and 'high-brow' versions of a religion which, like Dionysus-worship, came from somewhere outside the Hellenic World. The Orphic and Pythagorean doctrines, objectives, and prescriptions for attaining these objectives are identical in so many points with those current in India in the same age that it is incredible that the resemblance can be just fortuitous. A possible common source of these identical religious phenomena in India and in Hellas may be the Great Eurasian Steppe. In the eight and seventh centuries B.C. one of the periodical eruptions of the Eurasian Nomads swept some of them south-eastward into the Indus basin and others westward into the Danube basin, and they may have been the carriers of a religion that is still alive in Northern Asia. The fundamental tenet of this religion is that this world is not a soul's true home, and that life in the body is not its highest destiny. The true end of souls is to liberate themselves from the trammels of existence; but this supreme objective is also supremely difficult to attain, because existence is not limited to a single life-time; it is a sorrowful wheel of reincarnations which will succeed one another without end unless one has both the knowledge of the way of release and the resoluteness to follow it. The prophet-philosopher Pythagoras of Samos founded a community in the 'Great Hellas' in the 'toe' of Italy which was to put these beliefs into practice. It was a cross between a primitive religious fraternity and a modern Western scientific academy. The Master's word was gospel truth for his disciples. Like Muhammad and Calvin, Pythagoras obtained control over the government of a city-state, but, unlike them, he provoked a reaction which, at Croton, broke the Pythagorean community's power and dispersed the survivors into exile. Had Pythagoras and his followers been as successful in politics as they were in mathematics, Hellenic history might have taken a strangely different turn from its actual subsequent course.

The prophets of Hellas in the second quarter of the last millennium B.C. were not the spiritual equals of their great contemporaries in Canaan and in Iran. Unlike these, Pythagoras and Empedocles combined the prophet's role with the philosopher's and the natural scientist's, but they also differed from Isaiah, and perhaps from Zarathustra too, in combining it with the primitive magician's role as well. The Cretan prophet Epimenides may not have been much more than a connoisseur of archaic religious rites, and the adepts in Orphism fell into ill-repute for descending to this primitive level and for making money out of their clients' credulity. The Orphic, as well as the Pythagorean, movement missed its manifest destiny of becoming a Panhellenic church, and the Hellenes' need for a Panhellenic religious institution was met, in this age, by the oracle at Delphi in Central Greece.

The shrine at Delphi was shared by its original tenant, the primeval goddess Earth, with two successive intruders, Olympian Apollo and Thracian Dionysus; and the oracle drew its inspiration from this local alliance of three aspects of the godhead: the divinity of Nature embodied in the Earth, a divine power governing the Universe, represented by Apollo, and the demonic divinity of the subconscious psyche that was manifested in Dionysus. The oracle's pronouncements were uttered, in Apollo's name, by a prophetess in a state of ecstatic trance, and her utterances were edited in hexameter verse by the Delphic college of priests before delivery to the public. This public, which included city-state governments as well as private individuals, demanded information about the future, and the oracle could not afford to ignore this vulgar craving. It safeguarded its reputation for second sight by becoming a past-master in ambiguity, till, on the eve of Xerxes' invasion of European Greece, it mistakenly prophesied the apparently almighty invader's victory, and disgraced itself by advising its consultants not to resist. The Delphic priesthood attempted to re-establish its shaken prestige by putting into circulation a tale of Apollo's miraculous intervention against a detachment of the Persian expeditionary force that had been heading for his holy place; and this story was not openly impugned; but it fell flat in a new age of dawning rationalism. However, by that time, Delphi had fulfilled its real mission, which had been, not to tell dubious fortunes, but to give sage advice. Should we go to war? When should we make a *coup d'état?* Where should we found an overseas colony? Such questions were answered by the Delphic priesthood wisely on the whole. Its wisdom was born of long experience and good information. As a Panhellenic mentor, Delphi played a worthy part in the history of the Hellenic society in the age of its expansion overseas.

It has been mentioned already that Delphi was the meeting-place for one of the four recurrent Panhellenic festivals. Like the shrines with which they were associated, these meetings must have been religious in origin, but they had turned into competitions in individual prowess — in the fine arts as well as in athletics. All four were open to any freeman who could make good his title to call himself a Hellene; and, of all Panhellenic institutions, these were the principal expressions of a consciousness of membership in a common Hellenic civilization. All Hellenes had another common possession in the Homeric poems; and the popularity of these kept alive the memory of an earlier society which had not yet split up into the multitude of mutually antagonistic city-states that had subsequently divided the loyalty of the Hellenes between them. It was characteristic of Hellenism that it should have succeeded in expressing its common consciousness in poetry and in sport and not in politics or in religion.

The date and authorship of the *Iliad* and the *Odyssey,* as we know them, have been in dispute among modern Western scholars since the end of the eighteenth century, but there can be no doubt that these two masterpieces have behind them a poetic tradition that was as old as the age of the pre-Hellenic Völkerwanderung from which both poems have derived their themes and much of their setting as well. During most of the period of its incubation in the Dark Age of Hellenic history, this epic poetry must have been an oral art, since the art of writing, which had been in use in the Aegean area in the Minoan-Mycenaean age, had been lost there in the chaos of the Völkerwanderung and was not acquired by the Hellenes till the eighth century B.C. This recovery of literacy in the Aegean World was not made by way of a revival of the use of the syllabic Minoan script, which had been employed for writing Greek, among other languages, in Mycenaean times. This script had now fallen into oblivion everywhere except in Cyprus. Elsewhere the Hellenes made themselves literate by borrowing the alphabet from their Canaanite neighbours the Phoenicians. Under the inspiration of the old-established Sumerian and Egyptian systems of writing, new scripts had been invented, in the latter half of the second millennium B.C., by the Phoenicians and the Hittites, as well as by the Minoans, and the Hittites and the Phoenicians had never lost the use of theirs. The Phoenicians had reduced the number of the characters in their script to a minimum by isolating the consonants and recording nothing but these. But the Phoenician alphabet's gain over a syllabic script in conciseness was offset by a loss of precision, since there will be a number of alternative ways of supplying vowels for a word written in consonantal letters only. When the Hellenes borrowed the alphabet for writing Greek, Lycian, and Carian, they supplemented it by isolating the vowel sounds and devising letters to represent these. The consequent trifling loss in conciseness was out-balanced by an immense gain in both precision and clarity. This Hellenic vocalized alphabet is the easiest, as well as the most accurate, system of writing that has been invented up to date; and, in the form in which it was adopted by the Latins, it is still in use today in the modern Western World. Its invention brought the art of writing within everybody's reach — in contrast to the effect of the earlier invention of the Sumerian, Egyptian, and Chinese scripts, which were so complex and clumsy (they combined phonetic signs standing for syllables with older signs standing for particular words) that they were bound to be the monopoly of a handful of privileged specialists. By an early date in the fifth century B.C., if not before the end of the sixth century, literacy had become so wide-spread in Attica that a referendum could be taken by asking the voters to write on a potsherd the name of a politician whom they would like to see banished from the country.

This improved version of the alphabet gave the Hellenes another common institution which did much to foster a sense of Panhellenic solidarity. The Hellenic alphabet's excellence also commended it to the Hellenes' neighbours. It was rapidly adopted by the peoples of Anatolia west of the Central Desert and by the peoples of Italy as far north as Venetia inclusive for the writing of their local languages. Their reception of the Hellenic script made them receptive to the rest of the Hellenic civilization, and so paved the way for an enlargement of the borders of the Hellenic World by a process of peaceful conversion in lieu of forcible conquest and colonization.

V

THE RESPONSE TO THE CHALLENGE OF PHOENICIAN AND ETRUSCAN COMPETITION IN THE WEST

THE overseas expansion through which the Hellenic society had been solving the problem of over-population in its home territory was brought to a halt in the course of the sixth century by the effective resistance of competitors for the prize of colonizing the shores of the Black Sea and the Western Mediterranean, whose backward native inhabitants could not effectively resist the encroachments of any of the rival expanding Levantine civilizations.

During the early centuries of the last millennium B.C., when the Hellenic civilization had been bringing itself into existence in the Aegean basin by getting the better, there, of the anarchy left by the break-up of the Minoan-Mycenaean society, the nascent new civilization had been fortunate in not being under pressure from any neighbouring societies of its own kind. Like the anarchy with which the new order had to contend, this freedom from pressure was a legacy from the pre-Hellenic age of barbarism. The Völkerwanderung in the early years of the twelfth century B.C. had temporarily swept the Levant clear of great powers. Besides destroying the Mycenaean sea-power in the Aegean and the the Hittite land-empire in Anatolia, it had left Egypt exhausted by the effort of repulsing the barbarians from her threshold. This creation of a political vacuum had made it feasible for order to be restored in the Aegean, Syria, and Canaan by the formation of new political communities on the miniature scale of city-states. The new society in Syria and Canaan forged ahead of the new society in the Aegean in the first chapter of their contemporary histories. The Phoenicians had invented the alphabet, survived the twelfth-century Völkerwanderung, and discovered the Atlantic while the Hellenic civilization was still contending with anarchy; but the Phoenician, Philistine, and Hebrew communities in Canaan, the Aramaean communities in Syria, and the refugee Hittite communities there and astride the Taurus were, none of them, in a position to threaten the Hellenic society in its homeland. The most that the Phoenicians and the Hittites' maritime representatives, the Etruscans (Tyrrhenians), could do was to compete with the Hellenes for the command of the Black Sea and the Western Mediterranean; and, during the first two hundred years or so of this competition, the Hellenes were winning the lion's share of the spoils that all these rival Levantine adventurers were taking from backward native peoples.

By the end of the first half of the sixth century B.C. the Hellenes had won the competition for the Black Sea decisively. The only surviving traces of their rivals' activities in this quarter were the cult of Phoenician 'Great Gods' ('Kabirim') on the North-Aegean island of Samothrace and the survivors of Etruscan settlements on the island of Lemnos, just outside the entrance to the Dardanelles, who eventually took refuge inside it, at two places on the south shore of the Sea of Marmara. In the Western Mediterranean the Phoenicians had managed to retain only three bridgeheads on the island of Sicily, at its Western extremity, while the Etruscans' lodgement on the west coast of Italy had been hemmed in between a 'Great Hellas' in the 'toe' and 'instep' of Italy and a chain of Hellenic outposts, founded by Phocaea and her daughter

Massilia (Marseilles), that extended from the French riviera to the Catalonian *costa brava*. The whole eastern and southern seaboard of Sicily — the key to the command of the west — had been occupied by a continuous belt of colonial Hellenic city-states.

The Hellenes' victory over their Phoenician and Etruscan rivals in this first phase of the competition between them had been due to their enjoyment of three advantages: a superiority in numbers, a more favourably situated base of operations, and an immunity from attack by the first of the new great powers that were to arise, one after another, in South-West Asia.

In point of numbers, the five or six Phoenician mother-cities strung along the coast of Canaan and Syria between Mount Carmel and the mouth of the River Orontes were no match for the hundreds of Hellenic city-states in Asia, the Aegean Archipelago, and Continental European Greece; and the home base of the Etruscans must have been smaller still, since the Etruscan settlers overseas not only lost contact with it but did not even preserve any precise memory of where it had lain. We are left to guess that these speakers of a non-Indo-European language must have come from some secluded stretch of the south coast of Anatolia — perhaps the rock-bound seaboard of Western Cilicia — that had not been reached either by Luvian-speaking invaders at the beginning of the second millennium B.C. or by Greek-speaking invaders towards the end of it.

The situation of the Hellenes' base of operations — blocking their two competitors' access to the Black Sea and flanking their access to the Western Mediterranean — reinforced the effect of their superiority in numbers. But perhaps their greatest advantage was the negative one of being out of range of the Assyrian and Babylonian militarism by which the unfortunate peoples of Syria and

Canaan were repeatedly harried from the ninth century B.C. until the sixth. In the course of the sixth century, however, there were political changes in the Western Mediterranean and in South-West Asia that brought about a reversal of fortunes. In the first place the overseas Phoenicians in Western Sicily, Southern Spain, and North-West Africa did in the sixth century, under pressure of Hellenic expansion, what the mother communities in Syria and the Lebanon had once done for a moment when in 853 B.C. they had joined forces to foil the Assyrian invader in the Battle of Qarqar. In the sixth century the colonial Phoenician city-states put themselves permanently under the single command of one of their number, Carthage ('the New City'); and Carthage made an anti-Hellenic alliance with the overseas Etruscans, so that the Western Hellenes now found themselves confronted by their competitors' united forces. In the second place the fortunes of the Phoenician mother-cities along the coast of Canaan and Syria were retrived as a result of the replacement of the Assyrians and their Babylonian successors by the Persians. The conquest of the Babylonian Empire by the Persian empire-builder Cyrus in 538 B.C. brought liberation to the Phoenicians as well as to the Jews. But the Phoenician city-states gained still more from this political revolution than the Jewish exiles. The Persian imperial government took them into partnership with itself and endowed each of them with a miniature empire of its own. This association with the Persian Empire on terms of special privilege gave the Phoenicians a powerful military, political, and economic backing. Their hinterland had become friendly instead of hostile, and an immense field of economic enterprise, stretching eastwards into Central Asia and India, was now thrown open to them. This sudden improvement in the position of the Phoenician mother-cities must have strengthened the position of the Phoenicians overseas, since they, unlike the overseas Etruscans, had never lost touch with their homeland. These two revolutionary changes, together, tilted the balance against the Hellenes sufficiently to bring their overseas expansion to a halt before the sixth century closed. But, more than a hundred and fifty years before that, the increasing resistance that this expansion had been encountering had already begun to have an effect on the internal life of the Hellenic society.

The population of the Hellenic World was still increasing (it went on increasing until the second century B.C.), and the slowing-down and eventual stoppage of its expansion, without any increase in production per head or per acre, turned the pressure of the continuing increase in population inwards. The consequent social tension in the domestic life of the city-states was aggravated by a recent military innovation and a subsequent economic one. About the year 730 B.C. the phalanx (close order) formation for infantry warfare was introduced in the Hellenic World. About the year 650 B.C. coinage was invented somewhere on the Asian side of the Aegean, and its use spread to the rest of the Hellenic World from about the year 625 B.C. onwards.

Fighting in formation was a more efficient method of warfare for heavy-armed foot soldiers than single combats between champions, but it had not been a practical possibility so long as metal armour had been too costly for all but the richest members of the community. The replacement of expensive bronze by cheap iron, which had begun in the Aegean area about the time of the Völkerwanderung and had been completed during the subsequent dark age, brought within the means of the yeoman farmer an equipment that had previously been the monopoly of a small aristocracy, and the consequent large increase in the number of a city-state's heavy-armed fighting-men made it possible, for the first time in the Hellenic World, to make the weight of metal tell by substituting, for the chariot-borne champion, a phalanx of peasant infantry, whose virtue lay not in individual physical prowess but in drill and discipline and *esprit de corps*.

The least efficient piece of the Hellenic fighting-man's equipment had been the round shield. If it was kept small it was handy in the chariot but gave little protection in the field; if it was made large enough to cover the body from neck to thighs, it became so heavy that the left arm and hand had to be wholly employed in wielding it; and even then it bulged out superfluously beyond the left shoulder, while leaving the legs uncovered, so that these had to be encased in metal greaves that weighed the man down still more. In the new phalanx warfare the cumbrous round shield of larger diameter was made to serve the cause of military *moral*. In close-order formation, the leftward bulge of each man's shield gave cover to the next man to the left; so, in face of the enemy, it was safer to keep in formation than to break ranks, and a soldier who did fall out would be depriving himself of cover from the next man to the right, besides exposing his left-hand neighbour. Moreover, it was difficult to flee with so unwieldly an impediment dragging on one's arm, and it was therefore made a point of honour not to throw one's shield away. 'I trust that my son will return either with his shield or on it' is one of the many characteristic remarks that are attributed to Spartan mothers. The body of a soldier who had died an honourable death in the field was borne proudly home on the dead man's shield by his surviving comrades. The clumsy implement that had become the touch-stone of valour came to be known as '*the* armament' ('hoplon') *par excellence*, and the heavy-armed fighter in the phalanx as a 'shield-wielder' ('hoplitês').

The yeoman hoplite's close-order formation and *esprit de corps* put the aristocratic champion out of business. He tried to retain his paramountcy by copying from the Nomads (who in the eighth and seventh centuries B.C. had made one of their periodical eruptions out of the Eurasian Steppe) their latest equestrian trick of riding instead of driving. But the cavalry that replaced the traditional chariotry in the Hellenic World at the time of the introduction of the infantry phalanx did not become the premier arm till the age of Alexander the Great, some four centuries later. During the first three and a half centuries of phalanx warfare in the Hellenic World, the finest of all Hellenic hoplite phalanxes was the Lacedaemonian (Lacedaemon was the official name for the Spartan state, including its satellite communities of perioeci); and, as late as the fourth century B.C., the Lacedaemonian phalanx included a *corps d'élite* known as 'the Knights'; but in the fourth century these fought neither as old-fashioned charioteers nor as up-to-date cavalry. They took their places in the infantry line as the bodyguard of the Spartan kings, and they obtained these coveted places by military merit, not by aristocratic right of birth.

At Sparta the yeoman hoplite had come, perhaps as early as half-way through the seventh century B.C., to be recognised as the peer of his aristocratic comrade in the ranks. In other Hellenic city-states he was demanding what had already been granted to him at Sparta. Now that he had risen to be the community's military mainstay, he felt that he had acquired a claim to a share in the management of public affairs. When, so far from being given political satisfaction, he found himself suffering economically, he became determined to redress the economic balance in his own favour by winning the political rights to which his new military importance seemed to entitle him.

In an age when a recurrent shortage of land was making it harder for yeomen and agricultural labourers to make both ends meet, they were reduced to borrowing, at interest, from aristocratic landowners who still had a surplus to lend; and borrowing was facilitated by the invention of coinage. A coin is a piece of metal issued, as a medium of exchange, by a state whose image and superscription it bears. The state's hall-mark guarantees that the coin is of the value signified on the face of it. As its *quid pro quo* for giving the public this guarantee, the issuing state assumes a monopoly of the right to issue coinage within its own territory. What was new about this Hellenic invention was the intervention of states. Private individuals had used standard weights of metal as media of exchange since the dawn of civilization in the lower basin of the Tigris and Euphrates. But the new development of an old device made financial transactions easier — particularly the business of borrowing and lending — and, when the borrower saddled himself with obligations that he could not meet, this brought him and his household and his property into the lender's power. The peasant-proprietor had to mortgage his land, and the landless agricultural labourer had to pledge his and his children's personal freedom, as security; and, if they failed to meet their obligations, the peasant lost his land and the labourer became a slave whom his creditor had the right to sell overseas. The creditors were taking a grossly unjust advantage, and their victims turned savage. They demanded not only that their own liberty and land should be restored to them, but also that the large landowners' estates should be confiscated and divided up, with the dual object of breaking the large landowners' economic power and alleviating the land-shortage that had arisen from the slowing down of the Hellenic World's expansion overseas.

These pressures and grievances worked themselves out

in a sweeping transformation of society in the course of a hundred and fifty years. By the date, shortly before the close of the sixth century B.C., when overseas expansion was brought completely to a halt, the aristocracy in most of the leading Hellenic city-states had been deprived of its privileges; property-qualifications had been substituted for birthright as the basis of the political franchise; the larger landed properties had mostly been divided up; and there had been a revolutionary change in the Hellenic World's economy. This change had been the most important of all, because it had solved the economic problem created by the slowing down and eventual stoppage of the Hellenic World's expansion.

In most of the communities in which these changes had taken place they had been made by force through the agency of dictators ('tyrants'). There had been an epidemic of these dictatorships, beginning in the Isthmian states (Corinth, Sicyon, Megara) and spreading first to the Asian states (Miletus, Mytilene) and eventually to Athens. None of these dictatorships were long-lived. They were overthrown in the third generation at the latest. Sparta was singular in managing to get through without either falling under a dictatorship or making the economic revolution. At Sparta, as we have seen, commoners were provided with land-allotments at the expense, not of the Spartan aristocracy, but of Sparta's conquered Messenian neighbours; and the property qualification for ranking as a Spartan 'peer' was the minimal one of making the hoplite's contribution in kind to the rations of his mess out of the Messenian land-allotment that had been assigned to him. Sparta averted tension within her own citizen body at the price of creating tension between herself and her serfs; and she managed to maintain her hoplite army by exploiting her serfs' land and labour without departing from the old-fashioned economy of subsistence farming.

The existence of revolutionary dictatorships in neighbouring states seemed to the Lacedaemonian Government to be a menace to the peculiar solution of common social problems that Sparta had found for herself. Accordingly the Spartan authorities used their military power on land to overthrow dictatorships in Continental European Greece, as far afield as Athens inclusive. This was not a difficult feat, since these régimes had fulfilled and outlived their mission before Sparta took action against them. The Isthmian states now settled down under conservative régimes based on an entente between the hoplite yeomen and the business men who had previously supported the dictatorship as an instrument for deposing the former hereditary aristrocracy. These new régimes entered into permanent alliances with Sparta, which gave her the initiative in the making of the allies' common foreign policy. The sequel to the overthrow of the dictatorship at Athens in 510 B.C. was strikingly different. When Sparta intervened here for the second time, only two years later, at the call of the Athenian conservatives, her expeditionary force was compelled to capitulate and withdraw by a coalition between the Athenian hoplite yeomen and the non-land-owning majority of the population. The new régime was based on this coalition. It did not enter into an alliance with Sparta or accept Spartan leadership. It boldly went its own way, and it lasted for a hundred years, during which it made history.

Athens had already been going her own way since an early stage in the social transformation through which the Hellenic World had been passing for the last hundred and fifty years. A first attempt at establishing a dictatorship at Athens had miscarried. The contending parties had then tried to arrive at a solution that would be acceptable to both of them by agreeing, for the governmental year 594 B.C., to confer special powers on the chief annual magistrate, and to elect to this office a citizen in whose impartiality and disinterestedness they both had confidence. Solon, the man of their choice, lived up to their expectations. He staved off a violent revolution by cancelling the mortgages on debtors' lands and the enslavement of their persons, and he made it illegal for the future to give and receive loans on these securities. He also introduced a new political constitution, based on a gradation of property-qualifications, which was rather more liberal than the constitutions adopted in the Isthmian states a generation later. On the other hand he rejected the demand for the dividing up of the large estates, and thereby deliberately threw away a chance of abusing his trust by making himself dictator. He failed to save Athens from falling into the hands of a dictator in the next generation. The revolutionaries remained unsatisfied; and Peisistratus, who did not feel Solon's scruples, cast himself for the dictator's part and succeeded at his second attempt. Yet, for a dictator, Peisistratus, too, was a moderate. He ruled Attica, as Augustus was to rule the whole Hellenic World in a later chapter of its history, by manipulating the established constitution instead of openly subverting it. His economic policy, like Solon's, was important. We may guess that he took the revolutionary step, from which Solon had shrunk, of dividing up the large estates; but he also carried farther the constructive economic revolution which Solon had initiated; and it was owing to this that, after the expulsion from Athens of Peisistratus's son Hipparchus in 510 B.C., Athens did not go the same way as Sicyon, Corinth, and Megara.

The economic revolution was a change-over from an economic régime of farming for subsistence to one of specialized production, industrial as well as agricultural, for export in exchange for imports of foodstuffs and raw materials. An acre of Attic soil could support more

Athenian mouths if, instead of being sown with cereals for home consumption, it were planted with vines and olives producing wine and oil that could be exchanged for cereals grown in Sicily, Egypt, and the Ukraine. The net gain for the Athenian economy would be the greater if the liquid produce of the Attic soil were conveyed to the purchaser in attractively decorated earthenware containers. In this way the wheat-fields of the Ukraine, Egypt, and Sicily, the sheep runs of the Anatolian plateau, the mines of Etruria, and even Carthage's jealously guarded hinterland in North-West Africa and South-Western Spain could be annexed to the Hellenic World for commercial purposes, at a time when a halt was being called, by Carthaginian and Etruscan resistance, to the expansion of the area colonized by Hellenic settlers and cultivated by their hands. Solon understood this, because he was a business man. The permanent service that he did to Athens was the stimulus that he gave to the export of Attic-grown wine and oil and to the immigration of foreign-born potters and other skilled craftsmen.

Did Solon do this pioneer work for his own country only, or for the whole Hellenic World? We are in danger of over-estimating the role of Athens in Hellas during the sixth, fifth, and fourth centuries B.C. because so much of the story, as we now have it, comes, directly or indirectly, from Athenian sources. Down to Solon's day, Attica had been a backward country. It had played no part in the expansion of the Hellenic World by colonization overseas. At the opening of the sixth century B.C. business men were still rare in Athens; and one reason why Solon was singled out by his countrymen to act as a mediator was because the rare business man was a neutral figure in a still predominantly agricultural community. There will have been a larger business community in contemporary Miletus and Corinth; for, unlike Athens, whose home territory was unusually large, these two states owned only a minimum amount of cultivable land, and therefore they had been driven first into colonization and then into trade and industry. Miletus had learnt to make her living by trading luxury goods for Ukrainian grain and by spinning and weaving Phrygian wool; and pottery manufactured and painted at Corinth in the 'Proto-Corinthian' style made its appearance in the international market about a hundred years earlier than Attic black-figure ware, which did not begin to come on to the international market till about twenty years after Solon had given his stimulus to the Athenian potteries. Yet, before the close of the sixth century B.C., the Attic ware had captured the market, and the decoration of it had passed over to the more difficult red-figure technique. The enfranchisement of the non-land-owning element in the population of Athens after the overthrow of the dictatorship there is another indication that, by this date, the process of industrialization had already gone farther than it yet had in the Isthmian states, where the business men and the yeomen in concert were still able to keep the industrial workers out of power. It is true that, by comparison with the pre-revolutionary aristocratic régime, the post-revolutionary Athenian 'democracy' and Isthmian 'oligarchy' were merely variants of one and the same new constitutional pattern. The democracy established at Athens by Cleisthenes in 507 B.C. was a régime based on a property-qualification that had been reduced almost to zero. Similarly the Isthmian oligarchies were régimes in which so large a part of the adult male population had been enfranchised that it had become necessary, here too, as well as in democratic Attica, for public business to be dealt with first by a grand committee, representing a fair sample of the voters, before it could be brought before a plenary assembly in a form in which it could be handled by so unwieldy a body. Yet, notwithstanding the fundamental similarity between these two types of post-revolutionary constitution, the difference between them in the range of the franchise was all-important. In an industrialized Hellenic World towards the close of the sixth century B.C., the oarsman and the artisan had won the key position in society that had been won about two hundred years earlier by the yeoman-hoplite. This new military and economic fact was first translated into political terms in the Athenian constitution of 507 B.C. Athenian democracy was 'the wave of the future'.

Thus, in the course of the sixth century B.C., the political repercussions of the economic revolution had unseated the old hereditary aristocracy in most Hellenic states. Yet the aristocracy's prestige outlived its privileges for about a hundred years. Even in democratic Athens the radical politician Pericles, who was in power from 462 to 430 B.C., found it a political asset to be an Alcmaeonid on his mother's side; and a fifth-century Siceliot despot or Aeginetan business man would exert himself to qualify as an aristocrat by winning an event in one of the four Panhellenic festivals and commissioning the Theban poet Pindar to celebrate his victory in an ode.

The seeds of the economic revolution which attained its fulfilment at Athens had, no doubt, been sown as early as the beginning of the Hellenic World's territorial expansion overseas. Colonization presupposes navigation, and the navigators who opened the way for the farmer colonists will have been traders as well as pirates. Moreover, there were some Hellenic colonies whose location must have been governed primarily by commercial considerations. Cumae, the oldest Hellenic colony in the west and also the most distant until the foundation of Massilia, looks like the relic of an unsuccessful attempt to capture the mineral resources of Elba and the adjoining Italian mainland that were won by the Tyrrhenians. In the opposite quarter, Poseideïum, at the mouth of the Syrian river Orontes, was certainly a partially successful attempt to break the Phoenicians' monopoly of the trade between the Mediterranean and the Tigris-Euphrates basin. Yet, down almost to the close of the sixth century B.C., the dominant aim of Hellenic colonization was the acquisition of more agricultural land.

For example, when the Megarians colonized the shores of the southern end of the Bosphorus, they sited their first settlement at Calchedon, commanding the Bithynian riviera along the north shore of the Gulf of Ismid, and not at Byzantium, which has a barren hinterland. Calchedon was planted in 685 B.C., Byzantium not till 667 B.C. Herodotus, writing more than two hundred years later, relates that the Persian statesman Megabazus, when he passed that way in or after the year 513 B.C. and ascertained that Calchedon had been founded eighteen years earlier than Byzantium, nicknamed Calchedon 'the city of the blind'. How could its founders have allowed themselves to miss their chance of occupying the then still vacant site of Byzantium, with its incomparable harbour commanding the navigation of the Straits? The answer was, of course, that the seventh-century Megarians were in search, not of trade, but of fields, and that they would have been blind if they had occupied barren Byzantium in preference to the fertile Bithynian riviera. Whether the *mot* attributed to Megabazus was really his, or whether it was the invention of some fifth-century Hellenic mind, it is evidence that, by the date at which it was coined, the original purpose of Hellenic overseas settlement had been forgotten. The *mot* takes it for granted that commerce, not agriculture, is the principal source of an Hellenic city-state's livelihood. This had, indeed, come to be the fact before the close of the sixth century B.C., as a result of the economic revolution in the Hellenic World which that century had witnessed. But, if by this time the Hellenes had taken the result of the economic revolution for granted, they had not taken its political implications to heart.

By the end of the sixth century B.C. the Hellenes had solved the problem of providing for a still expanding population within a no longer expanding agricultural domain by transforming the economic structure of their world from a collection of minute water-tight compartments, each consisting of the territory of a single city-state, into an economic pool including, not only the Hellenic World itself, but most of the other regions, round the shores of the Mediterranean and the Black Sea, that were included, 500 years later, within the political frontiers of the Roman Empire. This international economic revolution had enabled the Hellenic city-states to ease the domestic tension which, within each of them, had been producing civil wars, political revolutions, and dictatorships. They had succeeded in recovering internal stability under new régimes which, whether they were called oligarchies or were called democracies, gave the franchise to a relatively large percentage of the adult male population by contrast with the former aristocratic régimes. But these solutions of the economic problem of the Hellenic World and of the political problem inside each of its component city-states were not enough, by themselves, to restabilize the Hellenic society.

The economic revolution had made the city-states economically interdependent while leaving each of them politically sovereign over its own little house, and this was a disharmony that could not last. Either the city-states must revert to being economically as well as politically self-contained, at the cost of a fall in their standard of living that would throw them back into starvation and civil war, or else they must surrender enough of their individual sovereignty to allow of the creation of some kind of Panhellenic political framework to match the Panhellenic economic régime that was now already a going concern.

The road to this now obligatory political goal was blocked by a religious obstacle. The Hellenic city-states had, as we have seen, come to be idolized by their citizens. Could these city-state-worshippers bring themselves to transfer their political allegiance from their deified city-states to a Panhellenic body politic? This would require a spiritual revolution. Could they make this, and make it fast enough to save themselves from disaster? At this critical moment the Persians gave the Hellenes a golden opportunity to solve the political problem that had arisen out of the solution of an economic one. The Persians drove the Hellenes to co-operate for self-defence by setting out to annex the whole Hellenic World to their empire.

VI

THE RESPONSE TO THE CHALLENGE OF PERSIAN AGGRESSION FROM THE EAST

THE Persians had suddenly impinged on the Hellenic World when, in 547 B.C., their first emperor, Cyrus II, King of Anshan, had conquered Lydia, in the immediate hinterland of Hellas-in-Asia. In the first half of the sixth century the Lydians had imposed their suzerainty on all the continental Asian Hellenic city-states except Miletus. The Lydians' Persian successors now compelled the Lydians' Asian Hellene subjects to submit to them in turn, and they succeeded in imposing their suzerainty on Miletus as well. In 525 B.C. the second Persian emperor Cambyses conquered Egypt, and about 513 the third emperor, Darius I, crossed the Bosphorus and succeeded in annexing South-Eastern Europe up to the south bank of the Lower Danube. These last two conquests placed the economic life of the whole Hellenic World at the Persians' mercy, since Egypt and the Ukraine (which was accessible to the Hellenes only through the Straits) had become the granaries of Hellas as a result of her sixth-century economic revolution.

Incorporation in the Persian Empire offered the same advantage to the Asian Hellenes as it offered to the Phoenicians. It opened up to them a vast commercial hinterland. Like the Phoenicians, again, and unlike the European Hellenes, the Asian Hellenes had suffered adversities that might have schooled them to appreciate the value of the Persian Peace. Though they had been just out of range of Assyrian militarism, they had been hit by the eruption of the Eurasian Nomads into South-West Asia in the seventh century B.C., and in the sixth century they had lost their independence to the Lydians. The Lydians, however, were neighbours who had been in process of Hellenization; the Persians were outlandish semi-barbarians from the far-away highlands of Southern Iran, and they made their suzerainty irksome by exercising it through the agency of local dictators just at the time when dictatorships were being overthrown in Continental European Greece. In 499 B.C. the Asian Hellenes deposed their dictators and revolted against their Persian overlords. The revolt spread northwards to the city-states along the shores of the Straits and south-eastwards to Cyprus and eventually also to Caria. It was not stamped out till 494 B.C., when the insurgents' fleet was defeated by the Phoenician fleet and Miletus, which had taken the lead in the revolt, was recaptured by the Persian land forces and was rendered impotent by the deportation of her people into the interior. In the first campaign of the war the insurgents had been aided by two European Greek city-states, Athens and Eretria. Darius concluded that the hold which he had managed to re-establish over his disaffected Asian Hellenic subjects would not be secure unless and until he had brought all the rest of the Hellenic World under Persian rule. Already, before the outbreak of the Asian Hellenes' revolt, he had sent a reconnoitring expedition as far west as the 'toe' of Italy under the guidance of his court physician Dêmocêdes, who happened to be a native of the Italiot Hellenic city-state Croton. Immediately after the suppression of the Asian revolt he re-established his authority over his continental European dominions and extended these as far west as Macedon inclusive. By 490 B.C. he was ready to retaliate against Eretria and Athens.

The contemporary political scene in European Hellas must have seemed to Darius to offer him a good chance of taking his intended victims one by one; for, in her political life, Hellas was still a house divided against itself. The two strongest states, Sparta and Athens, were not on friendly terms. Sparta was still resenting Athens' recent insubordination, while Athens still suspected Sparta of intending to reassert her claim to hegemony. Each of the two had also made enemies among its nearer neighbours. Sparta was at daggers drawn with Argos; Athens with Aegina, Thebes, and Chalcis. About the year 669 B.C., in the early days of phalanx warfare, Argos had inflicted on Sparta a signal defeat which may have given the Messenians the opportunity for their first great revolt. After Sparta had re-subjugated Messene and had turned herself into an armed camp, the balance of military power between Sparta and Argos inclined in Sparta's favour. In the sixth century, Sparta conquered from Argos the border district of Cynuria, along the east coast of the Peloponnese; and in 494 (?) B.C. the Spartan King Cleomenes I dealt her a crushing blow, which left her temporarily crippled but irreconcilable. The Argives would rather lose their independence to Persia than save it by fighting shoulder to shoulder with their Spartan arch-enemies. As for Chalcis and Thebes, Athens had made them both pay heavily for jointly attacking her just when she had adopted her democratic constitution. After defeating their united forces, she had annexed from Chalcis the Lelantine Plain, that had once been a bone of contention between Chalcis and Eretria; and she had established a protectorate over Thebes' former unwilling satellite the little Boeotian city-state Plataea, which commanded the westernmost of the passes leading out of Boeotia into Attica. The quarrel between Aegina and Athens was a commercial one. Like Athens, Aegina had started late but had then had a meteoric rise. She had been making her fortune in the trade with Egypt. These two parvenu states hated one another because each felt that there was not enough room left in the Hellenic World for both of them.

These Continental European Greek feuds had not yet involved the overseas Hellenic communities in the West; and, in the relatively young colonial society, where local loyalties had not yet had time to become hard set, two principalities, each comprising a number of city-states, were being built up round Syracuse and round Akragas respectively. The two dynasties of despots that were doing this constructive work were in good relations with one another. In concert they would be a power to be reckoned with. But Darius could count on their being immobilized by the threat of a Carthaginian attack on their home territory.

Yet, in planning the conquest of the still independent portion of the Hellenic World, Darius and his successor Xerxes made the same two miscalculations that proved disastrous to the British when they set out to conquer Afghanistan in 1839. The Persians underestimated both the spiritedness of their new adversaries and their readiness to suspend their family quarrels in order to make common cause against a foreign invader.

Up to this point the Persian Empire in South-West Asia and Egypt, like the British empire in India, had been built up rapidly and easily because, so far, the empire-builders had been dealing with peoples whose spirit had already been broken by harrowing experiences. The Persians had hitherto been following in the tracks of the Assyrians and the Eurasian Nomads; and the victims of these scourges had been ready for the rest-cure which was offered to them by the easy-going Persian régime. Even so, the newly built empire had nearly been broken up during the interregnum after Cambyses' mysterious death; and, from first to last, the Egyptians and Babylonians were too conscious of their past glories to be able to resist the impulse to revolt against the Persians whenever they saw an opportunity. In attacking the European Hellenes the Persians were challenging people who had not passed under either the Assyrian or the Scythian harrow. The enterprise was therefore much more hazardous than any of their comparatively facile past exploits; but they failed to realize this in advance, and so marched blindly into disaster.

The famous story must be summarized briefly. In 490 B.C. Darius sent an expeditionary force by sea which captured Eretria and deported its people but was then repulsed ignominiously from the shores of Attica on the beaches of Marathon by the Athenian hoplites under the command of Miltiades, the ex-dictator of the Gallipoli Peninsula (Thracian Chersonese), who had joined in the Asian revolt and had therefore had to flee to his native Athens. The Athenian phalanx won this victory with no aid except from the Plataeans; but it was significant that the Spartans sent help, though this arrived too late to take part in the action. First an Egyptian and then a Babylonian revolt delayed the next Persian attempt on European Hellas for ten years. When Xerxes marched in 480 B.C., he came in full force and advanced overland, across the Dardanelles and round the north coast of the Aegean, with his fleet accompanying him. This time the Persian preparations had been thorough, but the delay had been fatal; for a rich new vein of silver had been struck in the Attic mines at Laurium, and in 482 B.C. the Athenian statesman Themistocles had induced his countrymen to spend this windfall on building a large fleet of up-to-date three-oar-power warships, instead of frittering it away on a bonus for each citizen. By the time when Xerxes sighted Mount Olympus, this new Athenian navy was ready, and it proved to be the decisive factor in the war.

The Hellenic land-forces under Spartan leadership did not try to hold the invaders at the pass of Tempe, and failed to hold them at Thermopylae. This second pass had been turned before the Spartan King Leonidas and his three hundred men sacrificed their lives. Continental European Greece submitted to the Persians as far as Boeotia inclusive. The Thebans welcomed Xerxes for the sake of having their revenge on Athens. The Argives, who had been bled white in their latest battle with the Spartans and were also encircled by Sparta and her allies, remained non-belligerent, waiting to welcome Xerxes in their turn, when he arrived, for the sake of having their revenge on Sparta. Thus barely half the military and naval forces of Continental European Greece turned out to meet the common enemy. This remnant, however, summoned up just enough resolution, endurance, and cohesion to defeat him.

The Hellenic Allies' land forces, under Spartan command, did not attempt to defend Attica but retreated to the Isthmus of Corinth; but this exposure of Attica to invasion did not move the Athenians to submit. They evacuated the whole population of their mainland territory to the island of Salamis, and did not flinch at seeing the Attic countryside being ravaged and the city of Athens being sacked (the Persians burnt the temples on the citadel). The Allies' fleet covered Salamis by taking up a position in the narrow waters between the island and the mainland; and the crisis of the war came when the fleet's Corinthian commander proposed that the fleet, too, should withdraw to the Isthmus. This would have forced the Athenians to come to terms with Xerxes; and, since the Athenian navy was the mainstay of the Allies' fleet, the

Persians would have then secured a decisive superiority over the Peloponnesians at sea, and could have outflanked the Isthmus over the water, as they had outflanked Thermopylae overland. They could have landed their troops on the coast of Argos, and taken the Isthmus in the rear. These disasters were foreseen and forestalled by Themistocles. He slyly sent intelligence to Xerxes that the Hellenic fleet was in a trap, and inveigled him into blocking the narrow waters at both ends and then giving battle in the narrows, where numbers could not tell. The Allies won a crushing naval victory; the command of the sea passed to them; the Persian army's line of communications across the Dardanelles was now in immediate danger of being cut; and Xerxes withdrew to the Asian side, leaving part of his army to winter in Northern Greece with a view to taking the offensive again next year. Meanwhile, the Carthaginians had been making an attack on the Siceliot Hellenes and had been defeated in a land battle on the River Himera as heavily as the Persians in the naval battle off Salamis.

The Battle of Himera was decisive. It ended the war in the West in the Hellenes' favour; and the Carthaginian prisoners taken were so numerous that the Akragantines were able to convert the cultivation of their extensive countryside from subsistence farming to specialized agricultural production by turning their prisoners into plantation slaves — thus inaugurating in the West a new and sinister economic revolution which reached its climax three or four hundred years later. In the Aegean there was a second campaign in 479 B.C. In the spring of 479 B.C. the commander of the Persian army left in Northern Greece, Mardonius, offered the Athenians tempting terms if they would change sides. The Athenians rejected the terms and called on the Peloponnesians to help them, with their land forces, to save the mainland of Attica from being occupied a second time. But the Peloponnesians did not move; the Persian army reoccupied Attica; and the Athenians are said to have had to threaten to capitulate in order to bring their allies into the field. Upon the approach of the Allies' united land forces, Mardonius withdrew into Boeotia, and the decisive land battle of the war was fought in the territory of Athens' Boeotian ally, Plataea. Mardonius's army was destroyed, and on the same day the Allies' fleet destroyed the Persian fleet off Cape Mycalê, on the coast of Continental Hellas-in-Asia. The Asian Hellenes immediately revolted again, and the Hellenic sea and land forces spent the rest of that campaigning season in ejecting the Persians from the shores of the Straits. By the end of 479 B.C. the Persians had lost nearly all their European possessions except Byzantium and the fortress of Doriscus on the coast of Western Thrace; they had lost the command of the Dardanelles; and they had lost Hellas-in-Asia. Their north-west frontier now stood once more where it had stood before Cyrus had reduced the Asian Hellenes to submission in and after 547 B.C.

The Persians had not only failed to conquer the Hellenic World; they had now fallen into danger of seeing the Persian Empire conquered by the Hellenes. Their loss of the naval command of the Eastern Mediterranean in the battles of Salamis and Mycalê was not so serious for them as the establishment, in the battles of Marathon and Thermopylae, of the Hellenic hoplite's ascendancy over the Persian bowman. This archer, discharging a rain of arrows from behind a light oblong wicker shield that covered both body and legs when it was planted on the ground, ought to have been more then a match for the hoplite, with his heavy round shield and short one-handed stabbing spear. It was the hoplite's physical training that gave him the victory by enabling him, in spite of the impediment weighing on his left arm, to cross no-man's land at the double and engage the archer at close quarters before he had time to get in a murderous number of shots. Within a hundred and fifty years of the date of the battle of Plataea, the Persian Empire was, in fact, overthrown by an Hellenic expeditionary force. The result of the two campaigns of 480 and 479 B.C. was thus obviously a failure for the Persians; but, less obviously, it was a failure for the Hellenes too. While the Persians had suffered a serious defeat and a smarting loss of outlying territory, the Hellenes had failed to profit by their opportunity of achieving the political unity that was called for by the already accomplished economic unification of the Hellenic World. Their momentary co-operation had been, on the whole, exemplary. The Athenians had acquiesced in a Corinthian high command at sea, as well as in a Spartan high command on land. Athenian and Spartan hoplites, and Athenian and Aeginetan oarsmen, had gone into battle side by side. Yet this comradeship in arms had given new occasions for reciprocal suspicion and resentment; and, within less than fifty years, this discord engendered an Atheno-Peloponnesian war that wrecked the Hellenic civilization. The Persians had the satisfaction of watching the Hellenes bring themselves to ruin a hundred years before they met their own fate at Hellenic hands.

Meanwhile, the half-century (478–432 B.C.) that saw the Hellenic World heading through internal dissension towards self-inflicted disaster was also the time that saw the arts in Hellas burst into flower. They had been germinating ever since the darkness that had descended on the Aegean after the Völkerwanderung had been dispelled by the dawn of the age of expansion. They were now brought to a sudden florescence by the exhilarating effect of the apparently miraculous victory which had snatched the Hellenes out of the jaws of the deadliest danger that they had ever yet encountered. This outburst of creative genius was as brief as the blossoming of the Mediterranean scrub in spring-time, but its works became an everlasting possession for the Hellenes themselves and for posterity.

The stimulus was felt by all Hellenic peoples that had taken part in the struggle for life with the Persians. In a temporarily liberated Hellas-in-Asia the encounter with the far-flung Persian Empire and with the still farther ranging Central Asian Nomads expanded the geographical horizon and gave a proportionate stimulus to the intellect. The Carian historian Herodotus, who had been born a Persian subject and lived to write a history of the antecedents and outcome of the Perso-Hellenic war of 480–479 B.C., brought within his purview the greater part of the Old World, from the Straits of Gibraltar and the sources of the Nile to China — whose cultivated inhabitants had been labelled 'Trans-Northerlies' by some Hellenic explorer who had reached his far eastern objective but had lost his bearings on the way. On the island of Cos the same post-war period saw the rise of an empirical school of medicine associated with the name of Hippocrates. In contemporary European Greece the greatest achievements inspired by the common stimulus were, not scientific, but aesthetic. The Peloponnesian monument of the Panhellenic experience of exhilaration was the statuary on the temple of Zeus at Olympia. But the Peloponnesians were outshone by the Athenians, who had made both the greatest sacrifices in the common cause and the greatest contributions to the common victory. Attic drama, architecture, and sculpture all attained their peak within the span of those forty-seven years.

The fifth-century Attic drama ('ritual act') was a transfiguration of a traditional religious song and dance that was associated with the worship of the immigrant Thracian god Dionysus and was designed, not for the edification or amusement of spectators, but for the stimulation of the fertility of Nature by sympathetic magic. The original theme of comedy ('carnival opera') had been the god's marriage; the theme of tragedy ('goat opera') had been his death. These had been collective performances by dancing choirs of mummers, wearing masks like the performers in Japanese No-plays and masquerading as lecherous animals in order to stimulate Nature's procreative powers. This hallowed indecency was a common feature of comedy and the fourth (so-called 'satyr') play in a set of four tragedies.

Attic drama never lost touch with its religious origins. It was always performed in the theatre of Dionysus at Athens under the presidency of the god's Athenian priest; but in the course of three generations it was transformed by the genius of creative poets, of whom the two chief pioneers were Aeschylus (525–456 B.C.) and Sophocles (495–406 B.C.). These inspired innovators detached first one and eventually two or three individual actors from the choir and interspersed the choral dances with dramatic dialogues; and they did not confine themselves to the two traditional Dionysiac themes. They drew upon the whole range of Hellenic legend, and they brought on to the stage not only the heroes but the heroines of epic poetry. In an age in which the Athenian politician Pericles was telling the living women of Attica to make themselves inconspicuous, the legendary women of the age of the Völkerwanderung, impersonated by male actors, were holding the Attic stage. The playwrights had transformed an antique religious rite into a novel secular art. Their work reached its greatest heights while this tranformation was taking place.

Fifth-century Attic sculptors and architects found their

opportunity in the reconstruction of the temples and statues of the gods on the citadel of Athens that had been destroyed by the Persians in 480 B.C. The Propylaea ('Fore Gateway'), the temple of Wingless Victory (shorn of her wings to make sure that she should never fly away), the Erechtheum (shrine of the Earth-Shaker), and the Parthenon (shrine of the Virgin) still survive to testify to the genius of the architect Ictinus and his colleagues in translating timber-work into masonry. The genius of the sculptor Pheidias has to be taken on trust, as we have only inferior marble copies of his gold-and-ivory statue of Athênê in the inner sanctum of the Parthenon, and have even less evidence to go upon in reconstructing, with our mind's eye, his giant statue of Athênê Promachos ('Our Lady the Front-Line Fighter'). Presumably the Parthenon's beautiful metopes and frieze (now in the British Museum in London) were carved under Pheidias' superintendence.

The finest flower of Athens during 'the half-century' was not a statue, building, or play, but a soul. Socrates (470 (?)–399 B.C.) was a monumental mason in the hoplite income-group with a face like the mask of a mummer in a satyr-play; but, when you met him, you hardly noticed his features or thought of his profession; you were captivated by the personality behind the countenance, and you found yourself constrained to think the thoughts that he elicited from your mind by drawing you into conversation with him — especiallly when he fixed upon you his famous 'bull-like' stare. He had friends in all classes at Athens and also in many other states, including, for example, Thebes, which, in public life, was on bad terms with Athens during Socrates' life-time. But in making his personal friendships Socrates ignored national animosities, though he was punctilious in carrying out the military and other duties required of him, as an Athenian citizen, by Attic law. The feelings of affection and admiration that he inspired in people who knew him personally were tinged with awe; for the presence animating this quaint figure was no ordinary mortal's. The Delphic oracle once declared him to be the wisest of all human beings; and he was prompted by an inner voice which he used to call his 'familiar spirit' ('daimonion'). These promptings always took the negative form of telling him *not* to do something. He never disobeyed them. By 423 B.C. he had become famous enough for the playwright Aristophanes to make him the burlesque hero of one of his comedies. In *The Clouds* Socrates is presented as a professor of meteorology and sophistry (the art of manipulating words which had been invented, towards the end of 'the half century', in Sicily); but this caricature was the exact inverse of the authentic picture. At an early stage in his mental history, Socrates had turned away from the study of physical science which had been inaugurated in the sixth century B.C. by the Asian Hellenic philosophers, and which was best represented in Socrates' life-time by Hippocrates' observational school of medicine on the Asian island of Cos. Socrates had been struck by the findings of a contemporary Asian philosopher, Anaxagoras of Clazomenae, a distinguished physicist who had come to the conclusion that the ultimate reality was not matter but mind. Socrates directed his own attention to the study of human minds and human conduct, and he used the art of dialectic, not for getting the better of other people, but for making them his partners in a quest for truth.

One of Socrates' theses was that wrong-doing was due, not to wickedness, but to ignorance. If the wrong-doer had recognized that he was doing wrong, he would not have done it. Man is always trying to do right according to his lights. This Socratic view was also characteristically Hellenic; for an inclination to translate moral issues into non-moral terms was an Hellenic foible. In the idiom of the Greek language in Socrates' day, the usage of the word 'kalos', meaning 'beautiful', was stretched to stand for 'good' in the moral sense as well as in the aesthetic. This attempt to reduce moral issues to questions of taste or knowledge flew in the face of the evidence. It was challenged not only by the facts of everyday private life, but also by notorious contemporary public events. For example, the works of Pheidias and Ictinus on the citadel of Athens were manifestly beautiful, but it was also manifest that the action which had made these works possible had not been morally good, and, further, that this wrongful action had not been taken in ignorance of its true nature. In 443 B.C., when Socrates was about twenty-seven years old, the Athenian people had voted, at Pericles' instance, to pay for the replacement of the temples and statues, destroyed at Athens by the Persians in 480 B.C., by drawing on a fund collected from Athens' allies. This was dishonest, because the purpose for which the allies had originally agreed to contribute the money was the different one of providing for common defence against the Persian Empire. The Athenian people's action was also unjust, because they had been collecting the allies' contributions by force and were now misappropriating them without obtaining the contributors' consent. At the same time, the Athenians were seised of the moral issues involved, because the motion that they had passed at Pericles' instance had been opposed by Pericles' political opponent Thucydides son of Melesias. Thucydides had appealed to his countrymen's sense of honour; but they had voted in favour of Pericles' motion nevertheless, because its passage was going to ensure that the defence fund would still be spent on wages payable to Athenian citizens. They would be paid as quarrymen, carters, and masons, now that the conclusion of peace with Persia had put an end to their previous employment as oarsmen in the navy. This one discreditable transaction was sufficient proof that Socrates' analysis of human nature had been too sanguine.

VII

THE FAILURE OF SPARTA AND ATHENS TO ESTABLISH POLITICAL CONCORD

HELLENISM's half-century of florescence after the common victory over the Persians in 480–479 B.C. was cut short in 431 B.C. by the outbreak of a disastrous war between the Athenians and the Peloponnesians. The rest of the Hellenic World was drawn into the struggle, and the Hellenic civilization never recovered more than partially and temporarily from this self-inflicted wound. The disaster had its origins in the political and military history of the preceding fifty years; for this had been a golden age only in the fields of the visual arts and poetry. There had been a premonitory Atheno-Peloponnesian war in 459–445 B.C.; and, before that, the seeds of dissension had been sown during the very years in which the Peloponnesians and Athenians had been fighting side by side against the Persian invaders of European Greece.

In 480 B.C., Lacedaemonian leadership had been accepted by all states, including Athens, that had ventured to take part in the Hellenic resistance movement. Sparta's title to leadership of the Hellenic World was based on the superlative prowess of her hoplite phalanx and on the 'good neighbour' relation that she had established with her Laconian satellites ('perioeci') and her Isthmian allies. But the maintenance of Sparta's professional standing army of Spartiate 'peers' was dependent on the forced labour of her Messenian serfs, and the task of holding the serfs down left even a militarized Spartan community little strength to spare for action beyond Sparta's own frontiers. The Spartans' acquiescence in the humiliating failure, in 508 B.C., of their second military intervention in Athenian affairs is an indication that, before they were challenged by Persian aggression against Hellas, the Spartans were already aware that they had reached the end of their tether; and, when the role of leadership on a Panhellenic scale was thrust upon them by events, they accepted it only half-heartedly. The self-sacrifice of King Leonidas and his three hundred comrades at Thermopylae was, no doubt, the most romantic episode in the whole Helleno-Persian war; but it made no contribution to the Allies' subsequent victory; and, in sharp contrast to the Spartan soldier's war-record, the Spartan state's record was a poor one. After having failed to give Athens help in time in 490 B.C., Sparta nearly failed again in 479; and, all through, it was her policy to reduce commitments. At the critical moment in the campaign of 480 B.C. she did her worst to lose the war for the Allies by pressing for the withdrawal of the fleet from Salamis to the Isthmus. After the common victory in 479 had liberated Asian as well as Continental European Hellas, she proposed that the Asian Hellenes should be transplanted from their liberated homes to the ports of the European Hellenic states that had taken the Persian side, and that the fortifications of Athens should be left dismantled, to make sure that the Persians should not be able to use Athens as a base if they were to invade European Greece again.

Moreover, in 478 the glory won for Sparta by King Leonidas' heroic death in 480 was offset by the outrageous conduct of his temporary successor the Regent Pausanias. He had been in supreme command of the Allies at Plataea in 479; and, unfortunately for Sparta, he had not died on the field of honour, as Mardonius had, but had lived to take command of the Allies' siege of the Persian garrison in Byzantium. Here the Spartan Regent aped the behaviour of a Persian grandee and had to be recalled to Sparta in disgrace at the urgent demand of the Allies. Pausanias' débacle demonstrated that a Spartan 'peer', brought up under a peculiar national régime that repressed the normal workings of human nature, was in danger of becoming demoralized if he were given a taste of freedom and power through being sent on foreign service. This was a menace to the régime itself, as well as to Sparta's prestige in Hellas. Rather than risk a repetition of Pausanias' escapade, Sparta, followed by her Isthmian allies, withdrew from further participation in the war against the Persians, and acquiesced when the liberated Asian Hellenes placed themselves under Athens' leadership instead of hers.

If the Hellenic Alliance that had defeated the Persians in 480–479 B.C. had continued to hold together, this bloc of states, reinforced by the Asian Hellenes whom they had set free, would have been strong enough to grow into a Panhellenic confederacy. But the Asian Hellenes' transfer of their allegiance from Sparta to Athens in 478 B.C. left the Hellenic World divided between three blocs. There was the pre-war Peloponnesian bloc under the leadership of Sparta. There was the pre-war Sicilian entente between the two principalities of Syracuse and Akragas. And there was the new bloc under the leadership of Athens. This new alliance included the Asian Hellenic states, continental as well as insular; the islands of the Aegean Archipelago that had submitted to the Persians' suzerainty (that is, all Aegean insular states except Melos, Thera, and those on the island of Crete); and the states on the island of Euboea, which had been under Persian rule during the two years 480–479 B.C. only, but which had been partially occupied by Athens in 506 B.C.

The Athenians had earned their leadership of the

youngest and largest of the three blocs by the magnitude of their contribution to the common cause in 480–479. Their navy had done far more to win the war than the Lacedaemonian phalanx had; and the fortitude of their women and children in enduring the ordeal of evacuating their homes on the mainland was hardly less heroic than the self-sacrifice of Leonidas' three hundred, while it was much more effective in defeating the purpose of the Persian invaders. The Athenians had sacrificed their country for the sake of saving Hellas. The *beau rôle* had been, not the Spartans', but theirs. They had played it under the inspiration of democracy; and Athens' triumph made the fortune of the political régime with which she had identified herself. 'The half century' saw democracy sweep the Hellenic World. Argos sought to rejuvenate herself by going democratic about the year 470 B.C. Even Sparta's rustic ally Elis went democratic in 471–470 B.C. And Syracuse did the same in 466 B.C. — with the incidental consequence that the Syracusan principality fell apart again into its constituent Greek and native Sicilian city-states.

Here were all the makings of a conflict between Athens and Sparta, and the machiavellian Attic statesman Themistocles was accused of looking for some opportunity of forestalling future trouble by breaking Sparta's power. But the Athenians could not be persuaded so soon to turn and rend their late allies. When the Peloponnesians denounced Themistocles to his countrymen, he had to flee for his life and end his days as the Persian emperor's pensioner. This was a political victory for Cimon the son of Miltiades, whose policy for Athens was to keep on good terms with Sparta and to concentrate on prosecuting the war against Persia. Cimon won prestige at Athens by crushing a Persian counter-offensive in a decisive battle fought, in or about 466 B.C. on the banks of the River Eurymedon in Pamphylia, half-way along the south coast of Asia Minor. But the political career of Sparta's best friend at Athens was wrecked by a growing mutual ill-will between the Spartan and Athenian peoples.

In 464 B.C. a devastating earthquake at Sparta gave the helots their chance to make another of their recurrent insurrections. The Spartans called upon their allies to give them military aid, and Cimon persuaded the Athenians to send a contingent. They served reluctantly; for they did not see why they should go out of their way to assist the rival power in Hellas to recover her strength, and they disliked the task of helping to reimpose the Spartan yoke on the helots' necks. The Lacedaemonian Government became aware of their feelings and asked them to withdraw, and this rebuff precipitated a revolution at Athens. Two radical politicians, Ephialtes and Pericles, now caught the Athenian people's ear. On the home front a 'potsherd referendum' sent Cimon into a ten years' exile in 461 B.C. and some surviving constitutional restrictions on the free play of democracy at Athens were abrogated. At the same time Athens made ententes with Sparta's Peloponnesian neighbour and arch-enemy Argos and with the Thessalians. These were two of the three principal European Hellenic peoples that had sided with the Persian invaders in 480–479 B.C. Athens did not try to make friends with the third, which was her own neighbour and arch-enemy Thebes; but it would have been logical for her to make peace with the Persian Empire, now that she had made up her mind that Sparta was her 'enemy number one'. Perhaps Themistocles would have persuaded the Athenians to go to this length, if he had not been in exile already. But, under Pericles' leadership (the young politician's older and more fanatical associate Ephialtes had been assassinated), they pursued Cimon's policy of war with the Persian Empire on a more ambitious scale after having broken with the 'good neighbour' policy towards Sparta that had insured Athens against the risk of a war on two fronts. In 460 (?) B.C. the Isthmian city-state Megara seceded from the Peloponnesian confederacy to the Athenian; and, as long as she was on the Athenians' side, they would not have to fear a Peloponnesian invasion of Attica overland.

In 462 B.C. the Egyptians had made one of their recurrent insurrections against Persian rule; and in 460–459 B.C. the Athenians, in response to an Egyptian appeal, sent a large naval expeditionary force up the Nile and so committed themselves to protracted operations on the grand scale in this distant theatre. Soon after they had made this formidable commitment, the Athenians attacked the Peloponnese and blockaded their commercial rival Aegina. The Spartans and their Peloponnesian allies, on their side, retorted, in 457 B.C., by crossing the Corinthian Gulf into Boeotia and re-fortifying Thebes, whose city-walls had (we may perhaps infer) been dismantled as a penalty for her conduct during the Persian invasion. The Athenians replied by occupying the whole of Central Greece, except for Thebes and her territory, as far west as Thermopylae, and by forcing Aegina to surrender. But this triumph on a different front could not save Athens from disaster in Egypt. A Persian counter-offensive first blockaded the Athenian expeditionary force and then annihilated it in 455–454 B.C. After Cimon's return from exile in 451, Athens put him in command against Persia and freed her hands in Greece by purchasing a five years' truce with the Peloponnesians at the cost of renouncing her alliance with Argos. But, after Cimon had died without succeeding in turning back the tide of the Atheno-Persian war in Athens' favour, Athens made peace with the Persian Empire in 450/49 B.C. This relieved her of a war that, by then, she had been waging intermittently for fifty years. But that, again, did not save her from losing, in 447 B.C., all the conquests that she had made in Central Greece ten years earlier; and, when her truce with the Peloponnesians ran out in 446 B.C., she very nearly lost Euboea as well, and did lose Megara, which had seceded to her from the Peloponnesian confederacy in 460 (?) B.C. The revolt of Megara opened the way for a Peloponnesian invasion of Attica, and in 445 B.C. Athens had to make peace with the Peloponnesian confederacy. It was agreed that there should be peace for thirty years.

The truth was that, under Pericles' leadership during the sixteen years 460–445 B.C., Athens had been recklessly over-taxing her strength. A surviving inscription records that, in the single campaigning season of 459–458 B.C., one of the ten 'nations' among which the Athenian people had been distributed under the constitution of 507 B.C. had lost nearly 170 men killed in action in Cyprus, Egypt, and Phoenicia, in battle with the Persians, and at Halieis, in Aegina, and in Megara in battle with the Peloponnesians. Presumably the losses of the other nine Athenian 'nations' and the resident aliens in the same war year had been of the same order of magnitude; and this was a formidable rate of casualties, even if Athens' total male population of military age at this date, including resident aliens as well as citizens, were to be estimated as high as forty or fifty thousand. Pericles had now learnt his lesson about foreign policy; for the next fifteen years, down to his fall in 430 B.C., he did not lead his country into any war that he believed to be avoidable; but he did lead Athens farther down the path of converting the anti-Persian Hellenic confederacy into an Athenian empire, and this progressive change for the worse in Athens' relations with her former allies was the underlying cause of a second war between her and the Peloponnesian confederacy which resulted in the break-up of the Athenian empire and the breakdown of the Hellenic civilization.

The confederacy that had been established in 478 B.C., for mutual defence, between Athens and the Hellenic states liberated from Persian rule had had a good start. The first business on the new allies' agenda had been to settle the quotas that each state should contribute to the common cause and the form which the contributions should take. The negotiation of this business had been entrusted to the Athenian statesman Aristeides, and he had carried out his task with a fair-mindedness that had shone by contrast with the recent misconduct of the Spartan regent Pausanias. Two previous Persian acts of state had given Aristeides foundations to build on. After the suppression of the Asian Hellenic states' revolt in 494 B.C., Darius I's brother, Artaphrenes, had reassessed their tribute to the Persian Government and had also put pressure on them to make commercial treaties with one another in order that disputes over matters of business between citizens of different states might be settled by action at law in place of the former barbarous custom of distraining by force of arms on any property within reach belonging to citizens of the other party's country. Here was a ready-made basis for a voluntary confederation between Athens and the states that she had now liberated from Persian rule. The principal charge on the finances of the new confederacy would be the maintenance of a common navy; and it was obvious that the lion's share of the ships and crews would continue to be furnished by Athens, since she already had a great fleet in being. The larger and wealthier of the other states could also furnish naval squadrons. But the cost of building, fitting out, and maintaining even a single warship of the new and more expensive type put into commission by the Athenians since 482 B.C. was beyond the means of many, perhaps of most, of the confederate states. So, for the sake of both fairness and efficiency, it was agreed that any state, in lieu of furnishing a ship or ships, might pay an annual contribution in money, to be assessed by Aristeides, into a federal treasury that was to be set up on the holy island of Delos. This revenue was to be spent on subsidizing the Athenian navy, since Athens was furnishing the greater part of the ships.

These arrangements had been freely accepted with the best intentions on all sides. Aristeides' assessment had earned him the title of 'the Just'. But the new confederacy had soon run into trouble. When states members — especially those which, like the Euboean states and Naxos and Thasos, were now no longer the Persian Empire's immediate neighbours — had tried to secede, Athens had treated secession as high treason; had subdued the secessionists by force of arms; and, to ensure that they should not be able to try again, had deprived them of their warships and had imposed heavy annual money contributions on them. In 454 B.C. the confederacy's treasury had been moved from Delos to Athens (nominally on the ground that Delos was exposed to the danger of a Persian attack after the Athenian naval disaster in Egypt). By the time when Athens made peace with Persia in 450/49 B.C. there were only seven states left in the confederacy, apart from Athens herself, that were still furnishing ships: namely Samos, Chios, and the five states on the island of Lesbos. All the rest were now paying tribute.

The states on the west coast of the Asian mainland and on the adjoining islands had had (like Trieste in and after A.D. 1918) to pay a high economic price for their political liberation. This had cut them off from their commercial hinterland in the interior of the Persian Empire by the interposition of a military front. The Atheno-Persian peace treaty of 450/49 B.C. now placed them militarily at the mercy of both contracting parties by providing that their fortifications should be dismantled. No provision seems to have been made for the resumption of their lost trade with their Persian hinterland. But, now that the war was over, all the money-contributing states of the Delian confederacy expected at any rate to be relieved of this financial burden.

This reasonable expectation on their part produced an internal political crisis in Athens. One effect of the constitution of the confederacy of Delos, as it had operated in the course of thirty years, had been to make the earning of wages as oarsmen for the Athenian navy one of the main sources of livelihood for the landless urban majority of the population of Attica; and these wages had been paid out of the fund provided by the contributions of Athens' allies. There would be mass unemployment at Athens if the financial means could not continue to be found for providing the same wages for the same number of Athenian citizens in some alternative occupation to naval service. Could new work be found for which wages could be paid to the discharged Athenian naval crews? And, since Athens' own national budget would not run to bearing this formidable new charge permanently, would it be right to finance it out of contributions levied from the allies in peace-time? Pericles was a gentlemanly and cultivated politician (he was an aristocrat on his mother's side), and he owed his hold over the Athenian people to their appreciation of his superior qualities. But, in a democracy such as Athens now was, his leadership would not survive the calamity of mass unemployment. Pericles therefore took the line that the allies' monetary contributions to the common treasury were in the nature of annual premiums paid to Athens for insurance against the risk of a Persian re-conquest; and that, so long as Athens continued, whether by naval warfare or by treaty, to keep the Persian Empire's hands off its former Hellenic subjects, Athens was entitled to spend the money as she might think best. Pericles proposed that it should now be spent on rebuilding Hellenic temples destroyed by the Persian aggressors in 480–479 B.C. — i.e., in effect, the temples on the citadel of Athens. Aristeides' role was taken up in the Athenian national assembly by Thucydides son of Melesias; but, when the assembly had to decide between doing justice to the allies and providing for the continuance of remunerative public employment for its own members, self-interest prevailed. The consequences of this decision, taken in 443 B.C., were the creation of consummate Athenian works of art and the breakdown, decline, and fall of the Hellenic civilization of which these works were such outstanding products and monuments.

Another remunerative public employment at Athens was that of serving as jurymen (the juries were large and, for the trial of certain cases, were coextensive with the whole body of citizens entitled to vote in the assembly; and, on Pericles' initiative, they were paid for their services from 451–450 B.C. onwards). Since 478 B.C., Athens had been capturing more and more of the trade of the Hellenic World from her own Asian Hellenic allies and from the Isthmian allies of Sparta. This meant that an increasing proportion of actions at law between citizens of different states under bilateral commercial treaties were coming to be tried in Athenian courts. Athens now abused her power over her allies by compelling them to bring suits for trial to Athens even when the case was not a commercial one and even when the defendant was not an Athenian citizen. From the Athenian point of view this policy had two advantages: the economic one of bringing more pay into Athenian jurymen's pockets and the political one of giving opportunities for penalizing the well-to-do citizens of allied states, who were apt to be anti-Athenian because the tribute came out of their pockets, and for favouring the masses, who were apt to be loyal to

Athens because they had nothing to lose and much to gain by their country's alliance with the Athenian democracy.

By 451–450 B.C. the Athenian franchise had become so valuable that in that year, at Pericles' instance, the national assembly passed a law restricting the franchise to men who could prove that both their parents were Athenian citizens. The consequent purge of the citizen body was carried out harshly five years later.

Thus, within thirty years, the Athenian democracy had gone the way of its Spartiate predecessor. It had become a parasitic military 'ascendancy' with its own helots (the tribute-paying 'allies') and perioeci (the allies who were still privileged to contribute naval squadrons). Cleon, Pericles' ungentlemanly but unhypocritical successor in the political leadership of the Athenian people during the first bout of the second Atheno-Peloponnesian war, told his countrymen, with brutal frankness, that Athens had become a 'dictator state', and that her only hope of maintaining her now tyrannous rule lay in a policy of 'frightfulness'.

This degeneration of the confederacy of Delos into an Athenian empire was a tragedy. For, in this age, closer political union was, in itself, just what the Hellenic World needed, not only for defence against the Persian Empire but also, as we have seen, for providing the political framework for the already accomplished fact of economic interdependence. If the Athenians had resisted the temptation to abuse their trust, as the leading power in the confederacy, for their own narrow national advantage, the economic tide making for closer political union would probably have kept the confederacy of Delos in existence on a voluntary footing; and this might have led on, in time, to some kind of voluntary political unification of the Hellenic World as a whole. The course taken, at this critical time, by Athenian policy under Pericles' leadership led to a renewal of fratricidal warfare, the breakdown of the Hellenic civilization, and the tardy political unification of the Hellenic World by overwhelming Roman force.

The war between Athens and the Peloponnesian confederacy broke out again when the precarious balance of power, established in 445 B.C., was upset as the result of a conflict between a Corinthian colony, Corcyra (Corfù), and Corcyra's daughter city Epidamnus (Durazzo), which commanded, between them, the coastwise sea-route from Continental European Greece to the West. Epidamnus appealed to Corinth, Corcyra to Athens; neither power felt that it could afford to abandon its protégée at the other power's demand; and Sparta reluctantly decided to back her ally Corinth, partly for fear that Corinth might secede from the Peloponnesian confederacy, but mainly because the progressive conversion of the Delian confederacy into an Athenian empire was increasing Athens' power in a way that seemed to endanger the freedom of the Hellenic World as a whole. Athens gave fresh ground for this fear by putting economic pressure on a re-admitted member of the Peloponnesian confederacy, Athens' Isthmian neighbour Megara, as a penalty for Megara's refusal to change sides again. Megara's territory bestrode the Isthmus on the Athenian side of Corinth, and Pericles' object was to bar the land-route along which the Attic countryside could be invaded by the Peloponnesian army again, as it had been in 446 B.C. Since Athens was no match for the Peloponnesian confederacy on land, this was her Achilles' heel, and, when Megara held out, the Attic landed interest was as reluctant to go to war as Sparta was. But the landless urban majority of the Athenian voters had the last word in the assembly, and Pericles persuaded them to maintain their support of Corcyra at the price of war with the Peloponnesians, on the understanding that Athens was to confine herself on land to defending the perimeter of her gigantic fortifications — at the cost of seeing the Attic countryside devastated by an invader — and was to retaliate by naval raids, in the hope of tiring out the land-power as Miletus had once tired out Lydia.

In the ten-years-long first bout of the consequent war (431–421 B.C.) Pericles' hopes were more nearly fulfilled than the Corinthians', though the land-power of the anti-Athenian coalition was reinforced by the accession of Thebes. Pericles could not foresee the mortality that would be caused by a plague breaking out among the refugees from the Attic countryside who crowded for safety into the space between the walls connecting Athens with her ports (he himself died of the plague in 429 B.C., after having lived to be thrown out of office in 430). He also did not foresee that the Peloponnesians would succeed in invading overland not only the countryside of Attica but Athens' subject states along the distant north shore of the Aegean Sea. However, the Spartan commander Brasidas, as well as Pericles' successor Cleon, met his death in 422 B.C. at Amphipolis, before he had reached and cut Athens' life-line at the Dardanelles, through which she imported her supplies of grain from the Ukraine. In 421 B.C., peace was made on terms of *uti possidetis.* Except for the former subjects of Athens in Chalcidicê who had been liberated by Brasidas, the Athenian empire remained intact; and Sparta's Isthmian allies temporarily broke away from her in disgust. Yet, in spite of this further demonstration of the futility of war, Hellas did not settle down.

The nine-years-long second bout of the war (413–404 B.C.) was the sequel to a wanton Athenian act of aggression, in 415, against Syracuse, the strongest Hellenic state in Sicily. This adventure ended in 413 B.C. in the annihilation of the Athenian expeditionary force. Sparta then made war on Athens again, and this time she established a permanent base of operations on Attic territory at Decelea and also created a navy which, with the aid of a Syracusan squadron and a Persian subsidy, was strong enough to challenge the Athenian command of the Aegean. Athens postponed her inevitable defeat by her almost superhuman exertions, but, when, in 405 B.C., her last fleet was destroyed in the Dardanelles, she had to capitulate. Her remaining subjects were liberated, and the walls connecting the city of Athens with its ports were pulled down, as well as the walls round the ports themselves.

The only result was that Sparta inherited the maritime empire that Athens had lost, and at the same time made a land-empire for herself out of the confederacy in Continental European Greece of which she had for so long been the constitutional leader. The Spartan military governors (officially known as 'adjusters') proved to be far more oppressive than their predecessors the Athenian tax-collectors. After war had broken out between Sparta and Persia in 400 B.C. over the question of the future status of the Persian Empire's former Hellenic subjects, Athens intervened in 393 B.C. with a new navy built with the aid of a Persian subsidy, and in 387/6 another inconclusive peace was made on terms promulgated by the Persian Imperial Government. The Hellenic states on the Asian mainland (including the inshore island-state of Clazomenae) were abandoned to Persia by Sparta. In return, the Imperial Government ruled that every other Hellenic state was to be sovereign and independent (which meant that Sparta was to have a free hand to break up any anti-Spartan confederacies or coalitions). The Spartans did dissolve the Boeotian federation, in order to clip the wings of a now restive Thebes; and in 382 B.C. they occupied the citadel of Thebes itself by a *coup de main*. But this unprincipled Spartan move ended in the ignominious withdrawal of the

Spartan garrison in 379 and the sensational defeat of a Spartan army by the Thebans at Leuctra in Boeotia in 371. The Thebans followed up their victory by invading Laconia (the sharp-tongued Spartan women now set eyes on an invading enemy force for the first time on record, and they disgraced their country by giving way to panic). The city of Sparta did not fall to Theban arms, but Sparta's power was broken by Theban statesmanship. In 370 B.C. the Theban leader Epaminondas restored to the Messenian helots the liberty of which they had never despaired, and, to make sure that they should retain it, he helped them to organize themselves into an independent city-state with a strongly fortified civic centre round their historic pivot of resistance, Mount Ithomê. In 369 B.C. he sealed Sparta's northern frontier by organizing the little cantons of South-Western Arcadia into another new city-state with a strongly fortified civic centre at Megalopolis. Thus Epaminondas had made history before he lost his life in 362 B.C. in an inconclusive battle at Mantinea, in which the Spartans had the aid of the Thebans' old enemies the Athenians.

When Athens and Sparta had each failed, in turn, to impose political unity on the Hellenic World, Thebes could not hope to succeed. Her bitterest opponents were her Boeotian sister states, whom she tried in vain to absorb into her own body politic; and she was worsted in her attempts to impose her will upon Boeotia's backward western neighbours the Phocians, who made themselves a menace in 355 B.C. by seizing the accumulated treasure of the Panhellenic shrine at Delphi and spending it on hiring mercenary troops (by this time there was a plentiful supply of these from among 'displaced persons' uprooted from their homes by chronic warfare and domestic revolution). The Phocians had a shorter run than the Thebans. In 346 B.C. they were crushed by King Philip II of Macedon, acting on a mandate that he had procured from the Delphic Amphictyony. The overthrow of Phocis opened the way for a Macedonian advance into Central Greece. In 338 B.C. Philip won a decisive victory, at Chaeronea in Boeotia, over the combined forces of Thebes and Athens. At Corinth in the same year he organized a confederacy, under Macedonian leadership, which included all states of Continental European Greece except Sparta. This political union of Hellenic states under Macedonian leadership embraced a larger part of the Hellenic World than any of its predecessors; but, like them, it too was short-lived.

The damage done by the warfare that had been ravaging the heart of the Hellenic World for ninety-three years was not to be measured in material terms. The spiritual damage was the graver, as was pointed out by Thucydides son of Olorus, an unsuccessful Athenian naval commander who, in exile, started to write a history of the war that had begun in 431 B.C., until death overtook him before he had carried the story down even to the year 404. The war was a civil war between the partisans of conflicting political ideologies within each state, besides being an international war between two power-blocs. The international war was disgraced by atrocities: the destruction of Athens' Boeotian ally Plataea by the Thebans and their Peloponnesian allies in 427 B.C.; the Athenians' cold-blooded aggression, in 416 B.C., against Melos, a small and unoffending neutral independent state; the atrocious treatment of the Athenian prisoners of war interned in the quarries at Syracuse after the débâcle of the Athenian expeditionary force in Sicily in 413 B.C.; the Spartans' slaughter of their Athenian prisoners of war in 405 B.C. after the Battle of Aegospotami. Still worse crimes were committed in the course of civil war and domestic revolution: for example, the massacres of conservatives by radicals at Corcyra in 425 B.C.

and the murders perpetrated at Athens by the commission of thirty ('the Thirty Dictators') who were in power for eight months during the temporary eclipse of the democratic régime that followed Athens' naval collapse.

Partisans of the losing side in these domestic conflicts, when they escaped with their lives, became 'displaced persons'; and the number of these homeless and stateless exiles steadily grew until they became a permanent new element in Hellenic life — a class, outside the frame-work of city-states, that made itself a force through offering itself as a recruiting-ground for mercenary soldiers.

At Athens, in particular, from 431 B.C. onwards, there were increasing symptoms of a nervous tension that discharged itself in fits of hysteria. There was an increasing cult of foreign gods — not only the Hellenic god of healing, Asklepios, from Epidaurus and Cos, but the Thracian goddess Bendis and the Anatolian Great Mother Cybele. There was a witch-hunt at Athens in 415 B.C., when, on the eve of the departure of the great Athenian expeditionary force for Sicily, the busts of the god Hermes that crowned the posts at the street corners were defaced one night, by persons unknown. There were also persecutions of 'intellectuals' for 'impiety'. In this age Athens was still intellectually conservative by comparison with both Hellas-in-Asia and the colonial Hellas in Italy and Sicily. Athenian public opinion could easily be aroused by the cry that religion and morals were in danger; and there was a political motive for arousing it against 'intellectuals' when they happened to be protégés or associates of politicians who were 'on the spot'. The discredited Athenian politician Pericles' foreign protégé Anaxagoras of Clazomenae slipped away from Athens in good time. The punctiliously law-abiding Athenian citizen Socrates, who had once been an associate of Callias, the ringleader of 'the Thirty Dictators', stood his ground and met his death.

The judicial murder of the greatest citizen that Athens ever had was one of the acts by which the Athenian democracy signalized its recapture of the city from 'the Thirty Dictators' in 399 B.C.

VIII

MACEDON'S RECEPTION OF HELLENISM AND OPENING UP OF THE EAST

THE Macedonians, who imposed unity and peace on Continental European Greece in 338 B.C., were one of the unhellenized Greek-speaking peoples who occupied the mainland west and north of Delphi and Thermopylae. While the city-state civilization that had arisen to the east and south of that cultural frontier had been reaching, and passing, its zenith, Macedon had remained a relic of the 'heroic' — or barbaric — age which, in all parts of the Aegean area, had followed the fall of the Minoan-Mycenaean civilization. Macedon was still governed — in so far as it had a government — by an hereditary monarchy: an institution which, in the Hellenic World, had long since given way to republics and dictatorships. The king of Macedon's power was limited theoretically in law by some customary constitutional restraints; but in practice it depended much more on the personal ability of the king of the day to command the precarious loyalty of the nobles and commons in the country under his own direct rule, and of the chieftains of the highland principalities to the south, west, and north, who nominally acknowledged his suzerainty. When the throne was occupied by a king endowed with political capacity, vision, and, above all, a strong will, Macedon could make herself felt, in spite of her social and cultural backwardness. When her king was a minor or a nonentity, she could fall into anarchy and come within an ace of political extinction. Thus her fortunes depended largely on chance; and chance favoured her by bringing men of character to the throne at critical moments in Macedon's history. Alexander I, who was on the throne at the time of the Persian invasion of Continental European Greece in 480–479 B.C., and Perdiccas (reigned 440 (?)–413 B.C.) and his son Archelaus (reigned 413–399 B.C.), whose two successive reigns covered the period of the great Atheno-Peloponnesian war, were kings of outstanding ability. Philip II (reigned 359–336 B.C.) and his son Alexander the Great (reigned 336–323 B.C.) were men of genius — genius in two very different veins — and both would certainly have distinguished themselves in any walk of life at any time or place. But Philip was fortunate in coming to the throne of Macedon just after the ascendancy of Thebes in the Hellenic World had had its brief day; and Alexander the Great was fortunate in inheriting the power that his father had built up.

Macedon's fortunes were already linked with the international politics of the Hellenic World. Twice within the century and a half that had elapsed between the initiation of the Persian Empire's attempt to annex European Greece and the accession of Philip II in 359 B.C., Macedon had been saved from political extinction by the action of Hellenic states in pursuit of their own interests. For all that King Alexander I could have done single-handed, Macedon would have been permanently incorporated in a Persian province if Xerxes' defeat in 480–479 B.C. by the Hellenic Alliance under Spartan and Athenian leadership had not forced Persia to abandon all her acquisitions on the European side of the Dardanelles save for the single fortress of Doriscus on the coast of Thrace. Again, in 382–379 B.C., when Macedon was passing through a bout of anarchy and impotence between the end of Archelaus's reign and the beginning of Philip II's, the military intervention of Sparta saved her from being permanently incorporated in a federal union of city-states, along the north shore of the Aegean and in its hinterland, that was being built up by the Chalcidian colonial city-state Olynthus.

The master asset of the Kingdom of Macedon was the field for territorial expansion that lay open to any occupant of the throne who had the requisite power and the vision. The nucleus of the territory under the king's direct rule was the hill-country overhanging the western end of the plain traversed by the lower course of the River Axius (Vardar) on its way to the Gulf of Salonica. On three sides this domain was hemmed in by insubordinate autonomous Macedonian principalities with hereditary chieftains of their own. But, eastward, the king's domain could, and did, expand into open lowland country inhabited by Greek-speaking tribes — the wide-spread Paeonians, who were no match for the Macedonians because they were still less civilized that the Macedonians were. The seat of the king's government, which had originally lain at Aegae (Vodhená), on the brow of a precipice overlooking the Vardar plain, migrated to Pella (Yenijé Vardar), down on the plain, not far from Scydra, where Persian empire-builders had laid out the administrative centre for a short-lived European province. After the ebb of the Persian tide, King Alexander I carried the eastern frontier of Macedon up to the west bank of the River Strymon (Struma) along the river's lower course. But the colonial Hellenic city-states along the Macedonian coast and in Chalcidicê still easily maintained their independence, while, in the country immediately to the east of the Lower Strymon, the Athenians were now contending with the local Paeonian tribes for the prize of the gold mines on Mount Pangaeus. Philip II was the first king of Macedon to get this particularly valuable piece of territory into his hands. He secured his hold on it by founding there a city which he named Philippi after himself. Philip used the gold of Pangaeus, as Themistocles had used the silver of Laurium, to build up the necessary military power for seizing a political opportunity. Within twenty-one years from his accession in 359 B.C. he had incorporated in the Kingdom of Macedon all the Hellenic city-states along the coast (he annihilated the strongest of them, Olynthus, in order to intimidate the rest); he had brought the previously autonomous highland Macedonian principalities under his own direct rule; he had subjugated most of the Greek-speaking and Thracian-speaking tribes east of the River Strymon up to the Straits and the Black Sea and the lower course of the River Danube; and he had brought all the city-states of Continental European Greece, except Sparta, under his control.

What accounts for Philip's cnormous success? It was chiefly due to his character, to which high tributes were paid by his Athenian arch-enemy Demosthenes. In energy, wiliness, persistence, and patience, he was the equal of Augustus, who eventually performed a similar service for the Hellenic World on a larger scale and with more lasting results. The contemporary Chiot historian Theopompus is said to have called Philip the greatest man that Europe had produced so far, and so, perhaps, he was in the field of statesmanship. Demosthenes also put his finger on the masterly use that Philip made of his Pangaean gold. He bought with it some of the leading politicians of the leading Hellenic city-states, and he coined so much of it that, three or four hundred years later, coins stamped with caricatures of his image and superscription were being minted in far-away barbarous Britain. But there was another cause of Philip's success which Demosthenes did not see or would not acknowledge, and that was the Macedonian king's deliberate reception of the civilization of an Hellenic World that he succeeded in bending to his will.

In 430 B.C., in a funeral oration in honour of Athenian citizens killed in action in the first campaign of the great Atheno-Peloponnesian war, Pericles had boasted that Athens was 'the education of Hellas'. The abler kings of barbarian Macedon took Pericles at his word, not only in the way that Pericles had meant, but also in ways that he had not foreseen or intended.

Pericles might have been gratified, as well as surprised, if he had lived to see King Archelaus invite to his court at Pella the Athenian playwright Euripides, who was one of the most 'advanced' of the Athenian 'intellectuals' of his generation. He would certainly have rejoiced when King Philip II adopted the Attic, instead of his native Macedonian, dialect of Greek as the official language for his chancery (this Macedonian act of state may have done more than the literary genius of Euripides and the other great Athenian men of letters to make Attic Greek the lingua franca of the Hellenic World in the following chapter of its history, in which it expanded south-eastwards into India and north-westwards into Britain). Pericles would have approved of Philip's engaging the services of an Athenian by adoption, the eminent philosopher Aristotle of Stageirus, to be tutor to the Macedonian king's son and heir Alexander. But he would have been less happy when he heard that Philip himself, in his boyhood, had received an Hellenic education in the literal sense through living, as a hostage, within the walls of Athens' unloved neighbour, Thebes. And he would have been aghast at the military application that Macedonian kings had given to his dictum. Yet this was not really surprising; for notable improvements in military technique were one of the natural outcomes of the ninety-three-years-long bout of chronic warfare into which the Hellenic states had stumbled in 431 B.C.

Archelaus increased the efficiency of the Macedonian noble cavalry by giving them the Hellenic equipment of the day, and increased their mobility by building a network of military roads. Philip II gave the Macedonian infantry an up-to-date Athenian equipment and Theban formation. In 390 B.C., during Athens' war of revenge against Sparta for the débâcle of 404 B.C., the Athenian professional soldier Iphicrates had cut a Lacedaemonian division to pieces by bringing into the field, against its old-fashioned 'shield-wielder' armament and formation, a new-model light infantry armed with thrusting pikes that were more than a match for the 'shield-wielders' ' stabbing spears. The new-model soldier had both hands free for handling his pike, because his left hand had been relieved of the traditional heavy round shield. This had been replaced by a light target slung by a loop on his left arm. Philip armed his penurious peasant infantry with this Athenian equipment, which was commended by its cheapness as well as by its proved efficiency. But he did not marshal the new Macedonian targeteers in open order. The Theban captains Epaminondas and Pelopidas had routed the Lacedaemonians in 371 B.C. by a tactical development in the opposite direction from Iphicrates' innovation. Instead of breaking up the traditional phalanx into a screen of light-armed skirmishers, they had increased the number of its ranks, at one point in the line, to the depth of a column, and had broken through the Lacedaemonian line by staving it in with this human battering-ram. Philip marshalled his targeteers in a phalanx of Theban depth all along the line. This was a skilful combination of the two advantages of mobility and mass. The gold of Pangaeus also gave Philip the means for equipping one *corps d'élite,* the 'undershields', in the expensive traditional Hellenic style.

The arm which won Philip's and Alexander's victories for them was not this old-fashioned corps, and not their phalanx of targeteer-pikemen, but their cavalry. And, in the course of the century and a half that elapsed between the Macedonian victory in 338 B.C., at Chaeronea, over the Theban and Athenian 'shield-wielders' and the Macedonian defeat in 197 B.C. at Cynoscephalae at the hands of Roman swordsmen, the Macedonian phalanx, like its predecessors, grew unwieldly. A series of fratricidal wars between the successors of Alexander the Great brought phalanx into action against phalanx, and a consequent competitive increase in the length of the pike ended in making the arm almost unmanageable. But Philip's remodelling of the Macedonian infantry did have a lasting social and political effect. Now that the embattled Macedonian peasantry had become an effective military force, they acquired self-respect and a voice in public affairs. As the 'foot-companions' of the king, they were now on the same roll of honour as the 'companions' — the traditional name for the noble cavalry.

Besides his convinced opponents and his paid agents in the city-states, Philip also had disinterested supporters and genuine admirers. His Athenian supporter Aeschines was acting in the same good faith as his Athenian opponent Demosthenes. His Athenian admirer, the more academic publicist and man of letters Isocrates, saw in the union of all the states of Hellas, under the leadership of a single power in the hands of a single great man, an opportunity for at last carrying through the Panhellenic counter-attack on the Persian Empire which had been the unachieved aim of Cimon son of Miltiades. It might indeed have been expected that, after the failure, in 480–479 B.C., of the Persians' attempt to annex European Greece to their empire, there would have been an immediate resumption, with greater energy than ever, of the Hellenic penetration of Egypt and South-West Asia which had begun in the seventh century B.C. at the heels of the retreating Assyrians and had been cut short, in the sixth century, by the Persian Empire's sudden rise. The Persian Empire had been given a reprieve by the breach between Sparta and Athens. In 457 B.C. Sparta had stabbed Athens in the back when Athens was wrenching Egypt out of Persia's grasp. In 393 Athens had stabbed Sparta in the back when Sparta was driving the Persians out of Western Anatolia. For a united Hellenic World the conquest of the Persian Empire would present no military difficulties. This had been demonstrated, in 401 B.C., by the exploit of ten thousand Hellenic mercenaries who had been hired by a pretender to the Persian imperial throne. This modest force had marched, unopposed, from the west coast of Anatolia into Babylonia; it had won a pitched battle there against all the troops that the Imperial Government could muster; and then, when it had found itself left in the air by the death of its Persian employer in the battle, it had marched out again from Babylonia through unknown country to the Black Sea coast of Eastern Anatolia, in spite of the imperial army's efforts to cut off its retreat. Multiply the strength of the Panhellenic expeditionary force by three or four, with the backing of a united Hellas behind it, and the dazzling enterprise could not fail.

From the Hellenic point of view this grand design made sense. Why should the Hellenes go on fighting ruinous wars with one another when they could combine to subjugate and exploit the vast potential 'living space' to the east and south? In the fourth century B.C., as in the eighth, Hellas was suffering from over-population. Neither the colonization of the shores of the Western Mediterranean and the Black Sea nor the subsequent economic revolution had made permanent provision for the still increasing number of Hellenic mouths that had to be fed. A conquered Persian Empire would provide room for Hellenic colonists, and the colonists would serve to hold the conquered country down. It was practicable. But was it justifiable, apart from a dubious right of retaliation? In Aristotle's day there were Hellenic theorists who argued that the Hellenes had an inborn right of conquest, because Hellenes were born freemen, while non-Hellenes were born slaves. A hundred years earlier the writer of a treatise on the influence of physical environment on character (preserved among the writings of the Hippocratean school of medicine on the island of Cos) had shrewdly pointed out that non-Hellenes inhabiting rough countries were just as spirited and as freedom-loving as the Hellenes were; and the sequel to the Hellenic conquest of the Persian Empire vindicated the accuracy of this observation. The doctrine of the Hellenes' inborn right to exercise dominion over 'lesser breeds' was in truth a pretext for reproducing Sparta's oppression of her helots, and Athens' oppression of her tributary subjects, on an immensely enlarged scale.

In 336 B.C. Philip sent a small expeditionary force across the Dardanelles. Was this to be the advance-guard of a larger army? And how far did Philip mean to go? His young successor Alexander had to spend a year on intimidating the barbarians along the northern frontier of Macedon and crushing Thebes, which had taken the opportunity to revolt. Alexander crossed the Dardanelles with an army thirty-five thousand strong in 334 B.C. and systematically occupied the whole Mediterranean coast of the Persian Empire as far as the western desert of Egypt, in order to make sure that the Persian navy should not join forces with the Athenian navy to take him in the rear, as his forerunner, the Spartan king Agesilaus, had been taken in 394–393 B.C. In 331 he headed for the interior and routed at Gaugamela the Persian Empire's last field army, which had been waiting for him on the plains between the east bank of the River Tigris and the Assyrian city of Arbela. By 323 B.C. he had subjugated all the rest of the Persian Empire up to the line of the River Jaxartes (Sir Darya) and the former Persian possessions in the Indus valley up to the line of the River Beas, and had returned to Babylon to organize his conquests and to plan more of them.

The military triumph of Hellenic arms under Macedonian leadership had surpassed the dreams of Isocrates. For the Hellenes the sensation was something like what the modern Westerners felt when they discovered the Americas and the sea-route to India round the Cape of Good Hope. For the Persians and their subjects, it was like what the Incas and their subjects felt when the Castilian conquerors descended on them out of the blue armed with weapons irresistibly superior to theirs. In the series of Alexander's victorious campaigns there had been only one experience that, from the Hellenic standpoint, was disturbing. Though the battle fought in the neighbourhood of Arbela had been a decisive victory for Alexander, it had been a reverse for the cavalry that was the arm in which he trusted. The Hellenic cavalry equipment had proved to be no match for the mail armour (sheathing horse as well as rider) of the last Darius's Bactrian and Indian cavalry; and in the next phase of the war Alexander had met with a resistance that had surprised him when he had invaded this redoubtable cavalry's homelands in the Persian Empire's marches over against the Nomads of Central Asia. The wardens of these marches had shown that they were not born slaves. Alexander had paid them the compliment of marrying the daughter of the Iranian margrave who had given him the greatest trouble.

Alexander lived to rise above the low ideal of an Hellenic ascendancy over non-Hellenes to the lofty ideal of the brotherhood of all mankind. When he met the Persians he recognized and admired in them the virtues that had enabled them to govern so large a part of the world for more than two hundred years; and he dreamed, in his turn, of a world-wide empire governed by Persians and Hellenes in partnership. Yet this precocious idealist was also capable of murdering his friends and companions in fits of drunken rage, like the Homeric hero that the adolescent side of his nature aspired to be. And his habitual intemperateness was no doubt the underlying cause of his sudden premature death by sickness at Babylon in 323 B.C. He had had time to wreck a great empire, but he had only just begun to carry out the plans for reconstruction that were maturing in his mind.

The disaster of 323 B.C., and its still more disastrous aftermath, showed that Hellenization had been no remedy for Macedon's inveterate weakness. Her monarchical constitution exposed her to a risk from which city-states were exempt, whatever might be their shortcomings in other respects. It made Macedon's fortunes depend on the whims and lives of individuals who were fallible and mortal. At Alexander's death, as at Archelaus's, the cumulative achievements of two successive distinguished reigns dissolved in anarchy. But this time the collapse did not affect Macedon alone; it affected all Hellas and half the rest of the world.

IX

THE EMANCIPATION OF INDIVIDUALS FROM CITY-STATES

THE suppression of city-state sovereignty by the Macedonians brought relief to individual human beings in an age when citizenship had become a burden instead of a stimulus.

It is true that the warfare among Alexander's successors for the division of his heritage gave a number of city-states the opportunity to recover their sovereignty — for instance, Sparta and Rhodes and Cyzicus and Heraclea on the Black Sea coast of Asia Minor. Rhodes came to the fore partly thanks to her own action. In 407 B.C. the three small states among which the island had previously been divided entered into a politicial union; and the power which the Rhodians acquired through this act of 'synoecism' enabled them to take advantage of the key position in which their island found herself thanks to the expansion of the Hellenic World round the Eastern Mediterranean into Egypt as a result of Alexander's overthrow of the Persian Empire. Rhodes commanded the sea-routes from the Dardanelles, Macedon, and the Isthmus of Corinth to Alexandria. And she and other city-states that did succeed in playing independent parts in the great new world of kingdom-states which arose out of the partition of the Persian Empire, indulged their political ambitions at the price of reimposing the traditional servitude on their citizens. But few city-states were able to stay the course. Athens, for instance, fell out of the race once for all after the defeat of her attempt to defy the power of Macedon in the war of 267–262 B.C. When, in 229–228 B.C., she managed to buy out her Macedonian garrison, she settled down thankfully to lead a quiet life. Moreover, the citizens of city-states, still struggling to maintain their sovereignty, who found their state's demands upon them intolerable, now had the option of emigrating to Alexandria or some other of the non-sovereign Hellenic cities that were springing up in large numbers in the dominions of the Persian Empire's Macedonian successor-states. Here it was possible to enjoy the amenities, without the penalties, of the city-state way of life. And there was an influx of voluntary immigrants from exigent city-states, besides the influx of forcibly 'displaced persons' in search of new homes.

The ground had been prepared for this movement — a psychological movement as well as a demographic one — by the moral débâcle of the city-states during the discreditable years 431–338 B.C.; for this had already alienated from them some of the best of their citizens.

The crucial event had been the moral conflict between Socrates and Athens. Socrates was the first Hellenic martyr. In the name of a higher god he challenged, on a question of principle, the city-state that claimed to be 'the education of Hellas' and that was, in truth, the one that was the least unworthy of idolization. This challenge was impressive, because Socrates was no Archilochus. He had performed his military duty conscientiously and valiantly; and, when his conscience forebade him to do what the state demanded of him, it also forebade him to elude the death-sentence or to evade its execution by escaping from prison and fleeing the country. Unlike run-away Archilochus, Socrates was not seeking to save his life; he was insisting on losing it. And, in compelling Athens to choose between respecting his conscience and taking his life, he inflicted on her a defeat that was more damaging to her than her defeat by Sparta five years earlier. Athens' defeats at the hands of her Spartan conqueror Lysander and her Macedonian conquerors Philip II and Antigonus Gonatas were merely military defeats. Her defeat at Socrates' hands was a moral one. By casting her vote against Socrates in 339 B.C., the goddess Athene brought on herself as much infamy in real life as she had won glory on the stage by casting it in favour of Orestes in 458 B.C. Nothing did so much as the judicial murder of Socrates to detach Hellenic hearts from all city-states. For Athens had set herself up to be a pattern of what every Hellenic city-state should be, and Socrates had friends, admirers, and disciples in many states besides his own native country.

The emancipation of individuals from city-states was also assisted by Socrates' countryman and contemporary the Athenian playwright Euripides. In overtly discrediting the traditional presentation of the Olympian gods, Euripides was undermining the worship of city-states, since this had been projected, as we have seen, upon goddesses taken from the Olympian pantheon. Euripides was not the first Hellenic 'intellectual' to assail the Olympians. In Hellas-in-Asia, which had been intellectually more precocious than Athens, the late-sixth-century philosopher Xenophanes of Colophon had opened the attack at least two generations before Euripides' day. But Euripides' shafts did more execution because in his time the Hellenic public was in a mood to take such strictures to heart. In his rationalism, and likewise in his feminism and in his denunciation of the atrociousness of the institution of war, Euripides was the herald of a new age.

In the next two generations, Athens was the intellectual workshop of two men of genius — Plato (about 430–347 B.C.) and Aristotle (384–322 B.C.) — who were the greatest Hellenic minds, not only of their own time, but in the whole course of Hellenic history.

Plato, an Athenian citizen born just after the outbreak of war in 431 B.C., was alienated from his mother-country by the misdeeds of the Athenian democracy in his lifetime — above all, by the martyrdom of Socrates, whose devoted disciple Plato was. Plato could never forgive Athens, and also could never get over the shock of his disillusionment with her. In turning against democracy, Plato did not see beyond the city-state form of political life. He merely substituted for the Athenian political ideal an academic version of the Spartan one, with a visionary 'ascendancy' of Pythagorean philosophers substituted for the historic 'ascendancy' of the Spartiate 'peers'. Plato longed to translate his vision into real life, and naïvely hoped to find a short cut to this remote goal by persuading the contemporary despot of Syracuse, Dionysius II, to depose himself by imposing Plato's constitutional blueprint on his subjects. In his political ideas and activities, Plato was a child of his age. The Plato who towers above time and place is Plato the poet and the seer.

Aristotle did not suffer from Plato's spiritual torments, partly because he was a more prosaic soul and partly because he was born in a generation that was already better acclimatized than Plato's had been to living a noncivic life. Like a hermit crab, Aristotle could slip out of one social shell into another without discomfort. His native country was the obscure little colonial Hellenic city-state of Stageirus, on the east coast of the peninsula of Chalcidicê, which was annexed to Macedon by King Philip II in Aristotle's lifetime. Aristotle left Stageirus as a young man and divided his working life between Athens, the court of Hermeias, the despot of the petty Hellenic principality of Atarneus and Assos in the Troad, and King Philip's court at Pella. In spite of having lived both in Macedon and in the Persian Empire (Hermeias' principality lay in Persian territory), Aristotle, like Plato, had no eye for any kind of states except city-states; and he, too, produced a blue-print for a city-state constitution which was not essentially different from Plato's. At the same time Aristotle produced a collection of monographs describing the actual constitutions of historical city-states, and he studied these with scientific detachment as specimens, not as goddesses. Moreover, Aristotle, though he was so strangely blind to the political signs of the times, was in fact the intellectual harbinger of the post-city-state chapter of Hellenic history. His politics, like Plato's, were ephemeral. His greatness lay in his gigantic achievement of organizing the sciences — from logic to biology — into a coherent system that could be transmitted, as part of a comprehensive corpus of Hellenic culture, to non-Hellenes in process of Hellenization.

The Aristotelian philosophy was such a powerful and impressive intellectual instrument that it survived the dissolution of the Hellenic society and lived to impose itself on the Islamic World and on Western Christendom. The West did not emancipate itself from Aristotle's spell till the seventeenth century of the Christian Era, nearly two thousand years after Aristotle's own day. Yet in natural science, as in the study of human affairs, Aristotle's genius was unintuitive. Leucippus's intuition of the atomic structure of matter was followed up, not by Aristotle, but by his older contemporary Democritus of Abdera (another colonial Hellenic city-state on the north shore of the Aegean). And Aristotle did not anticipate his younger contemporary Heracleides Ponticus's intuition — followed up by Aristarchus of Samos (about 310–230 B.C.) — that the Sun, not the Earth, is the centre round which the planets revolve.

The new dispensation of Hellenic life, inaugurated by the revolutionary work of Philip and Alexander, gave reputable openings for individual careers that had been unknown under the old exacting city-state dispensation.

In the Hellenic successor-states of the Persian Empire — the Macedonian Kingdom of Egypt, established by Alexander's general Ptolemy 'the Saviour', and the Macedonian Kingdom of Asia established by his general Seleucus 'the Victor' — an Hellenic immigrant could find a career, not only in commerce, but in the liberal professions and arts. In Egypt's new maritime capital, Alexandria, which now superseded Athens as the commercial and intellectual centre of the Hellenic World, there was scope for him as an engineer or as a physician or as a man of letters, scholar, or scientist attached to the Museum (a publicly endowed research institute). In Seleucia-on-Tigris, which was the inland capital of the Seleucid monarchy, an Hellenic astronomer could collaborate with his Babylonian confrères. An immigrant into one of the new monarchies could also still call his soul his own if he took service with the Crown as a professional civil servant or soldier. The hundred years' war between the city-states (431–338 B.C.) had produced professional soldiers — the Athenian general Iphicrates, for instance, and the Spartan king Agesilaus — who had started their careers in the service of their native states and had ended as virtually independent powers, with private professional armies of their own, like the late medieval Italian condottieri. Such mercenary soldiers became less of a social scourge and public danger when they entered the service of the new monarchies; and they could enter it without ceasing to be free men; for, though Alexander and his successors were officially gods, it was possible to serve them on a business footing without being expected to pay them the sacrificial devotion that the city-state goddesses had demanded.

The new regard for private life was mirrored in the plays produced by the 'new school' of Attic comedy, which flourished during the time of transition from the old to the new age. The 'old school,' whose most famous master was Socrates' and Euripides' contemporary Aristophanes, had gone in for lampooning living people who were conspicuous in the public eye. Politicians were Aristophanes' favourite, though not exclusive, target; for he was producing his plays during the war of 431–404 B.C., when politics at Athens were even more than usually controversial (Aristophanes himself was a bold spokesman of the peace party). The new school — already nascent in Aristophanes' post-war plays, but best represented in the plays of the later playwright Menander (342/1–292 B.C.) — turned its attention to a comedy of manners in which the *dramatis personae* were imaginary characters and the social setting was the middle-class life of the day. The typical male character was a rentier — or his expectant heir — deriving his income from investments in real property. This was the state of life which the majority of the spectators would have liked to attain; and the fortunate minority that had succeeded in attaining it struggled grimly, throughout the remaining chapters of Hellenic history, to keep what they had got. The political régime introduced at Athens after the departure of the Macedonian garrison in 229–228 B.C. was based on the support of the rentiers and was designed to protect their property rights. So, too, was the political régime that was established throughout the Hellenic World by Augustus after his victory at Actium in 31 B.C.

While, in the New Comedy, the Old Comedy's obsession with city-state politics was conspicuous by its absence, female characters, which had been brought to the fore by Aristophanes as a *jeu d'esprit,* played, in the comedy of manners, a lifelike part which reflected a notable improvement in the position of women in society. The part played by domestic slaves in the New Comedy was even more prominent. The plot of a play often hinged on the zeal and ingenuity of a confidential slave in furthering the interests of his master; and, here again, the playwright's commonplace was a reflection of the realities of his day. The city-states, in their heyday, had been freemen's clubs into which there had been no admittance for women or for slaves. Under the post-city-state dispensation these two long disfranchised classes were now regaining something of the footing in society that had been theirs in the 'heroic' — or barbaric — age before the rise of city-states had left them out in the cold.

At Athens the position of domestic slaves had begun to improve as early as the fifth century B.C. thanks to the democratic régime's policy of making the rich pay for the maintenance of the Athenian navy. Costs not covered by the contributions of the subject allied states had been met by making the better-to-do Athenian citizens finance the fitting out of warships; and these compulsory capital levies (euphemistically called 'public services') had been so crippling that the victims of them had had to reduce their standard of living. One obvious form of economy had been to give up the luxury of retaining slaves for the owner's own domestic service, and to set one's slaves up in some remunerative business, in which they would earn profits for their owner instead of being a charge on his budget. But a live chattel that has been asked to go into business and make the business pay has been recognized, in the act, as being human after all. And a human being will not put his heart into earning profits for someone else unless he is allowed to pocket a fair share for himself. In striking their bargain with a slave whom they were releasing from domestic service in order to put him into business, financially hard-pressed Athenian slave-owners had found it most profitable for themselves to give the slave the strongest possible incentive to make the joint venture succeed, and the strongest incentive had been to allow the slave in business to purchase his freedom by instalments. In an acute critique of the Athenian democracy, written during the war of 431–404 B.C. by an anonymous Athenian observer, it is recorded that, in Athens at the time of writing, it was impossible to distinguish a slave from a freeman either by his dress or by his demeanour, and that to hit somebody else's slave was to ask for trouble, because a physical injury done to a gainfully employed slave would mean a financial loss for the slave's owner.

There were, on the other hand, at least three important elements in society that did not benefit by the collapse of a master institution that had become an incubus. While domestic slaves were gainers, agricultural and industrial slaves were losers. Slavery — the legalization of the treatment of human beings as chattels — is an inhuman institution at its best, and the only mitigation of its inherent atrociousness is the maintenance of a personal relation between slave and master, since it is not so easy to treat a human being as non-human when you are dealing with him face to face. For this reason, domestic slaves have usually fared better than agricultural and industrial slaves; and the agricultural and industrial slaves of the Hellenic World fared still worse than before when the increase in the scale of economic operations and the advance in technology, which were features of the post-Alexandrine age, made their relations with their owners still more remote and impersonal. The second element in society that was adversely affected was the vast agricultural labour-force of Egypt and South-West Asia, which had been annexed to the Hellenic society *en masse* as a result of Alexander's conquests. These labourers — legally freemen but practically serfs — had not fared so badly under the easy-going Persian régime. The landlords whom they had then had to support had been a sprinkling of barons and priests. But one of the objectives and achievements of the Hellenic conquest of the Persian dominions had been to plant a new crop of colonial Hellenic cities. Alexander himself and his successors — above all, the Seleucidae in Asia — had an unerring eye for choosing sites, and the colonists, too, had a genius for making their settlements thrive. Seleucia-on-Tigris and Dura-Europus-on-Euphrates lasted for five hundred years. Antioch-on-Orontes and Alexandria-on-Nile are alive today, and Alexandria is now once again a great city, with a large quota of Greeks in its population. Cities have never been founded in these numbers and with this success in any other time and place except, perhaps, in the Americas after the Castilian conquest of Mexico and Peru. For the Hellenes, the Hellenic colonization of South-West Asia and Egypt was a notable achievement; but for the native inhabitants it was a calamity; for the Hellenic rentiers were a heavier load on their backs than their former landlords had been. The Egyptian landworkers fared the worst; for in Egypt they had one omnipotent and omnipresent master, the Ptolemaic Crown. Isocrates had condoned the aggressiveness of his imperialist grand design by assuming that the conquered territories would benefit by 'Hellenic superintendence'. The Ptolemies organized the superintendence and took all the profits for themselves. Under their rule the native Egyptian landworkers were scientifically fleeced. The third element in society that lost by the new dispensation was the free peasantry of the older parts of the Hellenic World. In Sicily, by the end of the second century B.C., they were feeling worse off than the plantation slaves who were being goaded into armed insurrection by the ill-treatment that they were receiving.

Thus, after all, the beneficiaries from the collapse of the old city-state dispensation were only a minority in a now vastly enlarged Hellenic World. This minority was, however, the vocal element. The depressed masses were dumb, like sheep before their shearers; and, for the vocal minority, the experience of emancipation was a reality. Their gains, however, like all gains, had to be paid for. If the demands made on individuals by city-states had eventually pitched the tension of Hellenic life too high, the relief from this tension had robbed life of some of its former savour and significance. Individuals found themselves effectively emancipated from city-states without having yet formed any satisfying alternative attachment. Emancipation from the city-states' tyranny had been purchased at the price of a painful slackening of devotion and enthusiasm. Now that the old idols were shattered, what were the Hellenes' new gods to be?

Could the Hellenes of the post-Alexandrine age find worthy gods in the kings who had demonstrated their power by changing the face of the world, and their beneficence by changing it in ways that had given new scope to the Hellenic middle class? Alexander had been hailed as a god's son, and therefore a god in his own person, by the priest of the oracle of the Egyptian god Amun in an oasis in the Libyan Desert. For at least two thousand five hundred years before Alexander's own day, every pharaoh had been a god *ex officio,* and for at least two thousand of those years he had also been a son of the god Re, begotten by Re on the god-king's human mother. The Hellenes had identified Amun-Re with their own god Zeus, the leader of the Olympian war-band. And Zeus was credited with having begotten numerous sons — Hêraklês among them — on attractive women. But these older human sons of Zeus were all legendary heroes. A human son of Zeus here and now was a different matter. The only authentic human beings that the Hellenes had ever deified up to date had been the founders of colonies, and these had been deified only after their deaths and only in the cities to which they had given life. For Alexander's entourage — Macedonians and citizens of city-states alike — his assumption of the divinity that the Egyptian priest had imputed to him was a bad joke. If the portrayal of the Olympian gods in the likeness of the lawless barbarians of the age of the pre-Hellenic Völkerwanderung had long since become a scandal, it was appalling to see one of these barbarian gods descend from Olympus in the flesh in the person of a Macedonian king. Even the Persian Emperor, into whose shoes Alexander was also eager to step, had never claimed to be a god; he had tacitly disavowed any such pretension by claiming to be God's protégé and vicegerent. An Olympian god incarnate, armed with a Persian emperor's despotic powers! God save us from such a saviour of society! Here was a sinister self-assertion of an individual personality. To have allowed the city-states' oppressive divinity to be appropriated by kings might prove to be a fall out of the frying-pan into the fire. The Macedonian prince had come out of his Hellenic tutor Aristotle's hands as a still incorrigible barbarian under a veneer of Hellenism through which his unbridled passions might break their way at any moment with devastating effects. And the best of Alexander's successors were Alexanders writ small, whose latent barbarism was not redeemed by their great archetype's vision and idealism. They were, in fact, scions of the barbarian adolescent individualists in whose image the Olympians had been made. The type ran to demonic extremes in its female exemplars. The first of these viragos to make her mark was Alexander's own Molossian mother Olympias. In Laodice and at least three of the innumerable Cleopatras, the post-Alexandrine Hellenic World felt the full force of 'the monstrous regiment of women'.

Alexander's assertion of his claim to be a god was successful; and, when this precedent had been set, his successors inevitably usurped the title of gods as a corollary to proclaiming themselves kings. The official divinity of Alexander and his successors was made to serve one useful diplomatic purpose. An officially recognized god could dictate to those crypto-divinities, the city-states, without formally infringing their sovereignty. This constitutional fiction saved their citizens' faces, but it never gained a hold on their hearts. The cult of royal human gods could not fill the spiritual vacuum in Hellenic souls — not even when the deified rulers were no longer Macedonian war-lords keeping the world in turmoil as they scrambled for the spoils of the Persian Empire. Even the Caesars, who gave unity and peace to a world that Alexander's successors had torn to shreds, never succeeded in inspiring more than a lukewarm regard.

The deified king's claim to receive worship was made on the strength of his services to society as a saviour. But the ex-citizen of a discredited city-state could not be sure of finding a saviour-king on call. Still less could he be sure, if the king-god did make his epiphany, of finding in him a present help in trouble. If, after a disillusioning experience of idolized city-states, one has made up one's mind to look for salvation in individual, instead of in corporate, human power, perhaps it was better to depend on oneself — to be one's own saviour, if one could rise to that height. It would be an arduous undertaking, because here the god-king's political power — a euphemism for brute force — would be of no avail. Only spiritual power could help a soul to save itself; and a human being who succeeded in reaching this goal by this means must surely be the most godlike representative of the race.

Plato's fictitious philosopher-kings — imagined in a generation in which city-states were losing, but had not yet wholly lost, their hold — had been successful saviours of themselves who had reluctantly followed the call of duty by coming back into the world to save society as well. Two later sages — Zeno of Citium (about 335/3–261 B.C.), the founder of the Stoic school of philosophy, and Epicurus of Samos (342/1–270) B.C., who founded the complementary school called after his name — both lived to see the transformation of the Hellenic World completed, and both of them frankly repudiated the claims of society on the sage. The only state to which they offered their allegiance was the cosmopolis, a city coextensive with the Universe, or, short of that, with the whole 'inhabited world' (oecumenê); and, since the prospect of an Hellenic World-state, which Alexander the Great had momentarily brought within view, had been blotted out by his untimely death, the world's Stoic or Epicurean citizen was in no danger of being called upon to fulfil his admitted oecumenical civic obligations. It was not till all Hellenic and Hellenized lands west of the River Euphrates had been united in the Roman Empire, and until this would-be world-state had been in existence for nearly two hundred years, that, for the first and last time, the burden of ruling the world was shouldered by a Stoic philosopher-king, the Emperor Marcus Aurelius (reigned A.D. 160–180). The Stoic and Epicurean disciplines both concentrated their efforts on equipping an individual human being, detached from social ties, with a spiritual armament that would make him invulnerable to all the slings and arrows of fortune and imperturbable amid all the chances and changes of life, in a cosmopolis that, for all the sage's claims to have made it his spiritual home, was as vast and cold as interstellar space.

Spiritually self-sufficient philosophers were worthier models for gods in human form than politically potent kings. But they too were unsatisfying objects of worship. In attempting the *tour de force* of making themselves super-human, the Stoics and Epicureans made themselves inhuman. They could not make themselves invulnerable except at the cost of casting out love and pity for their fellow human beings, as well as patriotism and public spirit. And this studied callousness made it impossible for them to save either their neighbours or themselves. What then?

X

THE FAILURE OF MONARCHY AND FEDERATION TO ESTABLISH POLITICAL CONCORD

In 323 B.C., when Alexander had returned to Babylon after his completion of the conquest of the Persian Empire and of its former provinces in India, it looked for a moment — as it had looked in 479 B.C., after the expulsion of the Persians from Hellas-in-Asia, as well as from Hellas-in-Europe, by the Panhellenic Alliance — as if the Hellenic World had achieved political unity; and this time the apparent achievement was on a much larger scale. But in 323 B.C., as in 479 B.C., the hopes of peace and concord were immediately disappointed. Alexander's sudden premature death in 323 B.C. had the same effect as the breach between Sparta and Athens after 479 B.C. This time, once again, the Hellenic World broke up into contending camps.

Alexander's successors were blind to his vision of the brotherhood of the human race and were positively opposed to his moves for translating it into the practical terms of a partnership, on a footing of equality, between victorious Macedonians and conquered Persians. Alexander had insisted on eighty of his highest-ranking officers marrying Persian wives. After his death, Seleucus the Victor is said to have been the only one of them who did not repudiate the wife that had been wished upon him. In so far as the successors had any general ideas about what the relations between Hellenes and Orientals should be, they favoured the doctrine of the Hellenes' inborn right to rule. At any rate they acted as if this were their view. But they were not much concerned with theory. Each of them was intent on the practical objective of carving out for himself, by force of arms in conflicts with his colleagues, as much of his master's heritage as he could manage to seize and hold. The wars of the Alexandrine succession were fought with all the turbulence that was the Macedonian aristocracy's cultural inheritance from the barbaric pre-city-state age of anarchy, and with all the resources of the ransacked Persian Empire. In fact, the deadly fratricidal warfare in the Hellenic World, which had been waged on the city-state scale for ninety-three years (431–338 B.C.) and had then been suppressed for fifteen years (338–323 B.C.), now broke out again, after Alexander's death, on a vastly greater scale — as, in the history of Western Christendom, the fourteenth-century and fifteenth-century warfare between Italian city-states rankled into the higher-powered sixteenth-century warfare between the surrounding kingdoms. In both cases, Moloch's furnace was stoked to a fiercer heat by being fed with the rifled treasure of a conquered empire. The Persian Empire's, like the Inca Empire's, gradually accumulated hoards of bullion were suddenly put into circulation again in the form of soldiers' pay; and this had two untoward effects. Besides swelling the size of the contending mercenary armies, it devastated the aggressor society's economy by inflating the currency.

Thus the suppression of city-state sovereignty had not, after all, enabled the Hellenic World to attain the political unity that it so sorely needed. The life and death of Alexander undid the work of his father Philip by first expanding the Hellenic World to a colossal size and then breaking it up politically into a number of contending states which were chronically at war with one another like their predecessors, the city-states, but were war-machines of a far larger calibre. The political achievements of Hellenism in the post-Alexandrine age went no farther than the building of new local states of supra-city-state dimensions; and this was no compensation for the loss of the unity that Philip had conferred on Hellas before his death.

If Macedon's energies had not been immediately diverted by Alexander to the overweeningly ambitious enterprise of bringing the entire Persian Empire under his rule, Macedon might have had the strength to consolidate the Confederation of Corinth with one hand and to Hellenize with the other hand the northern barbarian peoples whom Philip had incorporated in his dominions. But, from Alexander's passage of the Hellespont in 334 B.C. onwards, Macedon was bled white — first by Alexander's own repeated calls for drafts to make good the losses of his original expeditionary force and to garrison the huge territories that he had occupied, and then, for a hundred and fifty years after his death, by the perpetual efforts of his successors on the throne at Pella to hold down European Greece and at the same time to hold the northern barbarians at bay with a man-power that had now been irremediably depleted to a degree that left it inadequate for sustaining a never-ending war on two fronts. It was an ironic sequel to Alexander's exploits that in 279 B.C., only forty-four years after his death, Macedon should have been overrun by Gallic barbarian invaders, and that one horde of these should have been able to cross the Dardanelles in Alexander's track and instal itself permanently in Phrygia, without any of Alexander's successors mustering the strength or resolution to dislodge them (a band that headed for the treasure-houses at Delphi was hurled back by Apollo — or perhaps by the Aetolians). When the Romans liquidated the

Kingdom of Macedon in 167 B.C., they found that numerous settlements of northern barbarians had been planted, by the Macedonian Crown's own action, in depopulated districts of the country adjacent to the northern frontier. Like a cancer, this alien element had replaced the native Macedonian peasantry which the wars had eaten away. Here was a local anticipation, in one war-ridden Hellenic state, of a social disease that was going to attack the whole perimeter of the Roman Empire four hundred years later.

Macedon, Ptolemaic Egypt, and Seleucid Asia were the only three Macedonian successor-states of Alexander's ephemeral world-empire that survived the struggle over the partitioning of it; and, of these three, the Seleucid monarchy displayed the greatest political originality. The Seleucidae succeeded in constructing an effective political framework — and this on a very large scale — within which a host of new non-sovereign colonial Hellenic cities could be set. The loyalty with which such cities in the far interior maintained their allegiance to the monarchy when the open country was being overrun by Oriental counter-attacks against the Hellenic 'ascendancy' was comparable to the loyalty of the majority of Rome's autonomous allies in Italy to Rome during the ordeal of Hannibal's invasion. This shows that the Seleucidae had established a relation with the Hellenic cities within their frontiers that was satisfactory to both parties. If the Seleucid monarchy had not been prematurely disabled by its collision in 192–189 B.C. with the Roman commonwealth, it might have evolved into a union of city-states held together by a common allegiance to a crown.

A more promising, because potentially more stable, method of achieving an organic union between city-states was by federation without employing the institution of monarchy as a political cement; and there were a number of promising Hellenic experiments on federal lines.

The earliest of these was made in Boeotia, where a federal constitution was an obvious expedient for trying to achieve a resolution of divergent local political forces: the tension between a persisting sense of common Boeotian nationality and a narrower loyalty to the city-states into which Boeotia had articulated herself, and another tension between the big city-state Thebes, which aspired to absorb the rest of Boeotia, and the smaller Boeotian states, which were determined to resist Theban attempts to dominate them. An elaborately equitable federal constitution was adopted in Boeotia in 447 B.C. after the liberation of the non-Theban parts of the country from the domination of Athens. Federalism in Boeotia afterwards went into a temporary eclipse during the brief period of the Theban ascendancy in Hellas. For a moment, Thebes fulfilled her ambition of annexing the rest of Boeotia outright. But, after Thebes had been humiliated by Phocis and crushed by Macedon, Boeotia became a federal state again till her federal union was dissolved, first in 171 B.C. and finally in 146 B.C., by Rome's fiat.

A long step in advance was taken in or about 432 B.C. in Chalcidicê, when, after the liberation of the country from Athenian domination, the constitutional device of dual citizenship was invented. The Chalcidian city-states entered into a federal union in which every citizen of every state-member automatically became also a citizen of Olynthus, the most powerful member and the seat of the federal government. This new type of federal constitution, under which all citizens were citizens of the federal union as well as of its component states, gave the union much greater coherence and vitality than if it had been merely a union of states and not also a union of human beings. The Chalcidian federal union displayed a great capacity for expansion. During the bout of anarchy in Macedon that set in after the death of King Archelaus in 399 B.C., the Chalcidians succeeded in absorbing large parts of Macedon into their own federal body politic. If Sparta had not broken up the Chalcidian federal union by force in 379 B.C., the Chalcidians might have done King Philip's work on a federal instead of a monarchical basis. They might even have forestalled the Romans in conferring political unity on the whole Hellenic World.

The institution of dual citizenship was adopted in the Aetolian and Achaean federations, which were formed successively in Continental European Greece in the third century B.C. as instruments for liberating this part of the Hellenic World from the domination of Macedon. It is significant that the nucleus of each of these new unions was a previously backward area, in which there were no memories of ancient local glories to deter the constituent cantons or city-states from merging their separate sovereignties and allowing a citizen to divide his loyalty between his mother-city or canton and the larger body politic into which she had entered. Athens never joined either federation. Sparta eventually joined the Achaean federation only under compulsion, and she seized her first chance of breaking away from it again. It was easier to attract the canton of Aeniania, in the Spercheus valley, into the Aetolian federation, and the recently 'synoecized' city-state of Megalopolis, in South-West Arcadia, into the Achaean federation. Both federations however, were joined by some older and more famous city-states.

The fortunes of the Achaean federation were made by the voluntary accession to it, in 251 B.C., of the adjoining Isthmian city-state Sicyon. The citadel of Sicyon had been recaptured from its Macedonian garrison by a daring band of Sicyonian citizens under the leadership of Aratus; and this Sicyonian leader proved himself a statesman as well as a soldier by persuading his Sicyonian countrymen that, in order to retain the liberty that they had recovered, they must join forces with their Achaean neighbours. Aratus became the political leader of the Achaean federation, and in 243 B.C. he capped his feat of arms in his home city by expelling the Macedonian garrison from the citadel of Corinth — one of the three 'fetters' with which Macedon had shackled European Greece — and bringing Corinth, too, and Megara as well, into the Achaean federation. The Aetolian federation likewise attracted to itself some old-established city-states: for example, Heraclea Trachinia, which had been founded by the Peloponnesians in 426 B.C. to command a passage, farther west than Thermopylae, between Central Greece and the North. These accessions were important strategically. Heraclea's entry into the Aetolian union cut Macedon's overland communications with Central Greece; Corinth's entry into the Achaean union cut Macedon's overland communications with the Peloponnese. But the chief significance of this fusion of advanced with backward communities was psychological and political. The acquisition of such distinguished new member-states gave the Aetolian and Achaean federations prestige; and it also did the new members credit, since it showed that they, at any rate, were not the prisoners of their memories of glorious independence.

The rise of the Achaean federation, with one of its strong points at Megalopolis on Sparta's doorstep, confronted Sparta with a painful choice. If she was not going to resign herself to losing her independence, she must at last make a break with her past, and this break must be a revolutionary one. By the middle years of the third century B.C., Sparta was faced with the same critical shortage of man-power as Macedon — a shortage which was not felt by the Hellenic World as a whole till a hundred years later. By this time the number of Spartiate families is said to have fallen to seven hundred, of which only about one hundred owned or held any land. The dwindling of the number of Sparta's military effectives was a matter of indifference to the rest of the world, which had long since ceased to reckon with Sparta as a military power. But it was pain and grief to a party in Sparta who had not yet reconciled themselves, as the Athenians had, to seeing their country become a nonentity in the field of international affairs. The remedy was not far to seek; for, even after the liberation of Messenia, Sparta's own territory (as distinct from the territories of her surrounding 'satellite' city-states) still comprised some of the most productive agricultural land in European Greece, and nothing had gone wrong with the soil. Sparta could never aspire to enter the lists against the post-Alexandrine great powers; but she could increase her military strength considerably — perhaps enough to enable her to hold her own against her new neighbour the Achaean federation — if she were to make her good earth maintain, once more, the full complement of soldiers that it was capable of supporting. There were landless Spartiates eligible for allotments; and the *élite* of the 'perioeci' could be given Spartiate citizenship and could be planted on Spartiate land still remaining over for re-distribution when all landless Spartiates had been provided for. This programme, however, would mean dividing up the estates of the surviving 'peers'; and any attempt to do this would arouse vehement resistance; for an increase in the surviving Spartiate landowners' average wealth per head had been the economic consequence of the diminution in their numbers, and this had reconciled the lucky minority to the accompanying decline in their country's military effectiveness.

The first attempt at carrying out this revolution in Lacedaemon was made by King Agis IV (reigned 244–241/0 B.C.). He was a tender-hearted idealist, and he suffered himself to be arrested and put to death by the counter-revolutionaries without making a fight. His widow was then married off to a younger man who was heir to the throne of the other Spartan royal house (at Sparta two kings of two different houses reigned side by side — a relic, perhaps, of the days before the 'synoecism' of the five Spartan villages). Queen Agiatis indoctrinated King Cleomenes III (reigned 237–222 B.C.) in her martyred first husband's ideals, and her second husband, who did not shrink from the prospect of using force and shedding blood, made up his mind to carry out the revolution effectively. This time it was the counter-revolutionaries, not the revolutionary king, who lost their lives. In 227 B.C. Cleomenes re-distributed the Spartiate land according to plan; and selected 'perioeci', as well as landless Spartiates, duly received their allotments.

The objective of this revolution at Sparta was not social justice. There was no question of enfranchising the helots (after the liberation of Messenia there were still helots in the Eurotas valley); nor was there any question of relieving the Spartiates, new or old, of the burden of the 'Lycurgean' system of penal military servitude. The increase in the numerical strength of the Spartiate contingent of the Lacedaemonian army was accompanied by a reform in the Lacedaemonian soldier's equipment. One hundred and sixty-three years after a Spartan division had been cut to pieces by a force of targeteer-pikemen organized by Iphicrates, King Cleomenes of Sparta re-armed the Lacedaemonian infantry with target and pike in place of shield and spear. From Cleomenes' point of view, the social effect of his reforms was merely incidental to their military purpose. But the social aspect of the Spartan revolution loomed larger than the military aspect in the eyes of Sparta's neighbours.

Now that a re-distribution of property had been started

at Sparta, where was this going to stop? The Achaean federation was an association for the mutual protection of private property as well as political independence. The Achaeans, in their turn, were now faced with having to make a choice between patriotism and middle-class interests. Could revolutionary Sparta perhaps be rendered innocuous by being brought into the Achaean union? A dangerous gamble; for Cleomenes had a dynamic and captivating personality. If once he were inside, the leadership might fall into his hands out of Aratus's, and the Achaean federation might find itself turning into a Spartan empire in miniature. Aratus, moved by his personal motive for keeping Cleomenes out and putting him down, played on the social and economic anxieties of his middle-class constituents. Cleomenes' overtures were rejected, and negotiations were opened with the reigning king of Macedon, Antigonus Doson. Antigonus's price for helping the Achaeans to settle accounts with Cleomenes was the reintroduction of a Macedonian garrison into the citadel of Corinth. Aratus persuaded the Achaeans to agree, though the liberation of Corinth had been one of his own two major feats. The Macedonian army marched south in 224 B.C.; yet this disturbance of the balance of power did not move Egypt to give Cleomenes military aid. Cleomenes' cause was lost before the new-model Lacedaemonian army was decisively defeated at Sellasia, on the north-eastern approaches to Sparta city, in 222 B.C.

Cleomenes and his family, with a few faithful comrades in arms, escaped to Alexandria; but his personality made him as awkward for King Ptolemy IV as a guest as he had been awkward as a rival for President Aratus. In the third century B.C., as in the seventh and the sixth, Egypt depended for her defence on a corps of Greek mercenaries. Cleomenes in exile at Alexandria became the hero of these Greek soldiers on foreign service. Many of them were his fellow Peloponnesians. Perhaps it might come into his head to woo their support for making a *coup d'état* and seizing Egypt as a base of operations for recovering Sparta. The Ptolemaic government felt it wise to intern the exiled king and his Spartiate comrades. The resentful prisoners broke out and charged through the streets of Alexandria, cutting down a luckless civil servant and calling on the citizens to rise in the name of freedom. The citizens were unmoved; if they had wanted any more of that, they would not have left their ancestral city-states to settle in Alexandria. Cleomenes and his comrades dramatically committed suicide. Their women and children were cruelly put to death by the Ptolemaic authorities. The life and death of Sparta's second martyr king, and of his martyred forerunner Agis, became a legend that lived on in the explosive underworld beneath the feet of the uneasily dominant Hellenic middle class.

The hostilities in the Peloponnese that had ended in 222 B.C. at Sellasia seemed like no more than a little war. But a bigger war was started in 221 B.C. when the Seleucid King Antiochus III attacked the Ptolemaic kingdom's possessions in 'Hollow Syria' (Coele Syria) — as Canaan was called in Greek, in allusion to the rift valley that runs down it from the Baqa' to the Gulf of 'Aqaba. In 219 a new local war broke out in Continental European Greece between the Aetolian federation and Macedon supported by her Achaean and other allies. And in the same year, on the distant Mediterranean coast of Spain, the young Carthaginian captain-general Hannibal son of Hamilcar besieged and captured the little native town of Saguntum — a Roman protectorate in an equivocal position on the Carthaginian side of the line of the River Ebro, which the two western powers had accepted as the boundary between their respective spheres of influence in the Iberian peninsula. These local fires were soon to run together into a Panhellenic conflagration. This was the nemesis of the Hellenic society's failure to preserve the unity that had been brought within its grasp, a hundred and twenty years back, by the work of the great Macedonian statesman Philip son of Amyntas.

XI

ROME'S RECEPTION OF HELLENISM AND OVERTHROW OF THE BALANCE OF POWER

THE political structures of the Achaean and Aetolian federations and the Seleucid monarchy looked like promising solutions for the post-Alexandrine Hellenic World's common problem of devising constitutions for states of a supra-city-state calibre; but the future lay with a new commonwealth to the west of the Straits of Otranto.

If any of the states in Italy and Sicily was to play a leading role in post-Alexandrine Hellenic history, this might have seemed to be the destiny of Syracuse; for Syracuse was one of the most populous, powerful, and cultivated of all Hellenic city-states, and Sicily had, as we have seen, been the region in which Hellenic statesmanship had achieved its earliest successes in combining city-states into larger political units. The creation of two principalities centring respectively on Akragas (Agriggentum) and Syracuse had been the local Hellenic retort to the antecedent union of the Phoenician city-states in the western basin of the Mediterranean under the supremacy of Carthage. In alliance, these two principalities had defeated, in 480 B.C., a Carthaginian attempt to conquer the western Hellenic colonial area. Carthage had embarked on a second attempt in 409 B.C., after the Hellenic portion of Sicily had been ravaged by the Athenian assault on Syracuse and the victorious Syracusan fleet had sailed away to take part in a counter-attack on Athens in the distant waters of the Aegean. This time the Carthaginians had come near to success. Returning to the charge in 406, they had overrun all Sicily up to the walls of Syracuse and had laid siege to Syracuse itself, when the Sicilian Hellenes' fortunes were retrieved by Dionysius, a friend of Hermocrates the leader of the Syracusan resistance to Athens. Dionysius turned the tide so dramatically that, for a moment, in 398 B.C., he succeeded in expelling the Carthaginians from most of their possessions in Sicily, including their islet-fortress Motya. After the tide had turned once again, and yet once more, the belligerents agreed in 392 B.C. to partition Sicily along a line that left only the north-west corner of the island to Carthage and gave the rest to Dionysius.

The new Siceliot despot's dominions thus embraced the former dominions of both Hiero of Syracuse and Thero of Akragas; and Dionysius went on to bring a number of the Hellenic colonial city-states in Italy under his rule and to establish a naval command over the Adriatic Sea. If the Hellenic principality that Dionysius had founded, west of the Straits of Otranto, had survived into the age of Alexander's successors, it could have held its own among the new Hellenic monarchies. Indeed, the principality re-founded in that age by Agathocles of Syracuse (reigned 317–289 B.C.) did successfully hold its own, though it was smaller and weaker than Dionysius's principality had been. Unfortunately for the future of Hellenism, Dionysius's principality was short-lived, like Hiero's and Thero's at an earlier date and like Agathocles' at a later one; and the disruptive forces to which these unions each succumbed in turn were the same. The Siceliots had acquiesced in their establishment as the only means of saving themselves from being conquered by Carthage; but the price of salvation had been the subordination of the smaller Siceliot city-states to Syracuse and the subjection of the Syracusans themselves, as well as the other Siceliots, to the rule of a despot. In Hellenic eyes this was a very high price to pay; so, as soon as an immediate threat from Carthage receded, the wish to re-establish republican government and local sovereignties usually got the better of the wish to maintain an insurance policy against foreign attack at the cost of paying so burdensome a premium. In 356 B.C., after Dionysius I had been succeeded by a son of the same name but not of the same ability, the Dionysian dynasty was overthrown, and its territory broken up, by a revolution made in the name of liberty.

The break-up of the Dionysian principality in 356 B.C. had more serious consequences for the western Hellenes than the break-up of the Hieronic principality in 466 B.C.; for, this time, Carthage was not the only aggressive neighbour whom the western Hellenes had to fear. Already, before their deliberate disbandment of their united forces, they had begun to suffer from the native peoples' counter-attack. After the previous disbandment, 110 years earlier, the city-state of Syracuse, without the aid of the other Siceliot Hellenic city-states whose resources she now no longer commanded, had proved strong enough to prevent the native Sicel peoples in the interior of Sicily from shaking off her domination. Moreover, the Sicels had rebelled against Syracusan rule in the name of the Hellenic ideal of liberty; and their failure to reconquer their political independence from a domineering Hellenic power did not alienate them from the Hellenic civilization or slow down the process of self-Hellenization on which they had embarked. By contrast, the second wave of the native counter-attack came from a distant hinterland along the east coast of Italy, north of the 'spur' above the 'heel'; and here Hellenism had so far made no lodgement except at Ancona, where Dionysius I had established a Syracusan naval base. Ancona was the only good natural harbour along this coast to the north of Brundisium (Brindisi), the future base for Roman operations across the Straits of Otranto. Hellenism made little impression on eastern Italy, north of the 'spur', till this region was incorporated in the Roman Commonwealth; and the Oscan barbarians who, from the later decades of the fifth century B.C. onwards, began to descend, from this remote region, upon the Hellenic colonies in Campania and in the 'toe' showed themselves as impervious to Hellenic culture as the Sicels had shown themselves receptive towards it. The principal Hellenic colonial cities on the coasts of Italy — for example, Tarentum, Locri, and Rhegium — managed to hold out. Even little Neapolis (Naples) on the Campanian coast did not fall. But cities that did fall, and many of the smaller Hellenic cities did, were temporarily lost to the Hellenic World. The break-up of the Dionysian principality opened the flood-gates wide. The extent of the danger was revealed when, in 289 B.C., the Siceliot Hellenic city of Messana, commanding the Sicilian side of the Straits between Sicily and the 'toe' of Italy, was seized, cleared, and colonized by a band of Oscan mercenaries, previously in Agathocles' service, who called themselves Mamertini after the name of the native Italian war-god.

Thus, after the break-up of the Dionysian principality, the western Hellenes' attempts to keep Carthage and the Oscans at bay were ineffective. The despot Agathocles, who re-established the Syracusan principality in 317 B.C., was energetic — he was the first champion of Hellenism to attack Carthage in her home territory in North-West Africa — but his work was ephemeral. And, when the principality was re-established again, for the last time, by a second Hiero (reigned 265 (?)–215 B.C.), its territory was confined to the west coast of Sicily, exclusive of Mamertine Messana, and it survived only so long as it submitted to a Roman protectorate. The western Hellenes also applied for help to their brothers east of the Straits of Otranto. In 344 B.C., for instance, Timoleon, a high-minded citizen of Syracuse's mother-country Corinth, came to Sicily in answer to a Syracusan appeal for deliverance from Dionysius II, who had regained possession of Syracuse in 347. Timoleon succeeded in eliminating Dionysius and other local despots, composing differences, and collecting an army to stem a Carthaginian attack. But he was too scrupulous to seize his chance of becoming a despot himself; and, after he had retired again into private life, the Siceliot city-states relapsed into another bout of anarchy which lasted till the rise of Agathocles.

Four successive champions from Continental European Greece came to the help of the Italiot city-states in answer to appeals from the Tarentines. King Archidamus III of Sparta came in 342 B.C., only to lose his life on an Italian battlefield in 338. Alexander, king of the Molossians — a North-Greek people in the interior of 'the Continent' (Epirus) opposite the island of Corcyra — crossed the Straits of Otranto one year after his Macedonian namesake had crossed the Dardanelles. The two Alexanders' united forces might have made Italy safe for Hellenism, but the Molossian adventurer was undertaking a more formidable military enterprise than the Macedonian with far smaller resources, and he met with Archidamus's fate. His intervention, too, was a failure; the Spartan prince Cleonymus's subsequent intervention in 303 was a fiasco; and, when a later king of the Molossians, the famous war-lord Pyrrhus, landed at Tarentum in 280 B.C. with more adequate forces than his predecessor the Molossian Alexander, it was already too late; for, by that time, Tarentum was confronted, not by semi-barbarian Oscan war-bands, but by Rome. Pyrrhus found himself unable to break the power of Rome, even with the united forces of Tarentum, the Lucanians, and the Bruttians behind him. Yet, with the Romans still in the field, Pyrrhus embarked on the hardly less formidable task of trying to expel the Carthaginians from Sicily. And all the time he was looking back over his shoulder to make sure of not missing any good chance of re-intervening in the scramble for the partition of Alexander of Macedon's vast and comparatively docile heritage. When, in 275 B.C., Pyrrhus withdrew to the eastern shore of the Straits of Otranto, it was clear that, if Hellenism in the west was to be saved, its one possible saviour was Rome.

Fortunately for the future of Hellenism there were continental native Italians on the west coast of Italy who were as receptive towards Hellenism as their insular cousins the Sicels were. On this side of Italy, as well as in the 'heel' below the 'spur', Hellenism struck root and spread. And its propagation here owed less to the local Greek colonies, old and important though some of these were, than to the adoption of the Hellenic civilization by peoples of non-Hellenic origin. Hellenism was adopted not only by the immigrant Etruscans, who had colonized the island of Elba and the neighbouring stretch of mainland coast (attracted, no doubt, by the rich deposits of minerals there); it was adopted also by the Etruscans' Latin neighbours in the lower basin of the River Tiber. The west coast of Italy, unlike the east coast, was well supplied with natural harbours, and it had a fertile and accessible hinterland. In the sixth century B.C. the Etruscans had pushed their way over the Appennines into the great basin of the River Po; and some of their settlements there — for instance, Mantua and Spina — had survived a subsequent deluge of Gallic barbarians from beyond the Alps.

If Hellenism was going to penetrate the European

interior of the Eurasian continent from one of the European shores of the Mediterranean and its northern gulfs, the coast that might have been expected to become the base-line for this expansion into the hinterland was the north shore of the Aegean, where the valley of the River Axius (Vardar) offered as open a road into the interior as the distant valley of the River Rhône in the hinterland of Massilia (Marseilles). But this 'Thracian' coast, as it was called, was cheated of its manifest destiny first by Sparta's act, when she broke up the Chalcidian confederation, and then by Alexander's, when he diverted the energies of Macedon from the organization of South-East Europe to the conquest of South-West Asia. And eventually it was the west coast of Italy — relatively distant though this was from the heart of the Hellenic World — that came to play the part in the Hellenization of Europe that was played, in the Hellenization of Asia, by the west coast of Anatolia. After the adoption of the Hellenic culture by the Latin city-states, one of these, Rome, followed up the Etruscans' abortive advance and carried her own advance far further. She eventually carried it eastwards, down the south bank of the River Danube, to the west coast of the Black Sea, and westwards as far as the eastern shore of the Atlantic on a frontage extending from Morocco to Britain and Batavia.

The Latins, Etruscans, and colonial Phoenicians continued to take the institution of city-states seriously at a time when the Hellenes were throwing it over in the hope of finding salvation in a revival of the archaic institution of monarchy. City-states were a native product in Canaan as well as in Hellas, and the colonial Phoenicians had brought the institution with them from their homeland. We do not know whether the Etruscans and Latins adopted this institution, like so many others, from the Hellenes or developed it independently. Rome is called 'an Hellenic city-state' by Aristotle's contemporary Heracleides Ponticus in a notice of her momentary capture by a roving Gallic war-band in 390 B.C.

During the seventy-five years 340–266 B.C., while the Macedonians were engaged in overthrowing the Persian Empire and in fighting one another for the spoils, Rome was uniting all Italy, south of the Appennines, into a commonwealth that was a new power in the Hellenic World. The kingdom of Macedon dated from the pre-Hellenic age of anarchy and the Carthaginian empire from the sixth century B.C., while the Seleucid monarchy in South-West Asia and the Ptolemaic monarchy in Egypt were, in effect, the respective successors of the Persian Empire and a dissident Kingdom of Egypt that had maintained its independence against Persia from 404 till 342 B.C. But no power, before Rome, had ever united all Cis-Appennine Italy. The Etruscans had had their chance in the sixth century B.C. and had missed it. The association between the Etruscan city-states was so loose that, when Rome set out to bring her neighbours under her control, she was able to master the Etruscan states one by one.

The structure of the new Roman commonwealth was heterogeneous, and most of its features had Hellenic precedents. Like Sparta and Carthage, Rome attached other city-states to herself by permanent political and military alliances under which they undertook to follow her lead. Like the Seleucid monarchy, she founded new city-states — the so-called Latin colonies — that were autonomous but were not sovereign. The Latin colonies, as well as Rome's other allies, had to do what Rome told them. The Latin colonies were planted on lands taken from defeated enemy states; but, like Sparta and Athens, Rome also enlarged her own city-state territory (its original nucleus was only about half the size of Attica) by annexing to it some of the lands taken from the defeated states. Indeed, in some cases she annexed a defeated state's whole territory. Like Athens she planted out settlements of her citizens on enclaves of annexed territory that were more than a day's journey from the city itself and were detached from the main body of the city's domain. The Athenian cleruchies (allotment-holdings assigned to Athenian citizens) were, however, linked with Athens, rather than sundered from her, by the sea, whereas the enclaves of territory assigned to the more recent of the Roman 'tribes' (meaning 'thridings' and corresponding to the 'nations' constituting the citizen-body of an Hellenic city-state) were sundered from Rome by the territories of autonomous allied states. But only a small part of the territories annexed by Rome was planted with Roman settlers drawn from Rome's ancestral territory. The greater part was left in the possession of its original inhabitants; and these became Roman citizens by acts of wholesale naturalization. By the time when Rome had brought the whole of Italy south of the Appennines into her commonwealth, she had also enlarged her own city-state territory by annexations that were so extensive that the 'ager Romanus', as it was called, now stretched right across Italy from sea to sea — running from the shores of the Western Mediterranean on either side of the mouth of the River Tiber to the shores of the Adriatic on either side of the territory of Rome's ally Ancona. The area of the 'ager Romanus' in 266 B.C. was, in fact, approximately the same as the area of the Papal States (minus the Emilia) in the medieval and modern age, before Italy was united into a single state in the nineteenth century.

The most significant tendency in the evolution of the Roman commonwealth was a steadily increasing application of the institution of dual citizenship.

Roman citizens belonging to the 'thridings' into which Rome's original territory had been divided or to the additional 'thridings' planted on parts of the subsequently annexed territories were, of course, citizens of Rome exclusively; and so, to begin with, were the compulsorily naturalized inhabitants of the backward cantons in the Appennines and on the Adriatic slope that had been annexed to the 'ager Romanus' without being colonized by Roman settlers. These new citizens were gradually educated in Roman life and law and in the Latin language, under the tutelage of magistrates sent from Rome, without at first being given either local autonomy or the rights of voting and of standing for election in the public assemblies of the Roman citizen body. Rome enjoyed, and took advantage of, a geographical situation like that which Olynthus had enjoyed but had been prevented from exploiting when Sparta had nipped in the bud the growth of the Chalcidian federal union. Rome, like Olynthus, was a city-state with a hinterland whose inhabitants were still in the pre-city-state stage; and these politically undeveloped populations were more easy to absorb into a more advanced body politic than the citizens of city-states that had merely been conquered in war without being the conquering city-state's inferiors in culture. Rome did also conquer and annex, in the lowlands along the west coast, a number of city-states that were her cultural equals; and she allowed most of these to retain, within the Roman body politic, the civic self-government that they had previously enjoyed while they had still been sovereign independent states.

It was here that the Romans applied the principle of dual citizenship, whether they were consciously following some Hellenic model or whether they had stumbled on the institution independently in the course of feeling their way towards a solution of their own political problems. In granting the privilege of local self-government to the compulsorily naturalized citizens of formerly sovereign city-states, they did this, to begin with, on one or other of two different bases. Where the people of the formerly sovereign city-state were alien to the Romans in language and culture — as, for example, the compulsorily naturalized citizens of the Etruscan city-state of Caere — the Romans excluded them, as they excluded the backward inhabitants of the annexed highland cantons, from the exercise of political rights that would have given them a voice in the self-government of the Roman Republic. Where, on the other hand, the new citizens were the Romans' own close kinsmen — as, for example, the compulsorily naturalized citizens of the formerly sovereign Latin city-state of Aricia — the Romans were more generous. Besides allowing them to go on governing their own city autonomously, they gave them the same rights in the government of Rome herself that the old citizens of Rome enjoyed.

Aliens naturalized on the less generous of these two different sets of terms were known as 'citizens without the suffrage' or alternatively as 'municipes', meaning people who were subject to the duties of a Roman citizen without enjoying the rights. Autonomous city-states within the Roman body politic whose citizens were 'municipes' were known as 'municipia' (the origin of the modern word 'municipalities'). The general tendency in the Roman commonwealth, from the fourth century B.C. to the third century of the Christian Era, was for more and more of Rome's allies and subjects to be given the Roman citizenship, and for more and more citizens of the lower category to be transferred to the higher. At times there were hesitations, halts, and even backslidings in the execution of this prevailing policy, and sometimes these had serious consequences. But, in the course of centuries, the process of enfranchisement went forward; and, after the promulgation of the Emperor Caracalla's comprehensive decree, the Constitutio Antoniniana, in A.D. 212, there were very few people left in the Hellenic World west of the Roman Empire's eastern frontier of the day who had not been granted Roman citizenship on the most favourable terms that could then be offered.

In her policy of giving her franchise to aliens, Rome was more generous than any power that had previously entered the arena of Hellenic international politics; and Rome was pursuing this policy at a time when Cis-Appennine Italy was populous and when her population was still increasing. Consequently Rome came to possess a reservoir of military man-power that none of her competitors could match. And her peasant soldiers, in their myriads, were not mercenaries, not subjects, and not barbarians. They were citizens of Rome herself and of her Latin colonies and Italian allies; and they were also willing apprentices in the arts of the Hellenic civilization. The citizen-soldiers of Macedon and of the Seleucid monarchy were mere corporal's guards in point of comparative numbers. Ptolemaic Egypt and Carthage had large conscriptable subject populations and were rich enough to supplement these by hiring mercenaries; and armies composed of these materials might be more efficient than a citizen militia (Hannibal's professional troops repeatedly defeated numerically stronger Roman armies); but 'native' troops and mercenaries would also be less trustworthy. They might have a sense of personal loyalty towards a particular commander — for instance, Hannibal; but they would feel no moral obligation to the state that had hired or exacted their services — for instance, Carthage, who nearly met her end after the close of her first war with Rome, instead of in her third, through provoking her mercenary troops into a mutiny by the meanness of the terms on which she proposed to pay them off. The outcome of the competition between the five great powers showed that, in her citizen soldiery, Rome held the winning military card in her hands.

The Roman army in this age, like the Macedonian, included infantry armed in the expensive and old-fashioned Hellenic way. But in the Roman army, too, these shield-and-spear troops were a small minority and did not play a leading part. The equipment of the bulk of the Roman heavy infantry was more antique than the Macedonian phalangite's Iphicratean target and pike. Like the heroes whose combats are described in the Homeric epic, the ordinary Roman infantryman first hurled a throwing-spear and then fought at close-quarters with a sword. His throwing-spear was short and heavy, and he went into battle with a couple of them. His shield, which was oblong and concave and was made of light materials, wood and leather, gave his body far better protection, weight for weight, than either the traditional Hellenic metal-plated round shield or the Iphicratean target. The Roman shield had not the target's advantage of liberating the left hand, as well as the right, for active use. Yet the Romans were more successful than the Macedonians had been, even in the best days of the Macedonian phalanx, in combining mass with mobility. A charging Macedonian phalanx could sweep away anything in its path — a Roman legion included — so long as the enemy did not perform any counter-manœuvre and so long as the phalanx's own formation remained unbroken. But a Macedonian phalanx was lost if a body of Roman swordsmen got behind its guard, as happened both at Cynoscephalae in 197 B.C. and at Pydna in 168 B.C.; for the Macedonian pikes were formidable only in a frontal engagement in close formation; and, if the pikeman found himself taken in the flank and compelled to fight individually, he had no weapon but an inadequate dagger to fall back on. The Roman soldier, on the other hand, was an individual fighter even when in formation; both of his offensive weapons were effective; and they were doubly so because they were used in co-ordination — the preliminary shower of throwing-spears being intended to 'soften up' the enemy before he was assailed, hand to hand, with the sword. The Roman army's formation was also more flexible. The heavy infantry was grouped in 'handfuls', each only 120 men strong; and these 'handfuls' were marshalled in three waves. This tactical order was a step in the direction of the device of holding back reserves to be thrown into action at the critical moment. Thus a Roman army in action had many moves that it could make before it need resign itself to defeat, and its risks were widely distributed, whereas the fate of a Macedonian army hung on the outcome of a single charge made by a single unit. After the disasters on the River Trebia and at Lake Trasimene, the Roman high command momentarily lost faith in the Roman army's own peculiar tactical genius, and drew up its troops at Cannae in a Macedonian-like mass. The results of this retrograde step, induced by a failure of nerve, were so appalling that the error was not repeated. After the lapse at Cannae, Roman tactics went on developing on lines of ever greater flexibility.

The Roman infantry was, in fact, potentially the best in the Hellenic military arena in the age of the contending powers, and its quality was rapidly improved by the experience of measuring itself against the other great military powers of the day. On the other hand, the Roman cavalry was, and remained, as inadequate as the Macedonian phalangite's dagger. The smallness of its numbers was not made up for by any superiority in its fighting power. For cavalry, the Romans preferred to rely upon their allies; and their neglect of this arm was one of the reasons for their inability to cope with Hannibal.

In bringing the whole of Cis-Appennine Italy under her control, Rome had inevitably involved herself in the international affairs of a wider world, since Italy included a number of colonial Hellenic city-states, and the most important of these, Tarentum, had appealed for help against Rome to an Hellenic power on the eastern side of the Straits of Otranto. Rome plunged deeper in when, in 264 B.C., she took under her protection the Mamertine occupants of the Siceliot city of Messana, who had provoked Hiero of Syracuse and the Carthaginians into joining forces against them. This venture overseas involved Rome in a twenty-four-years' war with Carthage (264–241 B.C.). The two western Powers fought this war on a scale that dwarfed the contemporary wars between the Ptolemies and the Seleucids and between the Ptolemies and Macedon; and, unlike these, the first Romano-Carthaginian war had a definite result. It ended in the expulsion of the Carthaginians from Sicily and the political unification of the island under the control of a single power for the first time since the beginning, five hundred years back, of the competition for the possession of the island between Phoenician and Hellenic colonists. The Carthaginian province in Sicily now passed into Rome's possession. The Mamertines and Hiero had already become Rome's allies. Rome had won her victory by the *tour de force* of improvising, in war-time, a navy that was able not only to engage the Carthaginian navy but to wrest from it the command of the sea. Rome was, of course, able to draw upon the naval experience of her Italiot Greek allies, and her own abundant man-power could provide crews for a very large fleet. Yet, considering the Carthaginians' skill and reputation in naval warfare, Rome's challenge to Carthage on Carthage's own element was as audacious as it was successful.

The restoration of peace after the simultaneous but unconnected wars in the western and eastern basins of the Mediterranean, like the restoration of peace in the Aegean in 445 B.C., gave grounds for hope that coexistence might prove a feasible alternative to catastrophe. But this time, as before, this hope was soon extinguished by dire events.

The second Romano-Carthaginian war (218–201 B.C.) like the second of the twentieth-century world-wars, was a war of revenge launched by a defeated great power that had been humiliated without having been permanently incapacitated. In its devastating effect the second war far surpassed its predecessor — devastating though the first war had been. The second war brought the winner of the first war to the brink of utter defeat, but ended in the previous loser's being defeated for the second time, and this time irretrievably. The second Romano-Carthaginian war also resembled the second Atheno-Peloponnesian war (431–404 B.C.) in engulfing the whole Hellenic World and in starting a chain-reaction of warfare and revolution.

In the first Romano-Carthaginian war the only commander on either side who had covered himself with glory had been Hamilcar 'the Lightning'. When the Carthaginians had been on the point of losing their last foothold in Sicily, Hamilcar had prolonged the Carthaginian resistance in the island for six years. When the war had been lost by Carthage through a conclusive naval defeat for which Hamilcar had not been responsible, and when Carthage had then been brought within sight of extinction by a mutiny in her mercenary army, Hamilcar had crushed the mutineers and had then gone off to Spain to conquer there for his country a new empire to replace the old Carthaginian province in Sicily that Carthage had been forced to cede to Rome in the peace-settlement. Hamilcar planned to nullify the effect of Rome's capture of the naval command of the Western

Mediterranean and to reverse the result of the first Romano-Carthaginian war by making the new Carthaginian empire in Spain a base of operations for an invasion of Italy overland. The plan was magnificently daring. It involved the crossing of two great mountain-ranges, the Pyrenees and the Alps, and one great river, the Rhône. The whole line of march would be through undeveloped and, indeed, unexplored country: but these formidable physical ordeals seemed worth risking for the sake of two immense military and political prizes that might be gained if the operation were carried out successfully. Once arrived in the basin of the River Po, a Carthaginian expeditionary force might expect to become a rallying point for the local Gallic and Ligurian peoples, who were already up in arms against the advancing wave of Roman colonization. Then, once across the Appennines with Gallic and Ligurian reinforcements at its side, the Carthaginian force might hope to set going a landslide of defections among Rome's Italian allies. To break up the Roman commonwealth through a decisive Carthaginian victory over Rome on land on Rome's own Italian ground was Hamilcar's ultimate objective; and its achievement would indeed have reversed the result of the first war; it might even have relieved Carthage permanently of the Roman menace by breaking Rome's power once for all.

Hamilcar died before his preparations were complete, and left the execution of his plan to his son. Neither the Canaanite nor the Hellenic society ever produced a greater soldier than Hannibal, and it was not his fault that, in the end, the plan miscarried. Hannibal duly marched from the Ebro to the Po, and from the Po basin into Cis-Appennine Italy; in three successive years he inflicted on the Romans three defeats in ascending order of magnitude; on the River Trebia in 218 B.C., on the shores of Lake Trasimene in 217, at Cannae in 216; and he held his ground in Cis-Appennine Italy for fifteen years: 217 to 203 B.C. inclusive. He was foiled by three adverse factors over which he had no control: the indomitable spirit of the Roman Senate and people; the unshakeable loyalty to Rome of the majority of her naturalized citizens and her allies (whose steadfastness far outbalanced the sensational defections of Capua, Syracuse, and Tarentum); and the huge reserves of citizen, Latin, and ally man-power on which Rome was able to draw.

The second Romano-Carthaginian war was brought to an end by a decisive Roman victory in 202 B.C. over Carthage's last army, commanded by Hannibal himself, at Naraggara, on African soil in the neighbourhood of Zama Regia. But, long before that, the war had spread from Spain and Italy and Sicily to European Greece and the Aegean. In 215 B.C. Hannibal had negotiated a treaty with King Philip V of Macedon, who wanted to eliminate a bridgehead that the Romans had established on his side of the Straits of Otranto during the inter-war years. In 211 B.C. the Romans had retorted by making an offensive alliance with Macedon's arch-enemy Aetolia. And the world-war did not stop when Carthage ceased fighting. Hostilities between Rome and Macedon, which had been suspended in 205 B.C., were resumed in 200 B.C.; and, this time, the Macedonians were decisively defeated by the Roman infantry and the Aetolian cavalry at Cynoscephalae in 197 B.C. Macedon was compelled to surrender all her possessions in Greece south of Macedon proper, and even to grant independence to the rebellious highland canton of Orestis within Macedon itself. Corinth was liberated from Macedonian rule by the victorious Roman commander Titus Quinctius Flamininus, thirty years after she had been retroceded to Macedon by Aratus (fifty years after Flamininus's generous gesture, another

Roman general laid Corinth waste, which no Macedonian conqueror had ever done). Next came the turn of the Aetolians, who fell out with Rome over the disposal of the ceded Macedonian territories, and of the Seleucid King Antiochus III, who fell out with her in attempting to re-assert the Seleucid crown's sovereignty over the ancient Hellenic city-states along the west coast of Anatolia. Antiochus rashly allied himself with the Aetolians against Rome and, still more rashly, went to meet trouble halfway by advancing into European Greece. He was misled by relatively easy past military successes. He had once marched into the interior of Asia as far as the Hindu Kush; and in 198 B.C., at the third attempt, he had conquered Coele Syria from King Ptolemy V. He had not reckoned with the Romans' fighting-power. In 191 B.C. he was routed at Thermopylae; in 190 he was routed again at Magnesia-under-Sipylus. The Seleucid monarchy was compelled to surrender all its possessions north-west of the Taurus mountains; and this was the beginning of its end—though, in 162 B.C., Roman commissioners were still so afraid of a Seleucid military revival that they hamstrung the war-elephants at the monarchy's military headquarters in Apamea-over-Orontes. The Aetolians at bay fought like wild cats in their mountain fastnesses, but in 189 B.C. they too were compelled to capitulate.

Thus, in thirty years (218–189 B.C.), Rome had overthrown all other powers that had tried conclusions with her; but the experience of Hannibal's invasion of Italy had left her tormented by a haunting sense of insecurity: and it took Rome two more bouts of severe fighting to reduce her already discomfited adversaries to a degree of impotence at which even she could no longer feel them to be a menace. Her continuing fear of Macedon was justified; for Macedon after her second war with Rome, like Carthage after her first, was bent on revenge; and in the third Romano-Macedonian war (171–168 B.C.) she put up a much more formidable resistance than in the second before she was brought to her knees — as she was, once again, by the inadequacy of her man-power and by the shortcomings of her valiant army's equipment and tactics. For Rome, this war was her most critical passage of arms since her defeat at Cannae. On the other hand, Rome's continuing fear of Carthage was no more than a nightmare; for, though Hannibal had been Rome's implacable and indefatigable enemy to the last, he had been driven to commit suicide in exile in 183 B.C., and, since the conclusion of peace between Carthage and Rome in 201 B.C., the Carthaginians had abandoned all ambitions and were seeking nothing more than just to be allowed to survive. Rome's assault on Carthage in 149 B.C. was one of the most cold-blooded acts of aggression in Rome's history; and it brought on her an immediate retribution; for Carthage in this final war with Rome (149–146 B.C.), which had been forced on her without provocation on her part, defended herself with the same desperate tenacity, in the face of inevitable doom, that her Jewish kinsmen in Palestine were to display in fighting the same irresistible Roman adversary in two wars (A.D. 66–70 and A.D. 132–135) which the Jews themselves had initiated. The Macedonians, whose spirit had not been broken by three defeats at Roman hands, rose in arms again in 149 B.C., and in 146 the Achaean and Boeotian federations foolhardily followed suit. Macedon was crushed, and in one and the same year Carthage and Corinth were blotted out and the Achaean, Boeotian, Euboean, Phocian, and Locrian federations were knocked on the head and disbanded.

No great power was now left in being in the Hellenic World except Rome herself; for the enfeebled Ptolemaic Kingdom of Egypt had tacitly submitted to a Roman protectorate as a lesser evil than annexation by her Seleucid rival. While the outcome of the third Romano-Macedonian war had still been hanging in the balance, the Seleucid King Antiochus IV had sought to compensate his monarchy for the loss of its possessions beyond Mount Taurus by adding Egypt itself to the Egyptian possessions in Coele Syria which had been annexed by his predecessor Antiochus III. When the news of the Roman army's decisive victory over the Macedonians at Pydna had reached the Egyptian theatre of war, a hovering Roman commissioner had pounced on the Seleucid invader with an ultimatum: 'Evacuate Egypt or we fight; and I want your answer on the spot.' Antiochus had had the sense to swallow his pride and obey. Rome's ascendancy was now unchallengeable within her infantry's effective range of operations from bases on the shores of the Mediterranean and its gulfs, till her advancing armies stumbled on the plains of Mesopotamia and the forests of northern Europe, where the terrain gave the advantage to other arms and other tactics. Meanwhile, within these limits, the world lay at Rome's mercy. Nothing now could be done without her sanction, and little except on her initiative. Rome's old friend Rhodes had been punished severely, after Rome's victory in her third war with Macedon, for having offered her good offices, while the military outcome was still in doubt, for arranging a peace settlement by negotiation. Rome was now the jealous mistress of the situation. What was she going to do?

XII

THE AGE OF AGONY

ROME did nothing — at least, nothing constructive on an oecumenical scale — for more than a hundred years after she had laid prostrate all the powers in the Hellenic World that could give her any grounds for anxiety. And this inaction of hers in a world that had been shattered by her own previous acts, and in which no other party could act without her, inevitably produced devastating effects. The age of agony, which had begun in the ominous years in which Antigonus Doson had marched on Sparta, Antiochus III on Coele Syria, and Hannibal on Italy, was drawn out from a span of 73 years (218–146 B.C.) to a span of 188 years (218–31 B.C.), and this was twice the length of the period of warfare and revolution that had followed the outbreak of the great Atheno-Peloponnesian war in 431 B.C.

Rome had been turned savage by her grim struggle for existence, and she had emerged from it in a vindictive mood. Her entry into the international arena had been inadvertent. She had been intent simply on making herself paramount in Italy, and her political horizon had not extended farther than that before she found herself at grips with Carthage and fighting, in the second round, on Italian soil for dear life. She had not wanted this alien world to close in on her in this frightful way, and, now that she had cut herself loose (so she thought) from the python's coils, she felt no responsibility for the world and wanted to hear no more of it. She had now made sure of her own security by eliminating every serious threat to this. She would leave the world to stew and would sit down to lick her own wounds. If she did give a thought to the world, it would be to plunder and exploit it.

Rome had grievous wounds to lick, for she had suffered cruelly — much more cruelly than the victor in the war of 431–404 B.C. After her decisive victory at Aegospotami, Sparta had restrained the vindictive Boeotians from going to all lengths in taking their revenge on a prostrate Athens. But Rome had suffered enough to stifle any impulse to be generous. She had not been the worst sufferer — as witness the names and dates Saguntum (219 B.C.), Syracuse (211), Capua (211), Coronea (171), Haliartus (171), seventy towns in Epirus (167), Corinth (146), Carthage (146). These cities had been put to the sack, and their unfortunate inhabitants had, at best, been robbed and ruined, if they had been lucky enough to escape being sold into slavery, or had escaped slavery by having met violent deaths. Except for Saguntum, all the places on this list had met their fate at Roman hands; and Saguntum's fate in 219 B.C. lay as heavy on Rome's conscience as Plataea's fate in 427 B.C. had lain on Athens's. Thus Rome's victims would have had worse sufferings to report than Rome herself. But her victims were no longer there to tell their tale; and, if they had been, their voices would have been of no effect. Rome's sufferings affected the world's destinies because Rome was the one sufferer from the world-war whose feelings now counted. The world was in the power of a victor who had been lacerated and whose wounds were aching.

Moreover, Rome's wounds went on festering after Hannibal had evacuated Italy and had been defeated at Naraggara and had been driven into exile and had been forced to take his own life. Of the many theatres in which the world war had been fought, the South Italian and

Sicilian theatres had been devastated the most thoroughly. Italy north of the River Volturnus and the 'spur' had got off comparatively lightly. Hannibal had traversed it in a single campaign (217 B.C.) and had not ever succeeded in re-invading it, except for his brief raid towards Rome in 211 B.C. The subsequent campaigns in North-West Africa, European Greece, the Aegean, and Western Anatolia had been short compared with the fourteen years (216–203 B.C.) of Hannibal's dire presence on South Italian soil. The Po basin and Spain were undeveloped regions in which there were limits to the material and psychological damage that it was possible to inflict. But the military operations, punitive measures, and reprisals of which Southern Italy had been the scene for those fourteen years had left their mark. At the end of the year 146 B.C., Carthage was an uninhabited heap of ruins, while Rome was then one of the great and growing cities of the Hellenic World. Yet, at the same date, the agricultural hinterland of Carthage was more or less intact, whereas in Italy the disastrous social and economic effects of Hannibal's sabotage were still working themselves out.

Southern Italy had been devastated not only by the fighting there but by its political aftermath. The peasantry in the communities — Roman, Latin, and ally — that had remained loyal to Rome had been chased away by Hannibal's ubiquitous cavalry. The peasantry in communities that had gone over to the Carthaginian side had been uprooted by the Romans when they had re-established their authority. Capua was treated with particular severity, because she had been juridically, not an ally, but an integral part of Rome's own body politic; but Capua was not the only victim. The re-subjugated allied states were punished by sweeping confiscations of land; and these confiscated lands were annexed to the 'ager Romanus'.

How was this depopulated land to be utilized by its new

owner, the Roman state? Rome had emerged from the war with a huge national debt to be paid off. She had to extract the maximum possible revenue from her national assets. Much of the confiscated South Italian land was intrinsically poor in quality, and to bring it back into cultivation would require a heavy capital outlay. To repopulate it with peasant proprietors would be a long-term investment yielding no immediate returns, and private capital was not interested in that. There was, however, plenty of private capital seeking investments that would be remunerative. This capital had been accumulated during the war by army supply contractors (the only Roman citizens who had been making money, and this sometimes by cheating the Government, at a time when all other classes were being impoverished). The old governing class, who still retained their landed estates, were now also being pushed into investing in the land by a law, passed on the eve of war, which debarred them from engaging in commerce. Speculators of these two classes were prepared to pay rent to the state for the use of the new empty public lands in the south if they were free to engage in either of two remunerative new activities: the grazing of sheep and cattle on the grand scale and the intense cultivation of fruit-trees — especially olives and vines — whose produce commanded a high market price.

The market was provided by the growth of the towns. 'Displaced persons' from the countryside were flocking into the towns in search of security, of the dole, and of the amenities of urban life. This was happening all over the Hellenic World, but most rapidly in Italy, where the devastation of the countryside had been the most severe and where the amenities were still an exciting novelty. The labour for supplying this new market was to be found in a vast new supply of slaves: unransomed prisoners of war and civilians kidnapped in the course of civil disturbances. After the death of Antiochus IV (reigned 175–163 B.C.) the Seleucid dynasty hastened its own dissolution by engaging in chronic civil wars for the possession of its rapidly shrinking dominions. Syria fell into anarchy, and the export of Syrian slaves, via a clearing house on the holy island of Delos, became the chief source of supply for staffing the new ranches and plantations in Southern Italy and in Sicily, where the new economic revolution was being carried out by native speculative capitalists. The rural domain of the Siceliot city of Akragas was, as has been noted, the place where the first experiment had been made — and this as far back as 480 B.C. — in using a slave-labour force for intensive farming. On a short view, slave-labour had two advantages over free labour. It could be worked to death and it was exempt from being conscripted for military service.

The second-century economic revolution was a continuation of its sixth-century predecessor in one respect. It was a move to increase the yield of the land by substituting cash-crops (animal as well as vegetable) for subsistence-farming. It was, at the same time, a new departure in two respects, both of which were sinister. In the sixth-century economic revolution a free peasantry had been the beneficiaries. The increased profits won from the land had flowed into their pockets. The second-century revolution put the peasants out of business by employing servile man-power. In the second century, as in the sixth, the increase in the yield from the land catered for an increase of population. But in the sixth century this had been an increase of the whole population, in the countryside as well as in the towns, whereas, in the second century, the population as a whole began to fall, for the first time in Hellenic history, while the increase in the urban population was continuing and, indeed, accelerating. This overgrowth of the towns at the cost of depopulating the countryside first opened the way for the second-century economic revolution and was then stimulated by it. This vicious circle was as intractable as the excessive growth of the towns was unwholesome.

It was not only in the South Italian war-zone that the peasantry had been prised off the land that their ancestors had been cultivating from time immemorial. The peasant man-power of the entire Roman commonwealth throughout Italy had been diverted from its agricultural business in vast numbers, and for many years on end, to fill the cadres of the enormous armies that the Roman Government raised and maintained from 216 B.C. until the conclusive defeat of Carthage on an African battlefield in 202. Even the abounding rural population that had been the strength of Cis-Appennine Italy until Hannibal's advent was depleted by these exorbitant demands upon it. If the demands had ceased after Carthage had given up the struggle, the peasantry might at least have had a chance of holding the line of the River Volturnus and the 'spur' against its new enemies the slave-ranchers and slave-plantations, as it had held it against Hannibal and the Italian communities that had deserted to his side. But the Italian peasant-soldier was given no peace. The demand made on him for waging the supplementary wars against powers east of the Straits of Otranto was not the most serious; for these wars were short and decisive, and even the most critical of them, the third war with Macedon, did not require levies on the scale of those that had been raised to fight Hannibal. The continuing drain on Italy's depleted military man-power was due to the demand made by three open frontiers adjoining the Hellenic World's boundless barbarian hinterland. These open frontiers — one in the Appennines and the Po basin, a second in

Spain, and a third along the inland borders of Macedon — had been left on Rome's hands by her overthrow of all the other powers.

The pacification of the Appennines and the Po basin was a military enterprise that brought in social returns in compensation for its contribution to the strain on the Roman commonwealth's social fabric. During the seventeen years ending in 173 B.C. a well-planned large-scale programme of peasant colonization between the Appennines and the south bank of the Po called into existence there a new peasant Italy to replace the peasantry's lost domain south of the Volturnus and the 'spur'. The Romans had no compunction in ousting the wild Ligurian highlanders of the Appennines or the implacably hostile Gallic Boii on the plains, who had thrown themselves into the war on the Carthaginian side. But decency forbade them to dispossess their loyal allies the Veneti or those temporarily disloyal Gallic subject peoples, between the Po and the Alps, that had more or less promptly resubmitted. The test case was a Roman commander's unprovoked aggression, in 173–172 B.C., against a small unoffending people in Southern Piedmont, the Statielli. The Senate at Rome, to its credit, took energetic action which assured other still independent barbarian peoples that they could come under Roman rule without being ejected from their lands and being sold into slavery; but, in the act, the Senate was also serving notice on Italian peasants who had lost possession of their ancestral holdings in Cis-Appennine Italy that their prospects of acquiring new holdings north of the mountains were soon going to fade away. In 173 B.C. the whole of the still unallocated residue of those Roman public lands in Italy and the Po basin that had been acquired by confiscation since 218 B.C. was, in fact, distributed to individuals in freehold allotments. In order to provide further lands for landless Roman agricultural workers, the only recourse now remaining would be to redistribute those public lands that had been leased to large-scale capitalist planters and cattlemen.

Frontier warfare had now come to an end on Cis-Appennine Italy's threshold, but it was still going on in the distant Spanish peninsula. The tribesmen on both sides of Rome's Spanish border were perpetually up in arms, and the only way of imposing peace on one militant area was to carry the frontier forward into another. For nearly two hundred years, dating from the landing of the first Roman army in the north-east corner of Spain in 218 B.C., the frontier gradually receded farther from the Mediterranean coast without ever being eliminated. When, after 31 B.C., Augustus set himself to put the world in order, he found the north-west corner of the peninsula still unsubdued. During at least the first three-quarters of this time, the burden of holding the Spanish frontier and pushing it forward weighed on the shoulders of Italian peasant-conscripts. Once shipped off to Spain, they might be kept under arms there for years on end, while their farms at home went to pieces. For the Italian peasantry the interminable colonial war in Spain was as baneful as the fourteen years' war for life and death against Hannibal in Southern Italy. The dominion in Spain that Rome had wrested out of the hands of Carthage proved, indeed, to be a shirt of Nessus. Meanwhile, the capitalists who had made their money in the Hannibalic war as army contractors now found a second lucrative source of profit in farming the taxes in territories — Sicily was the first of these and Spain the second — that the Roman Government had reluctantly taken under its own administration. Thus, in the 'cold war' on Italian soil between peasants struggling to keep their ancestral lands and capitalists seeking to wrest these lands out of their owners' grip, the scales were heavily weighted in the capitalists' favour; and larger and larger numbers of former peasant proprietors sank to being landless casual labourers, living from hand to mouth by seasonal employment on estates whose permanent labour force consisted of slaves. The Roman governing class was trying to manage an empire without either a professional army or a professional civil service, and this obstinate conservatism gave a bonus to predatory business men at the cost of ruining the peasantry that had been the military mainstay of the Roman commonwealth.

One consequence was a decline of Rome's military manpower in the course of the second century B.C. that was as serious, scale for scale, as the corresponding decline at Sparta in the third century B.C. In Rome, as at Sparta, this moved members of the governing class to embark on a radical agrarian reform. And events followed the same course. The pioneer reformer, Tiberius Sempronius Gracchus, who in 133 B.C. carried through the Roman national assembly a law for dividing up into peasant holdings the public land that had been leased to planters and cattlemen, was clubbed to death next year by a mob of senators (a portentous event for Rome, who had kept herself free from civil disorders since the beginning of her territorial expansion, more than two hundred years back). Tiberius, like Agis, lost his cause and his life through being too gentle-hearted to resort to force. His young brother Gaius, who came into office ten years later, had some of the ruthlessness of Cleomenes, and the burst of fighting in which he lost his life was a minor civil war. The redistribution of the public land, for which the Gracchi had given their lives, went forward, but it failed to produce the result that had been their objective; for, all the time, the resettlement of landless agricultural workers on new holdings was being offset by the continual uprooting of Italian peasant proprietors to do long-term military service on distant frontiers. So far from healing the Roman commonwealth's social sickness, Tiberius Gracchus's would-be remedial action plunged the commonwealth into internal disorders that, starting as murderous brawls in the streets of the capital, lighted up into full-dress civil wars which set the whole Hellenic World in a blaze and which were not brought to an end till a hundred turbulent years had passed since Tiberius's death.

This Roman hundred years' revolution was given its turn for the worse by a momentous change in the social composition of the Roman army that was made towards the end of the second century B.C. under stress of a sudden military crisis. An avalanche of North European barbarians was descending on the new domain that Roman arms had been reclaiming for civilization in the Po basin and Spain. To meet this threat the Roman commander Gaius Marius, a parvenu from a rural municipium, enlisted volunteers from among citizens who had lost their land and also, in consequence, were exempt from compulsory military service. This transformed the Roman army from an association of freeholders into a trades union of dispossessed freeholders in search of new holdings. And this, in turn, had the effect of transforming military commanders into political bosses who bought their troops' armed support for engaging in civil war with their rivals by promising to give the soldiers allotments of expropriated Italian land as the reward for winning victories over their own fellow-countrymen. The contending Roman war-lords drew on the resources of a conquered Hellenic World, as the contending successors of Alexander had drawn on those of a conquered Persian Empire. The worst of it was that, when victorious soldiers did receive allotments at the cost of the lawful owners, they found that, after all, they had lost the taste and aptitude for going back to work on the land.

The Roman civil wars were fought in two bouts (90–80

B.C. and 49–31 B.C.); and in both bouts the dispossessed peasants' demand for land and the 'political generals'' pursuit of power were entangled with a demand for Roman citizenship on the part of the Latins and the Italian allies. Roman citizenship was now the one effective safeguard against Roman tyranny. The demand for this, like the demand for land, was conceded by the Senate grudgingly, under *force majeure*. In 90 B.C. there was a secession of Italian allied states from the Roman commonwealth on a far larger scale than the secession after the Battle of Cannae. The lead was taken this time by states that had remained loyal to Rome during the second Romano-Carthaginian war and had therefore not had their strength broken by forfeitures of land. They ought never to have been driven to take these extreme measures for extorting an enfranchisement that was long overdue. The Roman aristocracy, which had justified its rule by building up the Roman commonwealth and then defeating Hannibal's attempt to disrupt it, was showing itself unfit to remain in power.

The Romans' savageness to one another was the nemesis of their callousness towards the rest of the world; but the agony that had goaded them into violence was world-wide, and it declared itself, not only in civil wars among the freemen of the Roman commonwealth, but in revolts of slaves, insurrections of subject Oriental peoples, and invasions of barbarians. The first recorded conspiracy of plantation slaves in Italy was hatched in 198 B.C., on the initiative of the slave-retinue of Carthaginian hostages interned in the Latin fortress of Setia. There was also one in Etruria in 196 B.C. After that, some premonitory outbreaks among the slave-herdsmen in Apulia (a big one in 185 B.C.) were followed — just about the time when Tiberius Gracchus was introducing his revolutionary legislation at Rome — by a revolt of plantation-slaves in Sicily

(134–131 B.C.), and by simultaneous revolts in the slave-mart on the island of Delos and in the Kingdom of Pergamum, Rome's satellite state in Western Anatolia, which had just become the property of the Roman people by the will of its last king. The insurgent slaves in Sicily massacred their owners and proclaimed their leader king (he called himself Tryphon, after a contemporary usurper of the throne of the Seleucids). The insurgent slaves in Anatolia found a king in Aristonicus, an illegitimate son of the last king of Pergamum. He called his followers 'Citizens of the Sun' — the just and benevolent god who bestows his light and warmth on poor and rich impartially. This movement was inspired by an anti-Roman nationalism as well as by the slaves' desire to win their freedom from their masters. All three revolts were suppressed by Roman arms; but in 103 B.C. the Sicilian slaves revolted again, and in 73 B.C. a band of gladiators (victims of an atrocious Etruscan sport) broke out of prison at Capua under the leadership of Spartacus (a name once borne by Thracian kings) and ranged for three years unchecked over the Italian countryside, gathering reinforcements from the slave-barracks on the plantations. The terror that they inspired was reflected, after they had been hunted down, in the ferocity with which the captured survivors were punished. The 6000 crosses on which they were crucified extended all the way from Rome to Capua along the Via Appia.

The most active suppliers of the international slave-market were pirates, who seized the command of the Mediterranean when, after the end of the third Romano-Macedonian war, Rome broke the naval power of Rhodes by ruining her economically. Rome did not care to maintain her own command of the Mediterranean when once her navy had served its purpose of helping to bring other powers to their knees; so the decay of the Rhodian navy left the Mediterranean unpoliced. The decline of the Seleucid monarchy enabled the pirates to acquire a secure base of operations along the rock-bound coast of the 'rough' western end of Cilicia, and they found accomplices in the rather disreputable city-states of Crete, which had so far never lost their independence. It amused the pirates, when they had the chance, to kidnap a Roman grandee: for instance, a provincial governor-elect on his way, with his staff, to take up his official duties. About the year 76 B.C. young Gaius Julius Caesar, on his way from Rome to Rhodes, passed some unpleasant days in the pirates' hands. If his captors had chosen to liquidate him, as he did liquidate them after he had purchased his release, the world's history might have taken a different course.

Aristonicus of Pergamum's short-lived 'City of the Sun' was only one of a number of militant nationalist movements in what had once been the dominions of the Persian Empire. Alexander the Great had left unconquered a great zone of Persian territory in the north and north-east of Asia Minor; and the pre-occupation of his successors, after his death, with their wars among themselves had given a number of Persian and native princes the opportunity, in this region, to found independent successor-states: Bithynia, Pontic and Inland Cappadocia, Armenia, Media Atropatene (Azerbaijan). Bithynia, and, to a slighter extent, the two Cappadocias, had been adopting Hellenism of their own accord without having been forced into this by a Macedonian conquest. Pontic Cappadocia and Armenia asserted themselves as military powers during the interval between the recession of the Seleucid monarchy and the onset of Rome. In 83 B.C. King Tigranes of Armenia occupied the Seleucids' capital, Antioch-on-Orontes. In 88 B.C. King Mithradates of Pontic Cappadocia overran the former Kingdom of Pergamum, now the Roman province of Asia. He presented himself as a liberator from Roman oppression; and, at his instigation, there was a general massacre, throughout Asia Minor, of Roman business men (the death-roll was said to have amounted to 80,000, including, perhaps, their native employees). Mithradates pressed on across the Aegean into Central Greece, and this time the Persian invader was welcomed at Athens with open arms. Mithradates had pushed his way into European Greece as far as the farthest point reached by Xerxes before his army, in its turn, was routed in Boeotia in 86 B.C. The Romans, preoccupied with their own civil war in Italy, had not been able to check Mithradates' advance at an earlier stage; and, though they now managed to push him back behind his own frontiers, he lived to challenge them again in 84 and 74 B.C. and was not put out of action till 66 B.C.

Even populations that had undergone the shattering experience of Macedonian conquest eventually recovered their *moral*. When the Seleucid King Antiochus III threatened Egypt's metropolitan territory in 218 B.C., the Ptolemaic Government, driven to desperation, eked out its defence force by taking the unheard-of step of arming and training native Egyptians to serve in the phalanx. When the Ptolemaic and Seleucid armies joined battle next year at Raphia (Rafa), Antiochus's well-trained Indian elephants routed their huge African cousins, but the improvised native Egyptian phalanx surprisingly won the day for its master Ptolemy IV by routing Antiochus's seasoned phalanx composed of troops that were Macedonian by descent. From that epoch-making moment onwards, the Hellenic 'ascendancy' in Egypt lost its prestige and the Ptolemaic Government's Egyptian subjects became unmanageable. There were armed insurrections *en masse*, and individuals discovered how to elude the Government's exactions by the tactics of 'non-violent non-co-operation'. They 'retreated' into asylums in the precincts of temples or in the desert, where they were beyond the tax-collector's and the overseer's reach.

The Seleucids' turn came next. Antiochus III's ignominious defeat by the Romans in the war of 192–190 B.C. became common knowledge among the monarchy's previously submissive subjects, and this nerved them to resist subsequent impositions on the Seleucid Government's part. Both Antiochus III and Antiochus IV are said to have met their deaths in popular *émeutes* provoked by attempts of theirs to appropriate the treasures of native temples up-country in Media and in Elam. After the onerous peace-settlement of 189 B.C. with Rome, the Seleucid Government needed money to pay its war-indemnity and national solidarity to reinvigorate what was left of its dominions. In the temple-state of Jerusalem, which was part of the Coele-Syrian territory that Antiochus III had eventually conquered from the Ptolemaic Crown in 198 B.C., an opportunity presented itself in 175 B.C. to his successor Antiochus IV of killing two birds with one stone. Joshua-'Jason', a 'philhellene' aspirant to the office of high priest of the local god Yahweh, bought the high priesthood from the Government at Antioch at the price of an increase in the annual tribute and a programme for converting his Jewish temple-state into a city-state on the Hellenic model. The younger Jewish priests and Levites were encouraged to go in for Hellenic athletics.

Similar measures of Hellenization had gone through smoothly in other places in the Seleucid dominions; but, in annexing the Judaean piece of Coele Syria, the Seleucids had caught a Tartar. The spectacle of priests of Yahweh taking exercise stark naked, or wearing nothing but Hellenic solar topees, gave mortal offence to conservative-minded Jews, and Jason's Hellenizing policy provoked armed opposition. Antiochus IV retorted in 167 B.C. by re-dedicating Yahweh's temple in Jerusalem to Olympian

Zeus, and setting up a statue of this Hellenic god in the Holy of Holies. 'The abomination of desolation, standing in the place where it ought not' was so shocking to the Palestinian Jews that it produced an explosion. Attempts at coercion provoked martrydoms; and the martrydoms provoked an armed rebellion, led by the Hasmonaean family (better known as the 'Maccabees'), which the Seleucid Government never succeeded in stamping out. The Hasmonaeans turned the Jewish temple-state into a warlike independent principality. They attacked and destroyed some of the colonial Hellenic city-states that had been planted by the Ptolemaic Government in the attractive hill-country to the east of the River Jordan; and they conquered and forcibly converted to Judaism two neighbouring native cantons, Idumaea and Galilee (the Samaritan remnant of the people of the long-since defunct Kingdom of Israel successfully insisted on continuing to worship Yahweh on Mount Gerizim in accordance with their own tradition). The world's history might have taken a different course if Idumaea and Galilee had not fallen into Hasmonaean hands; for, in that event, neither Herod the Great nor Jesus of Nazareth would have been born a Jew.

Hellenism's encounter with Judaism in and after 175 B.C. was the most portentous single event in Hellenic history. When Rome had overthrown the other powers of the Hellenic World, 'captive Hellas had captivated its savage conqueror and had introduced civilization into rustic Latium'. But conquering Hellas failed to captivate captive Jerusalem, and her attempt to introduce civilization, as she understood it, into rustic Judaea was indignantly rebuffed. In the end a frustrated Hellas came to terms with an unbending Judaea by adopting a Hellenized version of Judaea's fanatical religion. This stormy meeting and eventual mating of Hellenism with Judaism gave birth to Christianity and Islam, and these two Judaic-Hellenic religions are professed by half the human race today.

A suffering Hellenic World excited the cupidity of the surrounding barbarians. In the West European and North-West African hinterlands of the Western Mediterranean, Roman arms were successfully extending the domain of the Hellenic civilization in Latin dress in the teeth of barbarian counter-attacks — but this at a social cost to Italy which has already been noted. On other fronts the barbarians began to profit by Alexander's destruction of the Persian Empire as soon as the Persian Empire's Seleucid successor-state began to lose its grip. In Syria in the second century B.C., Arab tribes (advance-parties of the great Arab Völkerwanderung of the seventh century of the Christian Era) drifted out of the desert into the gaps between the walled cities and founded principalities there, as the Israelite tribes had done eleven hundred years earlier. On the north-east frontier — which the Persians had always defended more energetically and more successfully than their more remote north-west frontier over against the Hellenes — the Iranian-speaking Central Asian Nomads, whom the Persians had held at bay since the great Nomad Völkerwanderung in the seventh century B.C., now got on the move again.

In or before the year 248/7 B.C. the Parni, an insignificant tribe from what is now Türkmenistan (adjoining the present northern frontier of Persia, east of the Caspian Sea) moved into Parthia (Khorasan) and thereby cut the main road from Antioch-on-Orontes and Seleucia-on-Tigris to the north-eastern outposts of Hellenism on the plains of Bactria and Sogdiana, between the Hindu Kush and the River Jaxartes (Sir Darya). These outposts, which were now isolated, tacitly seceded from the Seleucid monarchy and set up an independent Hellenic kingdom of Bactria. Meanwhile, for the next ninety years, the Seleucid monarchy was able to hold in check the 'Parthians' (as the Parni came to be known after the name of the province that they had occupied). It held them at the Caspian Gates: the narrow passage where the great north-east road threads its way between the southern spurs of the Elburz mountains and the northern bays of the central desert of Iran. Between the years 161 and 142 B.C., Parthia suddenly raised herself to the stature of a great Power by pushing her south-west frontier forward from the Caspian Gates to the Euphrates. Babylonia, which thus passed into Parthian hands, had been the Seleucid monarchy's prime source of food and revenue. Two Seleucid attempts to reconquer Babylonia and Media ended disastrously in one Seleucid king, Demetrius II, being taken prisoner in 140 B.C. and another, Antiochus VII, losing his life in 130 B.C. A subsequent Roman attempt, under the command of Publius Licinius Crassus, to wrest the former Seleucid dominions, east of Euphrates, out of Parthian hands met with an equally disastrous end in 53 B.C. at Carrhae (Harran). The Roman infantry, rashly venturing out on to the Mesopotamian plains, was encircled and mown down by Parthian mounted archers supported by a camel train carrying copious supplies of ammunition.

Parthia adopted the 'philhellenism' of the Hellenic power that she had ousted. She respected the autonomy of Hellenic colonial cities left stranded by the Seleucid Empire's recession. She also did the Hellenic world a service by stemming a flood of other Iranian-speaking Nomad peoples, Sakas and Tokharians, from the heart of the Central Asian steppe, who overwhelmed the Hellenic kingdom of Bactria, in the upper basin of the River Oxus (Amu Darya), about the year 130 B.C.

The Hellenic World's agony did not prevent it from expanding; for in this age, as in the years 431–338 B.C., the art of war made progress at the expense of almost everything that was of value in life. The addition to Hellenism's domain in the age of agony that is best known in the modern West is the Roman conquest of the commercial hinterlands of Carthage and Massilia (Marseilles) in North-West Africa, Spain, and Gaul. In the first Romano-Carthaginian war the Romans had broken the 'wooden curtain' of Carthaginian sea-power that had closed Spain and North-West Africa to Hellenic enterprise for 300 years. In the second war Rome had embarked on the gradual conquest of Spain on which she was still engaged. In 126 B.C. Rome annexed a band of territory along the Mediterranean coast of Transalpine Gaul to fill the gap between her expanding possessions in Spain and her possessions in the Po basin. In 58–50 B.C. the rest of Transalpine Gaul, up to its Atlantic and Channel coasts and the left bank of the Rhine, was conquered by Gaius Julius Caesar with the military man-power that the new Italy in the Po basin could now provide. But the expansion of Hellenism into these barbarous western regions was not such an important event in Hellenic history as its expansion into India: a sub-continent with a civilization of its own that was appreciated by the Hellenes who came into contact with it.

Alexander's passage through India had been little more than a raid; but the spectacle of his destruction of one empire had inspired an Indian stateman to build another one by conquests on an Alexandrine scale. The strategic centre of Northern India was Bihar, where five or six great rivers meet, and, for about two hundred years before Alexander's passage of the Hindu Kush, wars of increasing violence in that commanding region had been thinning out the local states and bringing one of them, Magadha, to the fore. Chandragupta Maurya, King of Magadha (reigned 322–298 B.C.), now launched out on sweeping conquests. He easily overpowered the garrisons that Alexander had left in the Indus valley, and he obtained cessions of territory west of the Indus from Seleucus the Victor in exchange for Indian war-elephants to tip the scales in Seleucus's struggle with Antigonus 'One-eye', Alexander's lines-of-communication officer, who was making a bid to usurp the whole of his dead master's heritage. Chandragupta's grandson Açoka (reigned 273–232 B.C.) found himself, at his accession, master of the whole subcontinent except the one province of Kalinga. He rounded off his empire in a successful war of aggression, and was so horrified at the evil which he had let loose that he became a convert to the philosophy of Siddhartha Gautama the Buddha and devoted the rest of his life to propagating it both in India and in the Hellenic World. Under the Maurya empire India enjoyed the unity, peace, and order that South-West Asia had enjoyed during the better years of the Persian régime. But in 183 B.C. the Maurya dynasty was overthrown by a usurper, and Demetrius, king of the Bactrian Hellenic successor-state of the Persian Empire in the Oxus basin, crossed the Hindu Kush in Alexander's tracks and made conquests in India that were both larger and more enduring than Alexander's had been. For about sixteen years (183–168 B.C.) the vast region extending from the upper Oxus basin on the north-west to the upper Ganges basin on the south-east was united under the rule of a single Hellenic empire-builder. Then, in 167 B.C., a Seleucid expeditionary force under the command of Antiochus IV's cousin Eucratidas, which had made its way round the south-east corner of the Iranian desert, broke into Bactria and took Demetrius the usurper in the rear; and the Hellenic Far East broke up into splinter states which went on fighting each other until most of them were engulfed by invading Saka and Tokharian Nomads from Central Asia.

Thus, by the year 31 B.C., when the second bout of Roman civil wars was brought to an end by Octavianus

Caesar's victory at Actium over Marcus Antonius, Hellenism's agonies — which now looked as if they might be her last — had worked havoc as far afield as India and the Atlantic coast of Europe.

XIII

THE AUGUSTAN PEACE AND THE DECAY OF THE HELLENIC CULTURE

By the year 31 B.C. the Hellenic World had been in agony for 188 years, and society seemed to be at its last gasp when the sudden inauguration of the Augustan peace gave Hellenism an unexpected reprieve. This reprieve proved to be only temporary; the political concord that was now achieved had been due for 500 years; and overdue for 400, and the wounds that the Hellenes had inflicted on themselves during these centuries of incessant trouble were mortal. Yet the rally that Hellenism now made under Augustus's auspices was sustained for 265 years. It was not till A.D. 235 that the Hellenic World again fell into troubles comparable in severity and duration to those from which Augustus had salvaged it. And this quarter of a millennium was a long time of grace compared with the fourteen years' peace that had been won for the Hellenic World by Philip of Macedon's work, or the gleam of light that had flickered across the landscape on the eve of the outbreak of the world-war of 218–189 B.C.

The new political concord did not express itself in the establishment of a single world-state embracing the whole of the Hellenic civilization's contemporary domain from the Ganges to the Atlantic. But this vast area was now gathered up into no more than three great empires: the Roman Empire round the shores of the Mediterranean; the Parthian Empire in 'Iraq and Iran; the Kushan Empire, founded about eighty years later than the Roman

Empire, astride the Hindu Kush in the Oxus basin and in Northern India. None of the three ruling peoples were Hellenes by origin; but all three, in different degrees, had been initiated into the Hellenic culture. The Romans were thorough-going converts to the Hellenic way of life. The Parthians were benevolent patrons of it. The Kushans were Hellenes by adoption. They were one of the originally nomadic Tokharian tribes that had broken out of the steppes into the Hellenic kingdom of Bactria in the second century B.C. In the last century B.C. the Kushans had fraternized with Hermaeus, an Hellenic prince who was then still holding out in the fastness of the Hindu Kush in the country of the Paropanisadae. This entente had opened a way for them through the mountains into India, and there they had re-united under their rule most of the territories that Demetrius of Bactria had brought into the Hellenic World two hundred years earlier.

The three 'philhellene' empires' relations with each other were based on a common acquiescence in the prospect of 'co-existence'.

As between the Roman Empire and the Kushan Empire, friendliness was easy, since they were insulated from each other by the Parthian Empire overland, and therefore had no disputes over debatable territory, while at the same time there was an easy line of communications by water between Alexandria and the Kushan Empire's ports at the mouths of the Indus delta via the Nile-to-Suez ship-canal that had been cut by the Persian emperor Darius I. In the course of the last century B.C. and the first half of the first century of the Christian Era, Alexandrian seamen discovered, by stages, how to navigate direct across the Indian Ocean, from the mouth of the Red Sea to the Indus delta and even to Ceylon, by taking advantage of the monsoons. An Hellenic commercial emporium on the east coast of Southern India at Arikamedu, a few miles south of Pondichéry, has been re-discovered by modern archaeologists; and, within the frontiers of the Kushan Empire, the strength of the Hellenic cultural influence that commercial relations with the Roman Empire brought in their train is attested by works of art of a Hellenizing school that have been discovered in Gandhara, the country between Peshawar and Rawal Pindi, which was the heart of the Kushan Empire.

Roman-Parthian relations, when Augustus took them in hand, were still poisoned by the memory of hostilities in which Parthia, as well as Rome, had suffered reverses; but in 20 B.C. Augustus obtained a settlement that saved Rome's face and relieved Parthia of her anxieties. The previous trial of strength between the two empires had, indeed, demonstrated that it was beyond Rome's strength to eject the Parthians from Babylonia, and beyond Parthia's to eject the Romans from Syria; and these results of experience, on which the settlement made in 20 B.C. was founded, were confirmed when, in A.D. 113–117, the Roman emperor Trajan repeated Crassus's ill-judged attempt to break the Parthian Empire's power and win for Rome the Seleucid monarchy's long-lost dominions. Trajan escaped annihilation, but he was defeated by insurrections in his rear and by the inability of the Roman Empire to stand the strain of such an ambitious military adventure. The semi-conquered territories east of the Euphrates were promptly abandoned by Trajan's successor Hadrian, and from A.D. 117 till A.D. 224, when the Parthian Empire was supplanted by a re-born Persian Empire, neither Parthia nor Rome dreamed any longer of overthrowing her neighbour, though in Mesopotamia the oscillating frontier did, in the end, shift eastwards in Rome's favour.

In spite of these occasional lapses from a normal state of peace, there were few years during the quarter of a millennium running from 31 B.C. in which a Greek-speaking Alexandrian commercial traveller could not have made his way safely to Arikamendu or Taxila in one direction, or to Cadiz or Trier in the other, doing his business everywhere in his oecumenical Greek language. (Almost as much Greek as Latin could be heard spoken in the streets of Rome from the second century B.C. to the third century of the Christian Era.) Alexandria, like Edinburgh, could not reconcile herself to being no longer the political capital of a sovereign state, but she had the consolation of continuing to be the commercial, industrial, and scientific capital of the whole Hellenic World.

Meanwhile, Rome had at last begun to justify her political supremacy by taking responsibility for the damage inflicted on the world by her *laissez-faire* policy during the previous 188 years. When Augustus (Gaius Julius Caesar Octavianus) took the task of reconstruction in hand after his decisive victory over Antony and Cleopatra at Actium, he did not have to start quite from the beginning. The two foremost 'political generals' of the preceding generation, Gnaeus Pompeius (Pompey) and Augustus's own great-uncle and adoptive father Gaius Julius Caesar, had both been great organizers as well as great soldiers. In the year 67–62 B.C. Pompey, under mandates from the Roman national assembly that had given him almost plenary powers, had swept the pirates off the seas, expelled Mithradates from his hereditary dominions, and rescued the colonial Hellenic cities in Syria from the jaws of resurgent Jews and invading Arabs by turning the remnant of the Seleucid monarchy into a Roman province. Augustus's lieutenant Marcus Vipsanius Agrippa inherited these foundations, laid by Pompey, to build on when he completed the settlement of the Levant in the years 23–21 and 17–13 B.C. In 58–50 B.C. Julius Caesar had laid similar foundations in Transalpine Gaul. Augustus was not his adoptive father's equal in genius, but he had the advantage over both Caesar and Pompey in possessing just those gifts that the times required in a would-be saviour of society. Pompey had been lacking in political sense. Caesar had combined a generosity towards defeated adversaries with an impatience of venerable but anachronistic political institutions — a dangerous combination of virtues which had cost him his life. Augustus knew how to 'hasten slowly' and how to 'save face'; so he died in his bed and left behind him a new order which lasted for 221 years after his death in A.D. 14.

This new order was based on four master institutions: a deified saviour-king; a deified world-state in which the local city-states constituted the cells of the body politic; a professional army; a professional civil service. Not one of these institutions was a new creation. They had all been invented already in the post-Alexandrine age as expedients for filling the gap left by the collapse of Hellenism's previous master institution of sovereign city-states. But, in the age of Alexander's successors and in the subsequent age of agony, these substitute institutions had all missed fire. Augustus made them work, partly by the device of discreetly camouflaging them.

The Augustan saviour-king was a reclaimed Roman 'political general'. Augustus performed this metamorphosis in his own person. In fighting his way to the top, he had committed, perforce, the same crimes as his competitors and his predecessors. He had callously 'liquidated' political opponents (the 'liquidation' of the eminent barrister and immortal man of letters, Marcus Tullius Cicero, was perpetrated on Antony's initiative but with Octavian's consent). He had bribed his soldiers with allotments of land expropriated from the lawful owners. He had preyed on the world in his pursuit of his personal ambition. But, when his last competitor for supreme power had been eliminated, the victor at Actium deliberately mended his ways, whether or not he repented of his previous misdeeds; and, by the time that he had been styled 'Augustus' ('Sebastós' in Greek) and had been saluted as 'the father of his country', he deserved these honourable titles. He had, indeed, devoted his ill-gotten fortune to the common weal. The income from the vast private estate, amassed by Caesar and enlarged by Augustus himself through ruthless confiscation of their victims' property, had provided a supplementary revenue for financing the government of the new world-state.

Augustus understood the political expediency of being all things to all men. Looking east of the Straits of Otranto, he showed his face as a potent epiphany of the deified saviour-king with whose countenance the Hellenic World had been familiar since the self-deification of Alexander the Great. But, looking Romewards towards a once sovereign Roman people and a recently governing Roman aristocracy, Augustus wore a mask. In this direction he exercised his absolute and unchallengeable authority as a virtually perpetual holder of the combined constitutional powers of the principal magistracies of the Roman Republic. In combination these powers were as irresistible as the queen's combination of moves on the chess-board. This device of combining constitutional powers into a camouflaged supra-constitutional dictatorship had been anticipated in 67–66 B.C. by Pompey. With these constitutional cards in his hands, Augustus could be content to call himself, with studied modesty, 'the doyen (princeps) of the Senate'.

No doubt this camouflage was seen through by the classes towards whom it was directed, but it was taken as a sign of grace that the second founder of the empire, unlike his scornful adoptive father, should have been willing to take the trouble to make even a transparent pretence.

The senatorial nobility were resentful, and an academic republicanism was cultivated by some of them for seventy or eighty years after Augustus's death. But appearances were saved by Augustus's master-strokes of handing back to the Senate the control of provinces in which no garrisons were needed, and employing senators as governors of the provinces that he kept in his own hands—always excepting Egypt, which he governed through a non-senatorial deputy (no senator was allowed even to set foot in this arsenal of autocracy). As for the Roman middle class and the rest of the Hellenic middle class of all political categories — Latins, allies, and subjects — Augustus was making the world safe for them; they knew this; and they wanted nothing better. Augustus's camouflaged despotism did, indeed, give them security for 265 years, reckoning from the date of the battle of Actium till the eruption of the uncultivated under-world in A.D. 235. As for the great proletariat, which had been seething for the last hundred years, Augustus mitigated its sufferings just enough to bring its temper down below boiling point. The mere establishment of world-wide peace and order spelled the ultimate doom of plantation slavery, because it dried up the sources of supply. Pompey had already stopped the most copious source by putting down the pirates and removing the temptation for the survivors to resume their evil trade by giving them lands to cultivate and cities to live in. The insubordinate Egyptian peasants were brought back to heel by a judicious mixture of benevolence and sternness. Their intolerable Ptolemaic load was perceptibly lightened when they came under Roman rule, and at the same time they were over-awed by a Roman garrison which, unlike its Ptolemaic predecessor, could not be trifled with. They did not stir again till nearly five hundred years later, when Roman military power in Egypt began to weaken in its turn. In the city of Rome itself there was an unemployed proletariat of free Roman citizens (many of them freedmen or of freedman stock) who were still a potential danger to the newly established order because of their misery, their numbers, and their strategic position at the seat of world power. Augustus kept them quiet by keeping them on the dole on which Gaius Gracchus had put them. As a further insurance, he added rations of oil and wine to the basic 'bread and shows'.

The Augustan professional army had to be hammered out of unpromising Marian material. The armies with which the Roman civil wars had been waged had been bands of armed and organized claimants for land-allotments; and, at the close of the second bout of civil warfare in 31 B.C., Augustus had on his hands an inflated force of this type — partly raised by himself and partly bequeathed to him by his liquidated rivals Sextus Pompeius and Marcus Antonius. These unruly soldiers were a public danger, and Augustus dealt with them, as Pompey had dealt with his defeated and demobilized pirates, by giving them the means of leading a respectable life. Some of them were successfully resettled on the land; others were retained to serve in a professional standing army in which they were offered permanent employment with the prospect of provision for their old age. Professional military forces were not a new institution in the Hellenic World. City-state dictators and Siceliot despots, from the seventh century B.C. onwards, had usually won and kept their power over their fellow citizens by maintaining a professional body-guard. But this force had also usually been composed, not of citizens, but of foreigners, and it had been posted on the citadel of the city that it was holding down on its unconstitutional employer's behalf. Augustus, too, kept a body-guard, composed of German mercenaries, in his quarters in Rome on the Palatine. The novel features of his professional army were that it was mostly composed of Roman citizens and was mostly stationed permanently on the frontiers. It could, of course, be recalled at any moment to the interior, if the need arose, to deal with the insurrection of a subject people or with a republican movement in the Roman citizen body or with an attempt by some ambitious individual to oust Augustus and take his place. But 'out of sight, out of mind'. The public was content to see the unpopular army vanish beyond the horizon; and the army's normal duty, now, was, not to over-awe the public, but to protect it by holding the frontiers against the Parthians and the barbarians. Its location on the frontiers had the double advantage of posting it where it was most needed and of making it less obnoxious to the civilian population by making it invisible.

The reformed army's first task was to rationalize the untidy and disjointed pre-Augustan borders of Rome's scattered dominions by pushing forward to 'natural' frontiers. The military front in Spain that had been taxing the man-power of Italy for nearly two hundred years was now eliminated by subjugating the highlanders in the north-west corner of the peninsula up to the coastline (the highlanders in South Central Anatolia, who defied all attempts to subjugate them, were contained by a cordon of colonies of time-expired Roman veterans). The west bank of the Euphrates, where the river points an elbow towards the Mediterranean, was accepted as the frontier between Rome and Parthia. The hitherto isolated borders of Transalpine Gaul, Cisalpine Gaul (the Po basin), and Macedon (a Roman province since 146 B.C.) were linked up with one another along a new river-line extending from the North Sea to the Black Sea. The line that was Augustus's objective here was Danube–Elbe; but the successful resistance of the German barbarians in their forests forced him to be content with Danube–Rhine, and, unfortunately for his successors, this was the longest 'natural' frontier that could be found in Europe.

The Augustan professional civil service was an even greater masterpiece than the Augustan professional army; for the material out of which it was moulded was still more unpromising, if that was possible. The lower ranks were staffed with freedmen trained in the management of Caesar's private household and estate. The higher ranks were recruited from the progeny of those Roman aristocrats and business men who had preyed on the Hellenic World during its age of agony. The children were now enlisted for the beneficent service of repairing some of the damage that the fathers had done. The business experience acquired in such anti-social activities as tax-farming and money-lending was now applied to public administration; and the tradition of abusing power by misusing it in corrupt practices was broken partly by diminishing the temptation and partly by making an example of anyone who yielded to it. The new professional civil servants were paid fixed salaries on generous scales, and if they misbehaved they had to answer for it to Caesar. The wolves had been converted into shepherd-dogs. The imaginary 'guardians' of Plato's utopian city-state had made their appearance in real life to administer an empire on the scale of Zeno's utopian world-state; and their field of recruitment eventually came to be as wide as their field of action. During the last 150 years before the collapse in A.D. 235, the oecumenical civil service was adorned by Greek-speaking scholar-administrators — for instance, Arrian of Nicomedia and Dio Cassius of Nicaea.

The imperial administration's standing instructions were to do the minimum. Its function was to perform only such necessary services as could not be performed on a city-state scale by unpaid unprofessional elected magistrates serving for no longer than twelve months on end. The Roman Empire was a continuation of the Roman commonwealth, and it retained the commonwealth's constitutional structure. It was essentially still an association of self-governing, though non-sovereign, city-states held together by permanent relations, of several different kinds, with the paramount sovereign city-state Rome. Some of these city-state cells of Rome's body politic were Roman municipalities whose citizens were also citizens of Rome herself. Others were Rome's allies in virtue of having the status of Latin colonies or in virtue of being attached to Rome by treaty. Others were Rome's 'free' or tributary subjects. But all alike were expected to manage their own local affairs and to require no more than a minimum amount of supervision and intervention on the part of the imperial authorities. The objective of Augustus and his successors in the principate was to convert the empire by degrees into a body politic in which every cell would be a self-governing city-state and every one of these would also be a Roman municipality, so that every free male inhabitant of the Empire would be a citizen of two cities: his own city and Rome. This objective was attained, at least in juridical form, in the Constitutio Antoniniana of A.D. 212. It is not surprising that it took nearly two and a half centuries to complete the process of political enfranchisement, considering that this was conditional on initiation into the civic way of life that was the essence of the Hellenic civilization. Latin cities had to qualify for being raised to the status of Roman municipalities; allied and subject cities for being raised to the status of Latin cities; and the inhabitants of cantons and tribal areas for being raised to the status of citizens of cities of the lowest grade. These ex-barbarians in the Empire's outlying marches had to climb a ladder of at least three rungs in order to arrive at cultural and political parity with the

Roman citizens whose ancestors had brought their ancestors into the world-state by force of arms.

On the principle of letting the maximum amount of responsibility rest on the shoulders of the city-states, the Imperial Government made them serve, whenever possible, as tutors of the Empire's ex-barbarian subjects. This policy had been devised by Pompey when he had conquered Pontic Cappadocia and expelled King Mithradates. Pompey had realized that, if Mithradates was to be prevented from re-establishing himself in his ancestral dominions, something positive must be found to take the royal authority's traditional place. He found this in the local cities; and, as these were few and far between, he assigned to each of them an enormous territory to administer and civilize. This device of 'assigning' backward tribes to the tutelage of the nearest city-state became the general practice of the Roman Empire. For example, before the end of Augustus's reign, the city-state of Nemausus (Nîmes), in Gallia Narbonensis, had twenty-four tribal districts attached to it, and in the Emperor Claudius's time (reigned A.D. 41–54) the city-state of Tridentum (Trent), on the northern border of Gallia Cisalpina, had three.

Beyond the penumbra of the enlightened city-state world, in darkest Europe, where the quest for 'natural' frontiers had suddenly brought large numbers of outer barbarians within the world-state's fold, the imperial authorities found their regional educational agency in the army, which was the only representative of civilization in these outlying marches. Auxiliary units were organized, in which the Empire's ex-barbarian subjects were free to enlist; and, where they were good military material, they also found their way into the legions, though, officially, enlistment in these was reserved for Roman citizens. Within two hundred years of the establishment of the Empire's Danube frontier, the Illyrian provinces, along the river's right bank from the Wiener Wald to the Black Sea, had become the imperial army's principal recruiting ground. The Illyrians were inducted into civilization along this military road; and, in the crisis of A.D. 235–285, when the enemy was once again within the gates, Illyrian Roman soldiers saved the Roman common weal, as Italian Roman soldiers had saved it in the crisis of 218–203 B.C., by a self-sacrificing tenacity and an heroic refusal to despair of the republic.

In their policy of progressive enfranchisement, Augustus and his two great predecessors, Pompey and Caesar, were reviving the traditions of the Roman senatorial aristocracy in its best days, before the embittering and unnerving experience of the Hannibalic war had betrayed this former governing class into becoming untrue to its best self — with disastrous results for the world, for Rome, and for the aristocratic Roman régime. The new institutions, improvised by Augustus and perfected by his successors, enabled the principate to take over, in the Mediterranean basin and its hinterlands, Alexander the Great's mission of Hellenization, and to carry this out on a vast scale by a systematic, persistent, and effective use of the means employed by Alexander and his successors in the former dominions of the Persian Empire.

The first step was to heal the wounds inflicted on the Hellenic World, in its age of agony, by Rome herself in the course of overthrowing her rivals. Caesar had found time, between his victory in his civil war with Pompey and his assassination, to re-found Carthage and Corinth after having already refounded Capua; and the restoration of these three ancient and famous cities, all occupying key-positions in the geography of the Hellenic World, had been a symbolic gesture. But the desolate sites of the cities that Caesar had re-established had merely been the most conspicuous scars in a wider scene of desolation.

Since the second century B.C. the blight of depopulation had fallen upon Continental European Greece as far north as Macedon inclusive, and upon Southern Italy to within a hundred miles of Rome itself. After the country south of the River Volturnus and the 'spur' had been depopulated in the Hannibalic war, the adjoining highland cantons of Samnium (the Molise) had been depopulated in the civil war of 90–80 B.C. In the fourth century B.C. the Samnites had been Rome's competitors for supremacy in Italy; they had never forgotten nor forgiven their discomfiture at Roman hands; and in 82 B.C. they had come within an ace of taking a belated revenge in a fierce battle fought outside Rome's Colline gate, on ground that had been trodden by Hannibal in 211 B.C. The reactionary Roman dictator Sulla had retorted by laying Samnium waste; his work, like Hannibal's, had been done too thoroughly to be reversed; and the ruin of half Cis-Appennine Italy had not been fully counterbalanced by the post-Hannibalic Roman colonization of the Po basin south of the river or by Caesar's grant of Roman citizenship to the Romanized population on the north bank, who had been fobbed off in 89 B.C. with the niggardly grant of Latin status. Under the principate, one new Italy was called into existence in Baetica (Andalusia), and another in Gallia Narbonensis (Provence, Dauphiné, and Languedoc), to replace the old Cis-Appennine Italy; and a new Greece was called into existence in Anatolia — where the economic and cultural influence of Ephesus and the other ancient centres of Hellenic civilization along the west coast was able, thanks to the Roman peace, to radiate eastward into regions into which Macedonian arms had never forced their way.

Under the principate, Rome deliberately set herself to round out the edifice of Hellenic civilization which the Macedonians had left unfinished. Thrace, an obstinately barbarous region close to the heart of the Hellenic World and commanding the European shore of the Black Sea Straits, had been brought within the pale of civilization by Philip of Macedon for a moment, only to break away again after Macedonian energies had been diverted by Alexander to the conquest of the Persian Empire. From A.D. 46 onwards the Roman imperial authorities took in hand the Hellenization of this black spot. In Thrace, Greek, not Latin, was introduced as the official language, and a city-state, that still bears the name of its founder the Emperor Hadrian, was laid out on a site prepared for it by Nature herself at the confluence of the River Hebrus (Maritsa) with its principal tributaries. Hadrian (reigned A.D. 117–138) spent his time on tours of inspection round the Empire, repairing the work of his predecessors or carrying it to completion. He completed the building of the huge temple of Olympian Zeus at Athens, which the Athenian dictator Peisistratus had begun on a scale that was beyond even an exceptionally big city-state's resources, and which the Seleucid King Antiochus IV had also found too much for him when he had employed a Roman architect, Cossutius, to carry on Peisistratus's work. Like Caesar's restoration of Capua, Carthage, and Corinth, Hadrian's completion of the Olympieion at Athens was a symbolic act.

Thus the two respectable objectives of restoration and fulfilment were duly achieved by the benevolent and constructive policy of the Roman principate, but these achievements did not bring with them the rejuvenation that was the Hellenic World's vital need. In an exhausted society, tardily united under a world-government in which the oecumenical administration was autocratic and bureaucratic, life was dull. The artificial cults of the goddess Rome and the god Caesar could not fill, in human hearts, the place left vacant by the decay of the worship of the once idolized city-states: Athênê the Keeper of the City of Athens, Athânâ the Lady of the Brazen House at Sparta, and the rest. In the imperial public service there was a demand for efficient and conscientious soldiers, administrators, and jurists (the classical Roman jurists — most of them Syrian-born — flourished in the last generation of the principate); but there was no longer any room for serious politicians and public speakers. Orators were now reduced to giving academic talks on antiquarian subjects.

The dullness of life under the principate was reflected in the contemporary vogue of 'archaism'. People found no creative inspiration in the life of their own day, so they sought novelty in an affected aping of the past. This fashion expressed itself in a number of different media. Visual monuments of it were the careful copies of classical and pre-classical Hellenic works of art in Hadrian's villa near the road from Rome to Tibur (Tivoli). Its literary monuments were pedantic imitations of the accomplished Attic Greek style of the fourth century B.C. and of the rustic Latin style of the second century B.C. In the field of religion the same prevailing fashion expressed itself in the sedulous cultivation of obsolete religious rites: the boring ritual of the Arval Brethren at Rome and the brutal ritual of Artemis Orthia at Sparta. Augustus coaxed a sophisticated and sceptical Roman middle class into co-operating with him in a revival of the worship of Rome's national gods in exotic Olympian dress; and the public responded in the spirit in which the French middle class re-embraced Roman Catholic Christianity in the nineteenth century of the Christian Era. Moral rearmament was a tiresome but effective insurance for the sanctity of private property.

This nostalgia for the past might have been expected to benefit the Hellenic society's historic political institution: city-states. But it did not prove feasible, in the long run, to preserve the city-states' traditional glamour when once they had been made innocuous. In the early days of the Roman world-state the Jewish preacher of Christianity, Paul, was still proud of being a citizen of Tarsus besides being proud of being a citizen of Rome. But, now that city-states had been reduced — and rightly so — to being self-governing municipalities instead of idolized sovereign independent powers entitled to go to war with their neighbours if they chose, the price of thus drawing their teeth was to rob them of their charm as well. The scope, and, with it, the stimulus that they could offer to their citizens had been diminished, and their elected magistrates had now to deal only with formalities and frivolities, instead of handling, as they had done in the past, public affairs that were matters of life and death. Thus civic office, once the goal of high ambition, became psychologically unrewarding, while at the same time it remained financially onerous. The Athenian democracy had introduced the custom of making the rich pay for the privilege of being allowed to perform public services, and the staging of a show could cost an elected magistrate as much as the fitting out of a warship. Municipal magistrates became slipshod in the performance of their duties. Worse still, the most eligible citizens ceased to care to take office and eventually came to shun it as an unwelcome imposition. So civic efficiency declined *pari passu* with civic pride; and this decay of the institution of city-state self-government, on which the founders of the principate had counted for the provision of local administration, forced the Imperial Government's hand. The imperial civil service, which had been designed to play a supervisory role, found itself compelled, willy-nilly, to take over responsibility for the conduct of local government from the increasingly incompetent and corrupt municipal authorities. This made the imperial civil service top-heavy and expensive, while, for the public, it made life duller than ever.

As the public spirit and civic energy of the municipalities dwindled, they became less and less effective in the performance of their function of radiating civilization into the surrounding countryside. In return for this educational service, the peasantry had been called upon to contribute to the cities' upkeep by paying rates to their treasuries and rents to their land-owning citizens. But the cities now began to give the peasants less and less cultural value in exchange for the economic toll that they were still taking from them. Instead of continuing to serve as a stimulus, they were becoming an incubus on the peasants' backs — especially in the culturally and economically backward western and Danubian provinces, where city-states were something exotic and where the burden of maintaining them had always been disproportionately heavy. Thus in the Roman Empire, as in the Persian Empire's Macedonian successor-states, Plato's and Aristotle's blue-prints for ideal city-states on the parasitic and oppressive Spartan model were unfortunately translated into real life.

There was also a miscarriage of Augustus's policy of cantoning the Roman army on the frontiers and depending on it for the education of the ex-barbarian populations behind the line. Out in the wilderness, the soldiery no longer afflicted the civilized world with their burdensome presence, but, for this very reason, they became strangers to the city-state way of life in their distant rear, while they became attuned to the barbarian way of life on both sides of the line that they were holding. Moreover, as the army came to draw more and more upon regional sources of recruitment, there was a tendency for each corps to strike root in its own sector of the frontier, and that meant that the different regional corps became strangers to each other.

This was a new public danger, because it exposed the world to the risk of civil war every time that the principate fell vacant. The lack of any universally recognized and automatically applicable law of succession to the principate was an incurable infirmity that was one of the legacies of its revolutionary origin. The combination of constitutional powers which was the juridical source of the princeps' authority had to be conferred on him by the Roman Senate, representing the Roman people; but there was no constitutional machinery for electing the recipient, and, if an officer were acclaimed as 'imperator' by one of the frontier corps, the troops could extort from the Senate a retrospective ratification of their choice if they could win the race for Rome against other troops who had proclaimed competing pretenders. The corps quartered in Pannonia, in the angle of the River Danube, had the shortest march to make; and it was they who won the imperial throne for Vespasian in A.D. 69 and for Lucius Septimius Severus in A.D. 193. The civil wars of A.D. 69 and A.D. 193–7 between the contending frontier armies supporting rival aspirants to the principate were revivals of the civil wars of 88–31 B.C. between contending proletarian armies supporting 'political generals'. They were also forerunners of the fifty-years-long bout of anarchy into which the Hellenic World fell in A.D. 235. The epithets 'atrocious' and 'barbarian' that Virgil puts into the mouth of a Transpadane peasant whose fields had been given to a soldier by Octavian would have still more aptly described one of the soldiers who descended on Italy under the auspices of Vespasian and Severus and Maximinus Thrax; for, to these sons of the barbarian frontier, the civilized interior was virtually a foreign land, while, for the interior's horrified inhabitants, the descent of the frontier armies was virtually a barbarian invasion.

The original contrast between the Roman armies cantoned along the frontier and their barbarian 'opposite numbers' on the other side of the line did, indeed, gradually wear thin. And, while the legionaries were becoming assimilated to the barbarians, the barbarians were getting even with the legionaries by progressively learning from them their art of war. The barbarians could practise this, once learnt, more cheaply and skilfully than their involuntary instructors, since the frontier war-zone was the barbarians' native ground, and the barbarians were not burdened, like their opponents, with an elaborate organization and outfit. The balance might perhaps have been redressed in civilization's favour by bringing civilization's technical resources into play. Hero of Alexandria's toy turbine steam engine, applied to locomotion, could have solved the Roman army's logistical problems; and suggestions for eking out man-power by mechanization were presented in a Latin treatise on military questions written, by an author unknown, in the fourth century of the Christian Era. But the practical application of scientific discoveries never appealed to the Hellenic imagination. So the strain on the imperial frontier defence force increased with the passage of time; and this strain was transmitted from the frontier to the interior in the form of rising costs to the taxpayer for less efficient military protection.

The burden of frontier defence was also increased for Rome by an unexpected revolution beyond her eastern borders, in Iran. In A.D. 224 the slack and sluggish Parthian imperial régime was suddenly overthrown and replaced by one of its feudatories, the prince of Fars, the country that had given birth to the first Persian Empire. The second Persian Empire, thus founded by Ardeshir (Artaxerxes), of the House of Sasan, was as dynamic as the first; and, in a meteoric campaign worthy of Cyrus the Great, the new Persian empire-builder overran and annexed the Kushan Empire. He thus doubled his own empire's strength and upset, to Rome's disadvantage, a nicely adjusted balance of power that had maintained itself for nearly two hundred and fifty years. Moreover, the second Persian Empire, unlike the first, gave an official status to the Zoroastrian religion, and showed itself as fanatical as the first Persian Empire had been tolerant. Hellenism, which had lived on, under Parthian and Kushan auspices, in the vast region extending from the Euphrates to the Jumna, soon wilted away under the new Zoroastrian Persian dispensation. The emergence of this restless and aggressive power above Rome's eastern horizon added a heavy weight to Rome's military load.

The growing strain was widely spread. It was a strain on the peasantry to support the parasitic cities; it was a strain on the civil service to take over the decadent city-state governments' work in addition to its own; it was a strain on the taxpayer to support a growing civil service as well as a growing army. This multiple strain can be felt in the melancholy tone of the Stoic emperor Marcus Aurelius's private diary. The pressures were cumulative; and, within fifty-five years of Marcus's death in A.D. 180, they exploded in a general breakdown. The peasants in the countryside and soldiers on the frontiers revolted against their middle-class task-masters and pay-masters in the cities. The barbarians and the Persians broke through. In A.D. 251 one Roman emperor, Decius, was killed in battle with the Goths in Thrace; in A.D. 260 another, Valerian, was taken prisoner by the Persians in Syria (the Persian emperor Shahpur commemorated this dazzling feat of arms in two impressive bas-reliefs). The currency depreciated to zero. The world-state broke up. Rome had not found herself in such straits since her defeat by Hannibal at Cannae; but, against desperate odds and contrary to all reasonable expectations, she was pulled through by a series of Illyrian soldier-emperors: Aurelian, Probus, Carus, and titanic Diocletian. Unity was reimposed. The old frontiers were re-established except in two exposed salients that were not re-occupied. At grievous additional cost to the taxpayer, the stationary cordon of frontier guards was supplemented by the creation of a mobile field force to provide for defence in depth. Internal order was restored.

The Illyrians had salvaged the Roman Empire, but not the Hellenic civilization. The educated urban middle class, who had been the depositories and the propagators of Hellenism for the past six hundred years, had been ruined, and they never recovered. Under the Augustan principate, which had foundered during the fifty years of anarchy, the Hellenic middle class had been the Hellenic world-state's indispensable partner. What new staff could be found for the convalescent world-state to replace the broken reed? At this date it was taken for granted that the world-state's new partner would have to be some world-wide religious organization. The question was: which?

XIV

THE EASTERN RELIGIONS' RECEPTION OF HELLENISM AND DISSEMINATION IN THE HELLENIC WORLD

THE experience of the age of agony, and of civilization's subsequent reprieve and decay, inevitably had strong repercussions in Hellenic souls, and these launched the Hellenes on a long spiritual odyssey that ended in a surprising landfall.

This movement made itself felt first in the field of philosophy. In the post-Alexandrine age, Hellenic philosophy had split up into different schools, each concentrating on some particular objective. In the preceding age, Plato had taken the whole Universe for his field of inquiry, and had approached it not only as a rationalist but also as a poet and a seer. But even Aristotle had not spread his wings so wide, and Aristotle's third-century successors in his institute at Athens, the 'Promenade' (Peripatos), specialized in natural science and in scholarship, while Plato's successors in the Academy specialized in the theory of knowledge. When, in the next generation, Zeno of Citium and Epicurus of Samos endowed Athens with two more institutes of philosophy, the 'Porch' (Stoa) and the 'Garden', they and their successors specialized in the practical conduct of life, and discouraged the study of science, logic, and metaphysics beyond the minimum required as a background for the pursuit of ethics. Meanwhile, at Alexandria, the royal institute of arts and sciences (Museum), founded and financed by the Ptolemaic Government, put Aristotle's Athenian institute in the shade as a Panhellenic centre for scientific and philological studies.

The advent of the age of agony was followed by a change of spiritual climate in the Hellenic World which found its moving spirit in the Stoic philosopher Poseidonius of Apamea (about 135–51 B.C.). Poseidonius stood for a reconciliation of the intellectual differences in which the philosophers of the previous age had delighted, and apparently also for a return to a belief in, and dependence on, a transcendant god, in contrast to Zeno's and Epicurus's ideal of teaching human beings to raise themselves, by their own efforts, to a godlike level of self-sufficiency. This tendency towards a fusion of doctrines and a revival of supernatural religion, to which Poseidonius had given an impulse, reached its culmination, some three hundred years later, in the Neoplatonic school founded by Plotinus of Alexandria (about A.D. 203–262). Plotinus treasured the doctrines of all the historic schools of Hellenic philosophy and wove them into a unity; but, for him, the paramount pursuit, for a philosopher, was not intellectual work but contemplation, and the crown of contemplation was the mystic experience of the human soul's union with God.

Less ethereal souls than Plotinus's or Poseidonius's were attracted, from the second century B.C. onwards, by the pseudo-science of astrology. It won addicts even among the cultivated minority of the Hellenic society. This vulgar flight towards superstition was a reaction to the same experience as the arduous pursuit of the mystic's goal. In the age of agony, Hellenic souls were conscious of being at the mercy of destructive forces in society — and in themselves — which they did not know how to control. This spelled the bankruptcy of man-worship. It discredited the ideal of the self-sufficient philosopher as well as the ideal of the saviour-king. The consequent spiritual vacuum was too great for either mysticism or astrology to fill. So these two significant new bents in Hellenic minds gave two new openings for the entry of eastern religions into the Hellenic World.

Even in Hellenism's age of growth, the unsatisfactoriness of the Olympian pantheon had opened the door to non-Hellenic influences. These had made themselves felt in the worship of Dionysus and in the Orphic and Pythagorean movements. This tendency had been accentuated after the outbreak of the great Atheno-Peloponnesian war in 431 B.C. The world-war of 218–189 B.C. had given another cruel turn to the screw. And, now that vast African and Asian territories had been brought within the bounds of the Hellenic World by the successive conquests of Alexander of Macedon and Demetrius of Bactria, eastern religions had a greater opportunity than ever before of making Hellenic converts. There were, however, three conditions that they must fulfil if they were to have any success. They must win their way peacefully, by persuasion, without resorting to force (at least until they were securely in the saddle); they must have something to offer that answered to the Hellenic World's contemporary spiritual needs; and they must commend themselves to Hellenic hearts and minds by presenting themselves in Hellenic dress.

The militant insurrection of the proletariat against the Hellenic ascendancy in the age of agony had partly expressed itself in religious forms. The kings elected by the insurgent Syrian slaves in Sicily had won their hold by a display of supernatural powers; and the original driving-force of the Jewish revolt against the Seleucid monarchy in Coele Syria had been a zeal for the traditional Jewish way of worshipping the national god Yahweh when this had been threatened by Antiochus IV's policy of forcing all the local religions in his dominions into a uniform Hellenic mould. But the outcome of the age of agony had shown that, in the Hellenic World, there was no future for eastern religions that turned militant. They could not contend with the strength of the Hellenic middle class, now united and organized by the Augustan principate. When, in disregard of Herod the Great's warnings, the Jewish zealots insisted on quarrelling with the Hellenic world-state and took up arms against it as boldly as they had taken them up against a decadent Seleucid power, they brought upon themselves the crushing disasters of A.D. 66–70 and A.D. 132–135. Palestinian Jewry was blotted out, save for two remnants — the school of the Rabbi Johanan ben Zakkai and the Christian Church — which had both renounced the use of force as an instrument of religious policy.

It was even more significant that Zoroastrianism, too, forfeited its chance of converting the Hellenic World when it followed a militant Judaism's example. Zoroastrianism was not blotted out. Its homeland Iran was, unlike Judaea, beyond the effective range of Roman arms; and Zoroastrianism enjoyed the patronage, first of the later Parthian kings and then of the Parthians' dynamic supplanters the Sasanid founders of the second Persian Empire. But for Zoroastrianism, as for Judaism, the price of allowing itself to be used as a national religion was the loss of its chance to make a wider appeal. Zoroastrianism remained secure within the frontiers of the Persian Empire, but it did not spread beyond them till it was carried into China and India by refugees after the overthrow of the Persian Empire by the Arabs in the seventh century of the Christian Era; and its history after this dispersion was the same as that of Judaism round the shores of the Mediterranean. It proved to be a marvellous social cement for holding together a community that had been uprooted from its ancestral homeland; but it remained a national religion, and, as such, it had little attraction for mankind at large. The array of eastern missionary religions that competed with one another for the conversion of Hellenic souls did include one Iranian religion, Mithraism, and one Judaic one, Christianity; but both of these had broken out of their national bonds.

Each of these missionary religions offered spiritual insights and aids that answered to the needs of human souls in all times and places, and not least to their needs in the Hellenic World in its age of temporary convalescence after its age of agony. The blessings bestowed by the Augustan peace were negative. They were an absence of war and an absence of revolution. These alleviations did not bring with them any positive scope or stimulus for action, so that the Hellenes escaped, as we have seen, from agony only to be afflicted by dullness. Under the Augustan peace they were living in a spiritual vacuum. They had lost their previous objects of worship, and had found nothing to replace them except archaism: the fantasy of mentally retreating into a past for which they felt a nostalgia now that they had been rescued from its horrors. This spiritual bankruptcy of Hellenism gave the missionary religions an opportunity. They had a still greater opening for addressing themselves to the proletariat of the Hellenic World, to whom Hellenism, even in its heyday, had given so little in compensation for the heavy toll that the Hellenic ascendancy exacted from its victims. Christianity, in particular, also appealed to the women; for, though the status of Hellenic women had been improving in the post-Alexandrine age, they had not attained the standing and influence that were attainable, in the social life of the Christian Church, by women who won respect for their personalities through devoting themselves to the Church's service at the price of renouncing the satisfaction of their sexual nature.

In the Indian province of the Hellenic World of the day the field was occupied by a metamorphosis of the Buddhist philosophy — called 'the Great Career' (Mahayana) by its adherents — which was virtually a new religion. During the agonizing centuries that had preceded Chandragupta Maurya's establishment of an Indian world-state towards the close of the fourth century B.C., the Buddha's successors had practised a philosophy that was an Indian counterpart of Stoicism and Epicureanism — except that the Indians were more clear-sighted and whole-hearted than the Hellenes in their pursuit of the common aim of spiritual self-sufficiency. The Buddhist sage worked to rid himself, not just of love and compassion, but of all desire; and the complete extinction of desire solved his spiritual problem by extinguishing the self. Yet this selfish pursuit of selflessness left the spiritual athlete morally unsatisfied; and it was also discountenanced by the life-history of the Buddha; for, after his enlightenment, he had forborne for forty years to pass out of existence into Nirvana, and the motive for this self-sacrifice had been a compassionate desire to show to his suffering fellow-beings the way of release that he had found for himself. The master's example generated the ideal of the bodhisattva — a self-sacrificing saviour who has deliberately postponed his own release for aeons upon aeons in order to help his fellow-beings to find the road. This 'Great Career' of spiritual release may have been first essayed in Southern India. Nagarjuna, in his monastery on the banks of the River Kistna, was one of the founding fathers. But, before the end of the second century of the Christian Era, the Mahayana's main field of action had shifted north-westwards into the recently founded Kushan Empire, and it was from here that it was disseminated outside India. The establishment of the new Persian Empire, with Zoroastrianism as its official religion, headed the Mahayana away from the heart of the Hellenic World in the Mediterranean basin. From the Kushan dominions to the north of the Hindu Kush it travelled eastwards through the Tarim basin and found its destiny in Eastern Asia.

In the heart of the Hellenic World the first eastern missionary religions to make their way were the worship of the Anatolian goddess Cybele, the great mother, and the Egyptian goddess Isis, the devoted wife of the martyred vegetation-god Osiris. These two 'primordial images' had a universal appeal; but there were two other religions — the worships of the self-chastening Iranian god Mithras and of the self-assertive storm-god of the Syrian city of Doliché — which had a special appeal for the professional soldiers in the Augustan principate's standing army. While Isis and Cybele were making their conquests by sea — advancing from the ports into the cities in the interior of the Hellenic world-state — Jupiter Dolichenus and Mithras made their way north-westward from the western bank of the Euphrates overland, along the world-state's military frontier in Europe, till they reached its remote north-western marches in North Britain.

The appeal of Christianity combined in itself the appeals of each of the other competing religions. The god of Christianity was the omnipotent One True God of Judaism and Zoroastrianism; and, in this awe-inspiring aspect, the Godhead might seem almost unapproachable. Yet, for Christians, the Jewish God of Righteousness was also God the loving Father, and in God the Son the Godhead joined hands with its worshippers in the human figure of Jesus. Like a bodhisattva, God the Son was a self-sacrificing saviour, the devoted shepherd of a wayward human flock; but the sacrifice that he had made was a more arresting one. Out of love for his creatures he had voluntarily 'emptied himself' of his divine power and bliss in order to become the mortal man Jesus and to suffer a criminal's death by torture. Like the gentle Spartan martyr king Agis and the gentle Roman martyr aristocrat Tiberius Gracchus, Jesus had given his life for his people without resorting to force even in self-defence. But, unlike those two high-minded representatives of the Hellenic ascendancy, Jesus was a child of the proletariat — a carpenter's son from a village in the Coele-Syrian district of Galilee — and his people was the whole of mankind. Like Agis and Tiberius and the Sicilian slave-king Tryphon and the insurgent gladiator Spartacus, he had been done to death; but, like the slain vegetation god Osiris-Adonis-Attis-Tammuz, he had conquered death by coming to life again (Christ crucified might be foolishness in the eyes of Hellenic 'intellectuals' but not in the eyes of Hellenic peasants and Hellenic women who still cherished a pre-Hellenic agricultural religion). Like Augustus, Alexander, and every pharaoh, Jesus was the son of a god by a human mother; but Jesus's Heavenly Father was not just one member of a pantheon; he was the One True God; and Jesus himself was the One True God too in an aspect of the Godhead in which its other name was Love. Like Mithras, again, he had overcome his lower nature in resisting first the temptation to embark on the career of a proletarian political leader, and then the greater temptation to quail at the ordeal of crucifixion. Like Hadad the storm-god of Dolichê, he would come again in power, riding on the clouds. And all the time he was also the Eternal Creative Reason (Logos), in which Hellenic intellectuals, since the generation of Anaxagoras, had recognized and revered the ultimate reality behind the phenomena of the Universe.

This unfathomable figure of God incarnate in Jesus gave Christianity an impetus that would have availed, unreinforced, to ensure its victory in its competition with its rivals. But Jesus's human mother Mary was in reserve, waiting for her time to take the place of Isis and Cybele as the Great Mother of God (the Theotókos, meaning 'the God-bearer'). And soon the tombs of the Christian martyrs would be supplanting those of the Hellenic heroes. The heroes were legendary figures or, if historical, they had been unedifying barbarian war-lords in the pre-Hellenic age of anarchy. The martyrs were plain men and women of the current age who had given their lives in order to bear witness to their Christian faith. In the competition between cults of the dead, who would not choose to pay his devotion to the martyrs?

In thus combining, in one synoptic view, the vision of the Godhead in Hellenic polytheism with the vision of it in Jewish monotheism, Christianity made a compelling appeal to Hellenic souls. Yet even Christianity might have found it hard to make headway in the Hellenic World if it had not, like its competitors, presented itself in Hellenic dress. Judaism and Zoroastrianism were not competing, so they felt no need to pander to Hellenic tastes — though the philosophical works of Philo of Alexandria and the decorations of the synagogue in Seleucus the Victor's city Dura-Europus on the Euphrates testify that Judaism did set foot on the road that the missionary religions followed farther.

All the missionary religions, including the Mahayana, expressed themselves in the Hellenic style of visual art. The earliest known pictures of Jesus by Christian hands portray him in the likeness of the legendary Hellenic seer, poet, and musician Orpheus, charming the beasts of the field with his lyre in a naturalistically depicted landscape. The anthropomorphic representations of the Buddha would appear (though this has been disputed) to derive from the conventional representation of the Hellenic god Apollo which must have come into India at the heels of Demetrius's invading army in the second century B.C.

Three hundred years later, when the Mahayana was making itself at home in the Kushan Empire, it found, as we have seen, a visual vehicle in the style of art called after the Empire's metropolitan province Gandhara. This Helleno-Indian style — perhaps generated by the maritime transmission of artistic influences from Alexandria-on-Nile — set its mark on the Buddhist art of Eastern Asia; and thus the eastward march of the Mahayana conveyed at least a tincture of Hellenism to the eastern extremity of the Old World.

All the competing missionary religions except the Mahayana, which opted for Sanskrit, went on to use the Greek and Latin languages for their liturgies, scriptures, propaganda, creeds, and expositions of theology. From the moment when Saint Paul began to correspond in Greek with his Hellenic converts, it was certain that, sooner or later, Christian beliefs would be formulated in creeds; for the standard Attic Greek that was the Hellenic World's lingua franca from the post-Alexandrine age onwards carried a heavy freight of philosophical terms in its vocabulary; and Greek philosophers in the post-Alexandrine age of intellectual controversy had become accustomed to setting out their 'views' (dogmas) in systematic form. The Christian propagandists of the second century sought to commend Christianity to the educated minority of the Hellenic public by presenting it as the crown of all known philosophic systems. And this minority could not be won for Christianity without translating Christian beliefs into Hellenic philosophy's technical terminology — a procedure that had never been applied to Judaism or to any of the Hellenes' native religions.

In contrast to the worships of Cybele, Isis, Mithras, and Dolichenus, Christianity was singular in building up for itself a world-wide administrative organization, instead of letting each local group of converts go its own way.

Here again the Christian Church was adapting itself to the institutions of the society that it was seeking to convert. It based its structure on that of the Hellenic world-state. The local communities of Christians were autonomous without being sovereign. They were cells in the body of a 'Universal' (Catholic) Church, as the municipalities were cells in the body of the Roman Empire.

There was, however, one Hellenic institution with which the Christians were unwilling to compromise, and that was the worship of the world-state's collective human power symbolized in the goddess Rome and the god Caesar. While the Christian Church was progressively converting Hellenic souls, it was perpetually at war with this latest and most beneficent, but also, on that account, most formidable, of all the successive versions of Hellenic man-worship.

XV

CHRISTIANITY'S VICTORY OVER THE WORSHIP OF THE HELLENIC WORLD-STATE

IN A.D. 64, about forty years after Jesus had been put to death, the Roman Imperial Government became aware that Christianity was something more than a new sect of Judaism. They had no sooner come to this conclusion than they proscribed Christianity and made the profession of it a capital offence. This law was not assiduously enforced. For long periods at a time it was deliberately allowed to be a dead letter — in so far as the Christians themselves were willing to co-operate with the public authorities in making this official connivance possible without causing the Imperial Government to lose face. Yet the law remained on the statute-book for 249 years till it was abrogated by the Emperors Constantine and Licinius in A.D. 313. This was something exceptional in the history of the Roman Government's religious policy.

It is true that the Roman Government had always been on its guard against eastern religions and, at times, had taken drastic measures to check their dissemination in Roman territory. In 186 B.C., for example, it had repressed, with great harshness, the worship of Dionysus, which had been gaining ground in the Greek colonial cities of Southern Italy since their harrowing experiences during the second Romano-Punic war. This was carrying anti-Orientalism to extremes; for by that date the Thracian god Dionysus had been naturalized in the Hellenic World for at least 500 years. At the sanctuary of Delphi he had been admitted to partnership with Apollo and Earth, and in his theatre at Athens the Attic drama had flowered under his auspices. It was less unreasonable that, when, in 204 B.C., on instructions from the Delphic Oracle, the goddess Cybele had been brought to Rome in the shape of the holy black stone of Pessinus as a talisman to procure a Roman victory in the second Romano-Punic war, the Roman Government should have taken steps to insulate the outlandish goddess's new temple at Rome, with its Anatolian priests, from the Roman public. It was also not surprising that, when the Syrian priest-emperor Elagabalus (reigned A.D. 218–222) tried to impose his own holy black stone of Emesa on the Roman pantheon, this imprudent act of fantacism should have cost him his throne and his life. On the whole, however, the Roman Government's religious record was one of tolerance; and this was what was to be expected, considering the Romans' own religious outlook. A spirit of tolerance was the bright side of Hellenic polytheism; and, in the course of Rome's reception of Hellenism, the Olympian pantheon had been grafted, partly by Etruscan hands, on to the primitive Latin worship of countless impersonal spiritual presences (numina) representing the still unexplored and unsubjugated forces of Nature. How, indeed, could intolerance have been practicable in a world in which each local community worshipped a troop of divinities and each of these local troops had a different composition?

The Roman Government's characteristically Hellenic tolerance came out strikingly in its policy towards Judaism. While it was merciless to the Jewish zealots, in whose belief their religion required the re-establishment of a militant Jewish state, it granted generous terms to the school of Rabbi Johanan ben Zakkai. In return for a renunciation, on the Jewish side, of the use of force, the Roman Government, on its side, not only gave the Jews freedom to practise their own religion in their own way under Roman rule; the Government went so far as to accept the Jews' contention that it was incompatible with Judaism to perform the conventional acts of worship in honour of the goddess Rome and the god Caesar. This Jewish conscientious objection, which the Roman Government respected with such remarkable liberality, had been inherited from Judaism by the Christian Church; and the Christians had abjured militancy, no less than the Jewish followers of Johanan ben Zakkai. Why, then, did the Roman Government refuse to the Christians the *quid pro quo* which they were willing to grant to the non-militant remnant of the Jews?

In deciding on this extreme and, at first sight, arbitrary difference of treatment, the Imperial Government was acting on an accurate intuition of the respective political consequences that would follow from a policy of toleration in the two cases.

Judaism, when once it had renounced its aspiration to refound a Jewish state by force of arms, was no danger to the order of things established by Augustus. It was not much concerned to make converts; its overriding concern was to preserve the separate identity of the Jewish community in dispersion; and, even if Judaism had actively entered the Hellenic mission-field, its cherished beliefs and practices would have ensured its failure there. Judaism's intransigent monotheism was repulsive to Hellenic sensibilities. To reject all gods but one was tantamount, in Hellenic eyes, to atheism — as the Emperor Julian realized when he used the nickname 'atheists' to denigrate the Christians. Even more unattractive, if possible, was the obligation to observe the irrational and onerous commandments of the Mosaic Law. This was incumbent on converts to Judaism; and for male proselytes, in whose case the obligation included circumcision, the demand was virtually prohibitive. Judaism in dispersion was bound to insist on the meticulous observance of the Mosaic Law, since, after the destruction of the Jewish state, the Law was the Jewish nation's sole remaining life-line. But a requirement that had now become a necessity of Jewry's national life made it certain that Judaism would not convert the world. The Jews themselves had now seen to that; and this made it superfluous for the Roman Government to take any precautionary measures.

On the other hand, Christianity had broken away from its parent Judaism by making concessions to Hellenism that from the Jewish standpoint were scandalous and from the Imperial Government's standpoint disquieting. In contrast to what was the order of priorities for Judaism, the first concern of the Christian Church was, not just to preserve itself, but to convert the rest of mankind. As soon as the Church began to win non-Jewish converts, it dispensed these, not only from the rite of circumcision, but from the obligation to observe the Mosaic Law except for a perfunctory minimum of tabus. And it also made itself attractive to Hellenes by breaking the first two of the Ten Commandments. As the Jews saw it, Christianity broke the First Commandment in a characteristically Hellenic way by deifying a man and associating him with Yahweh on equal terms as one of the persons in the Godhead. (The Lord's Anointed — in Greek Khristós — whose advent the Jews were expecting, was to be, not a deified man, but a strictly human vicegerent of God, like the Persian Emperor.) The Christian Church broke the Second Commandment by using Hellenic visual art as a medium for religious propaganda. In Jewish eyes, these sweeping concessions to Hellenism on points of fundamental religious principle were disgusting; from the Imperial Government's point of view they were alarming.

If Christianity's surrender to Hellenism had gone the length of abandoning the vein of exclusiveness and intolerance that was the dark side of Jewish monotheism, Christianity might have been no more obnoxious to the Imperial Government than the other eastern missionary religions with which it was in competition. But, while Christianity opened its arms wide enough to Hellenism to tempt hungry Hellenic souls to seek spiritual sustenance in the Church's bosom, the Church showed an unmitigated Jewish intransigence in rejecting everything in the Hellenic way of life that she did not see fit to adopt. Thus Christianity was as pernicious for Hellenism as it was alluring for Hellenes. The Imperial Government had correctly gauged its potentialities when it refused to extend to it the toleration that it readily granted to non-militant Judaism. Yet, in proscribing Christianity, the Government was unintentionally playing into the Christian Church's hands.

The strength of all the missionary religions was their power of giving back to Hellenic life some of the significance and the zest that it had lost. When the Christian Church adopted Hellenic visual art, the Greek and Latin languages, Hellenic philosophy, and Roman political institutions as a means of putting itself *en rapport* with prospective Hellenic converts, it not only succeeded in providing itself with effective instruments of communication; it also revivified these instruments by breathing new Christian life into dry Hellenic bones. In this age of boredom, Hellenic intellectuals who were as yet untouched by the missionary religions were searching for themes and finding them, if at all, in an artificial revival of the Hellenic past. By contrast the Christians felt an abounding urge to depict, to expound, and to organize. The search for themes and tasks was no problem for them. They had no sooner taken over the instruments of

Hellenic culture than they made use of them up to the hilt; and this Christian creativity was not confined to the field of art and thought. In an age in which, in the cities of the Hellenic world-state, municipal self-government was in decay, ecclesiastical self-government was developing, on an Hellenic pattern, in the local Christian communities.

Thus, in contrast to the Hellenes in the age of the principate, the Christians did not suffer from lack of stimulus; and the crowning stimulus was given to them by the Imperial Government when it made the profession of Christianity a capital offence. One of the reasons for the prevalent insipidity of life in the Hellenic world-state was that the belated establishment of world-peace deprived most people of the opportunity of risking — and, if it so fell out, losing — their lives for the sake of a cause that transcended their petty personal interests. Before the Christians were made subject to martyrdom, the only inhabitants of the world-state who found themselves in this exhilarating position were the soldiers whose duty it was to guard the frontiers against the Parthians and the barbarians. As soon as Christians had to go in danger of their lives, an element — and this a growing one — in the population of the cities of the interior regained the boon of living dangerously which had been enjoyed by the citizens of these same cities in the age when they had called upon their citizens to hazard their lives in their service. These new heroes were recruited, surprisingly, from the lower middle class, which the Hellenic upper middle class and aristocracy had despised; and there was a difference between their heroism and their citizen-soldier forebears' heroism that was to the Christian martyrs' advantage. The citizens of the former city-states had been required to sacrifice their lives for public purposes that were often trivial, sometimes immoral, and always anti-social. The Christian in the interior of the Hellenic world-state, like the soldier on the frontiers, could feel that he was laying down his life for a worthier cause. The soldier was laying his down for the sake of saving a peaceful and cultivated society from rapine and murder at the hands of outer barbarians. The Christian was laying his life down for the sake of bearing witness to the truth that there was no god but God and that his loyalty to the One True God, including in the Godhead the person of Jesus Christ, had a greater claim on him than his loyalty to Rome and to Caesar.

The documentary evidence shows that during the 'Indian Summer' of the world-state, which lasted from the death of the Emperor Domitian in A.D. 96 almost to the death of the Emperor Marcus Aurelius in A.D. 180, it was usually the policy of the Imperial Government and its local representatives to avoid sentencing convicted Christians to death if this could be contrived. This policy was inspired partly by feelings of humanity — for this was the least inhumane age of Hellenic history — and partly by political wisdom; for the Imperial Government did not need to be told by the African Christian barrister Tertullian that 'blood is seed'. Some of the surviving records of proceedings in court that appear to be authentic show the Roman magistrate pleading with the Christian prisoner in the dock to cast a few grains of incense on Caesar's altar, on the ground that this ritual act was just an innocuous formality, and the Christian forcing the magistrate's hand — sometimes with an almost offensive truculence. The Christian aspirant to the martyr's crown was determined to obtain a death-sentence so he parried the magistrate's well-meant attempts to avoid passing it. Logically, the unyielding Christian had the better of the argument. For, if the required act were truly regarded by the public authorities as being an empty form, why should they have made non-compliance a capital offence? The Christian's aggressive intransigence was both sublime and perverse, and, in both these aspects, it was Judaic. But, throughout the age of the principate, this Judaic Christian intransigence remained pacific. Like the Jewish followers of Johanan ben Zakkai and unlike the Jewish zealots, the Christians did not ever take up arms against the Imperial Government. Their intention was to conquer, not by a *coup de force,* but by a progressive process of conversion. Yet, when they did eventually achieve their end in their own non-violent way, the régime of toleration for all religions, instituted in A.D. 313 by Constantine, the first overtly pro-Christian emperor, lasted for no more than sixty-eight years. In A.D. 381 the fanatically Christian emperor Theodosius opened a campaign for the extirpation of all non-Christian religions in the Roman Empire; and, on the surface at least, this objective had been attained by A.D. 390.

Meanwhile, during the 'Indian summer' of Hellenic history in the second century of the Christian Era, the enforcement of the law proscribing Christianity under pain of death was spasmodic and half-hearted. At the same time the Christians were unpopular among the still unconverted majority of the Hellenic society, and this for at least two reasons. In the first place their obstinate refusal to go through the formalities of Caesar-worship was condemned as a discreditable exhibition of a fanaticism that was felt to be a public danger because it was irrational. According to the spirit of the Hellenic religious tradition, an act of public worship did not carry with it even an implicit declaration of any religious beliefs; but it did have the force of a declaration of loyalty to the community. To refuse compliance was therefore an antisocial act, while the plea of a conscientious scruple was not a valid excuse. In the second place, the worship of the goddess Rome and the god Caesar, though it left Hellenic hearts lukewarm, did awaken in them some feeling of indignation when it was flouted. This worship was, after all, an expression of society's gratitude for the blessings of peace and concord which it had taken the Hellenic World five hundred years to achieve since the date — before the end of the sixth century B.C. — when some form of political unification had become due. The gratitude was genuine — as is illustrated in a striking passage in one of the works of Philo, in which this Alexandrian Jewish philosopher eulogizes Augustus as the saviour of society in terms that go to the verge of hailing him as a god. As a Jew Philo might be expected to be jealous for the exclusive divinity of Yahweh; as an Alexandrian he might be expected to feel some resentment against a Roman conqueror who had deprived Alexandria of her proud status as the capital of a great empire. If Philo felt as grateful as he evidently did feel for the establishment of the Augustan peace, Hellenes who were neither Alexandrians nor Jews are likely to have felt the same and felt it more strongly.

This smouldering conflict between Hellenism and Christianity burst into flame as soon as the Hellenic world-state began to fall into adversity. Already, before the Emperor Marcus's death, there were sporadic anti-Christian riots. In A.D. 177 there was a sharp local persecution at Lyons. The crisis came when the world-state dissolved into a temporary anarchy after the murder of the Emperor Alexander Severus in A.D. 235. In the 'fifties' of the third century, mass-persecutions of Christianity were running a race with mass-conversions to it. Hellenes who felt the foundations of the Hellenic society giving way beneath their feet were feeling tempted to seek refuge in the new society which the Christian Church had built on an apparently solid rock. And, just for this reason, other Hellenes, fighting with their backs to the wall to salvage and rehabilitate the old order, were feeling dismayed and outraged at the spectacle of the Christian Church erecting itself into something like a counter-state within the world-state. Since A.D. 212 almost all the inhabitants of the world-state were also citizens of it. A citizen had duties as well as rights; and surely his paramount duty was to rally to the support of the world-state and the Hellenic civilization when both were threatened with destruction. In this hour, solidarity was the citizen's first duty and society's first need. Dissidence in any field was now a crime; and it was most criminal of all in the field of religion; for here it was an offence against society's ancestral gods, whose favour must be recaptured if society was to be saved.

No doubt, in the eyes of a sophisticated minority of the Hellenes, these ancestral gods had been discredited for the last seven hundred years; but these intellectuals were the first victims of the social breakdown; and the saviours who had stepped into the breach were the Illyrian professional soldiers from the Danubian frontier. Late converts to Hellenism, and then receiving it only in its crude Latin dress, the Illyrians were as uncritical of their adopted civilization as they were proud to devote themselves to its service — if necessary at the sacrifice of their lives. As they live for us today, in their busts, with their close-clipped military beards and their care-worn yet indomitable countenances, they command our respect and excite our sympathy. But their fatal shortcoming was an hereditary barbarian naïveté that was unequal to coping with the problems of a civilization, even when this had relapsed to a semi-barbarian level. The classical example of this Illyrian defect is afforded by the Emperor Julian, who tried to put the clock back after his uncle the Emperor Constantine had had the clear-sightedness and common sense to come to terms with Christianity. Julian was two generations removed from an Illyrian simple soldier, and he had received a high Hellenic education from an accomplished tutor. Yet he embarrassed the more sophisticated among his anti-Christian contemporaries by the credulity and sentimentality with which he idealized the whole mixed bag of the Hellenic heritage. His notion of what Hellenism was, and his attitude towards what he supposed it to be, would have astonished an educated Hellene of the age of Hellenic rationalism (fifth century B.C. to third century of the Christian Era).

The still more naïve Illyrian soldier-saviours of the first generation, a hundred years before Julian's day, sought to solve the problem of Christianity by the desperate measure of trying to stamp it out — a solution that had never proved practicable even when the principate had been at the height of its power and prestige. In A.D. 250 the Emperor Decius — the heroic defender of his fellow citizens against the invading trans-Danubian barbarians — decreed that every inhabitant of the world-state must be able to produce, on official demand, a voucher (tessera) certifying that he had duly performed the officially prescribed act of sacrifice to Caesar's genius. This drastic measure ought to have brought to light all contumacious Christians, and it should have been followed up by their wholesale execution. Many Christians did give way; but others sacrificed their lives and the Church lived on after Decius had met his death in A.D. 251. The Emperor Valerian's tactics, in A.D. 257, of arresting, deporting, and executing Christians in prominent positions were no more successful, and the persecution was tacitly suspended when Valerian was taken prisoner by Shahpur in A.D. 260. It was not renewed in the 'seventies', when the indefatigable Illyrians were gradually mastering the military and political crisis by driving the barbarians back beyond the frontiers and putting down the splinter world-states that had sprung up at Palmyra and in Gaul. Now that the Christian Church had thus survived a systematic attempt to extirpate it, it was bound to take control of the Hellenic World sooner or later. This process of social and spiritual transformation might have been accomplished peacefully if Decius's ill-starred policy had not been taken up again, in A.D. 303, by the associate emperor Galerius against the better judgment of his senor colleague Diocletian — the prosaic Illyrian man of genius who had finally put the fallen world-state on its feet again and had then underpinned it with a new military and administrative organization.

In A.D. 303 the Imperial Government had no justification, either moral or legal, for proscribing a religion to which perhaps more than a third of its subjects now adhered. The world-state and society were no longer in danger; and Caesar-worship was no longer the world-state's official religion. The Illyrian emperor Aurelian (reigned A.D. 270–275) had concluded, from the spectacle of deified emperors being butchered by their soldiers, that for an emperor to be a god in his own person was no safeguard against the risk of his being liquidated; for the same sword would finish off man and god at one stroke, leaving no god alive to take vengeance on the dead god-man's murderers. Aurelian had preferred to reign, not as a god in his own right, but as the vicegerent of a non-human god — Aristonicus of Pergamum's Unconquered Sun — who was beyond the reach of the soldiers' weapons. This momentous change in the theoretical basis of the emperor's authority did not, after all, save Aurelian from being assassinated in his turn. But it did deprive Galerius of the traditional ground for declaring Christianity to be incompatible with loyalty to the world-state.

Galerius and his policy met the fates that they deserved.

Galerius lived to rescind the edict of A.D. 303 in A.D. 311, a few days before he died on a sick-bed. After that, it was certain that some Illyrian vicegerent of the Unconquered Sun would blazon Christ's cross over the Sun's disk. The Dardanian emperor Constantine showed his awareness of the realities in his day by choosing to be the agent of this inevitable revolution.

XVI

HELLENISM'S COLLAPSE

If the word 'death' could be used to describe the passing-away of an institution, the 'death' of Hellenism would be a case of suicide, not of murder. 'The triumph of religion and barbarism', which was Gibbon's theme in his history of the decline and fall of the Roman Empire, was not the slaughter of a living victim; it was a walk over a corpse. Before Christianity had become the official religion of the Hellenic world-state, and before the barbarians had established their successor-states on what had formerly been Hellenic ground, Hellenism was already dead; and it had died of the Hellenes' own failure to respond to a challenge with which they had been confronted as far back in their history as the fifth century B.C. After their economic revolution in the sixth century B.C. had made the local communities of the Hellenic World economically inter-dependent, the Hellenes had failed to achieve the political unity that their new economic circumstances required. And the nemesis of this failure had been the international and civil warfare that had devastated the Hellenic World, with hardly a breathing-space, for four hundred years dating from the outbreak of the great Atheno-Peloponnesian war in 431 B.C. When peace and order had been re-established at last by Augustus, the sequel had shown that the wounds which Hellenism had already inflicted on itself were lethal. The inability of the once idolized city-states to retain their hold over their citizens' hearts after they had been deprived of their disastrous power to go to war made it evident that the establishment of an Hellenic world-state had been, not a cure for Hellenism's malady, but merely a temporary palliative. And, when the Hellenic World's consequent relapse into anarchy in the third century of the Christian Era had ruined the Hellenic middle class, the Hellenic civilization had gone under with it.

The collapse of Hellenism in that age of anarchy is manifest in the subsequent policy of the Illyrian soldier-statemen who gave the Hellenic world-state a new lease of life. Diocletian deliberately completed the process of transferring administrative responsibility from the municipal magistracies to the imperial civil service, and Constantine deliberately took the Christian Church into partnership in place of the Hellenic middle class, which, under the Augustan principate, had been the Imperial Government's associate in the management of the Hellenic World's affairs. The Illyrians were conservative-minded, and they did not take their revolutionary action by choice. They were simply making use of the most serviceable materials on which they could lay hands for shoring up a tottering social structure. The old materials continued to prove their worth in so far as they remained intact. In Asia Minor, Syria, and Egypt, where the Hellenic middle class and civic institutions had struck root, the Hellenic world-state, which the Illyrians had rehabilitated before the end of the third century, survived into the seventh century of the Christian Era, while it broke up two hundred years earlier in the backward western provinces, where the Hellenic form of urban life had been something exotic. But the precious residue of the Hellenic society's stamina in the Levant was squandered by the Emperor Justinian in an effort to reconquer the world-state's lost western provinces, and by Justinian's successors in two long and exhausting wars with the Persian Empire, which opened the door for the conquest of both parties by the Arabs.

The weakness, in the last chapter of Hellenic history, of the Hellenic society's will to live is revealed by the feebleness of its attempt to fight Christianity with Christianity's weapons. Christianity's victory over the worship of the Hellenic world-state had not been a conclusive trial of strength between Christianity and Hellenic religion, since the worship of the goddess Rome and the god Caesar was an artificial cult which had been instituted to serve a political purpose and had left Hellenic hearts cold. In the third century of the Christian Era a Neoplatonic philosopher, Iamblichus of Chalcis in Coele Syria (about A.D. 250–325), took a new step forward in the movement that had been initiated by the Syrian Stoic philosopher Poseidonius in the second century B.C. Poseidonius had stood for a rapprochement between contending philosophies and for a revival of religious feeling. Iamblichus now thought of combating Christianity by organizing all the living non-Christian religions and philosophies of the Hellenic World into an anti-Christian counter-church; and this programme was put into action by two Illyrian emperors: Galerius's uncultivated lieutenant Maximinus Daia (reigned A.D. 305–313 in the East), and Constantine's highly educated nephew Julian (reigned A.D. 361–363).

Maximinus controlled the eastern provinces only, but he enjoyed the advantage of making his attempt before Constantine had given the Christian Church official recognition. Julian controlled the entire empire, but he laboured under the disadvantage of attempting to undo what, by his time, was an accomplished fact. It is significant that both attempts alike fell flat. Iamblichus had put his finger on two sources of the Christian Church's strength — its universality and its organization — and it was logical to fight Christianity on its own ground; but this was also an admission of Christianity's superiority to Hellenism, and it was a demand upon Hellenism to go counter to its own traditional genius. The spirit of Hellenic religion had remained on the whole polytheistic, in spite of the eventual imposition of a superficial unity in the form of Caesar-worship; and it also remained on the whole tolerant, in spite of occasional impulses to impose religious conformity by persecution — as, for example, at Athens during the great Atheno-Peloponnesian war and in the Seleucid monarchy during the reign of King Antiochus IV. A philosophically educated Hellene in the fourth century of the Christian Era might dislike Christianity and dread the prospect of its prevailing, but he would feel himself placed in a false position when he was asked to assume the role of pseudo-bishop in the hierarchy of an artificial counter-church. The only religion of their own to which the Hellenes had ever given a wholehearted devotion had been the worship of collective human power in the form of idolized city-states. The rest of Hellenic religion had been losing its hold since the fifth century B.C.; and in the third century of the Christian Era the process of decay had gone with a run. In Iamblichus's own day, the time-honoured practice of consulting Delphi and the other historic oracles of the Hellenic World had fallen into disuse. The Olympic festival was celebrated for the last time in the year A.D. 396. The Emperor Julian became a laughing-stock among his own supporters for his superstitious piety, and this was more fatal to his cause than the Christians' execration of him as an apostate.

Julian's counter-church died with him; and, when the Constantinian régime of toleration for all religions, which had been re-established by Julian's successors, was abandoned by the fanatically Christian Spanish emperor Theodosius (reigned A.D. 378–395) in favour of the militant policy of using the Imperial Government's power to stamp out all remnants of non-Christian religion within the world-state's frontiers, the Hellenes' resistance was ineffective. Eugenius's armed revolt in the west (A.D. 392–4) was easily suppressed by Theodosius, though the percentage of Christians in the population was then still small in that half of the Hellenic World; and the Roman Senator Quintus Aurelius Symmachus's peaceful protest against the suppression of traditional religious institutions by the secular arm was harshly overridden. In a public controversy with Saint Ambrose, Symmachus made a memorable declaration in which he was expressing the spirit of Hellenism more faithfully than it had been expressed by Iamblichus. 'There must,' he wrote, 'be more than one line of approach to the heart of the great mystery of the Universe.' This challenge to the Judaic vein of exclusiveness and intolerance in the spirit of Christianity has remained unanswered down to this day. If, in Symmachus's day, Hellenism had still had life in it, persecution would have stimulated it as it had stimulated Christianity in the age of the principate and Judaism in the reign of Antiochus IV. But, when the Hellenic society was subjected to a similar ordeal, it dwindled into a band of single-minded but cranky devotees, who read sublime symbolic meanings into the most extravagant and benighted non-Christian religious practices.

In the year A.D. 529 the Emperor Justinian closed the four institutes at Athens in which the doctrines of the four principal schools of Hellenic philosophy had been handed down, by that time, for the best part of a millennium. Seven of the professors who were thus thrown out of employment were unwilling to renounce their Hellenic religion under duress; and they sought and obtained asylum at the court of the Persian Emperor Khusraw I. But, in a long-since de-Hellenized 'Iraq, they soon found themselves homesick for their recently Christianized native land. Khusraw did not take their homesickness amiss; and he chivalrously wrote into a peace-treaty that he was negotiating with the Roman Imperial Government a stipulation that the seven Hellenic refugees should be allowed to go home with a life-long guarantee of exemption, by special privilege, from compulsory conversion to Christianity.

These seven professors were the last Hellenes on whom the Christian Roman government had its eye. But, three hundred and fifty years later, the worship of the Olympian gods was still going on, not far from Athens, on the secluded Taenarum peninsula: the central 'prong' of the three southern 'prongs' of the Peloponnese. Here the rustic descendants of some of Sparta's former 'satellites' had never heard of Xenophanes' and Euripides' strictures on the Olympians' misdemeanours or of Theodosius's and Justinian's penal laws against the practice of non-Christian religions. And, soon after Justinian's death, their fastness had been sealed off from Christendom by an influx of heathen Slavs into the Peloponnese from the far-away Pripet marshes. By that time, Illyricum had been depopulated by three hundred years of military exertions, as Macedon had been depopulated in the post-Alexandrine age; and the flood of the Slav barbarian Völkerwanderung washed over the empty countryside of South-Eastern Europe up to the walls of a few fortified towns on or near the coasts. This revolutionary change in the population towards the end of the sixth century of the Christian Era has left its mark in the Slavonic languages that are spoken in Bulgaria and Jugoslavia today, and in the numerous Slavonic place-names in present-day Rumania and Greece. But in the ninth century of the Christian Era the heathen Slav settlements in the Peloponnese were subjugated by a revived Greek

Christian Roman Empire; the heathen Greek worshippers of the Olympian gods on the Taenarum peninsula were discovered; and their Hellenic religion was suppressed by their Christian Greek conquerors.

By this date the word 'Hellene' had changed its meaning in Christian Greek-speaking mouths. The Hellenes themselves, in their heyday, had divided mankind into 'Hellenes', meaning 'civilized men', and 'barbarians'; Greek-speaking Christians divided mankind into 'Romans', meaning themselves, and 'Hellenes', now meaning 'heathen'. Thus, as a result of the triumph of Christianity, the connotation of an historic name had boxed the compass. A word that had once signified the children of light had now come to signify people sitting in outer darkness. In fact, the word 'Hellene' had acquired the ill odour that had formerly attached to the word 'barbarian'. This dramatic change in the usage of a Greek term showed that people could cease to be Hellenes while continuing to speak the Greek language as their mother tongue.

Greek Christendom broke away from the traditions of Hellenism by making radical innovations in a number of fields. The Bible supplanted the Homeric epic as *the* book for readers of the Greek language. Accentual metres replaced quantitative metres in the rhythm of Greek poetry. Christian Greek liturgical and devotional poetry was re-modelled in the seventh century on a Syriac Christian pattern. Christian Greek secular poetry adopted the accentual metre known as 'city' verse — presumably because it had originated in Constantinople. For Greek-speaking Christians, *the* city was no longer Hellenic Rome or Alexandria or Athens; it was the city founded by Constantine, which had been Christian from the start. The Hellenic type of building — an oblong hall with a gable roof and an outer colonnade — was replaced in the sixth century by the Byzantine type: a square hall crowned by a dome, with its columns secreted in its interior. The new style was dramatically antithetical to the old one. The Hellenic temple expressed an extroverted mental attitude, the Byzantine church an introverted one. Even the mountains of Hellas lost their famous Hellenic names. On the European mainland many of them were re-named by the incoming Slav barbarians in their Slavonic tongue; on the islands, which escaped the Slav invasion, prominent peaks were christened with the name of the Prophet Elijah. The Israelite hero's legendary ascent into heaven was familiar to Christian imaginations that had forgotten the tale of the Hellenic hero Heraklês' legendary ascent from Mount Oeta.

Christianity superseded Hellenism; but it did not, and could not, repudiate the elements of Hellenic culture which it had previously adopted as instruments for furthering its own original aim of converting the Hellenic World. The Christian Church's scriptures, liturgy, and theological literature were written in the Greek and Latin languages. Its creeds were formulated in the terminology of Hellenic philosophy. And it picked up and carried along with it a body of pre-Christian Hellenic literature, Greek in the east and Latin in the west, to serve as models of literary style and as canons of metaphysical reasoning. The quantity and range of the Hellenic literature that the Christian Church took under its aegis was actually much greater than the minimum required for strictly utilitarian purposes. This generous appreciation and preservation of an Hellenic literary heritage does the Christian Church credit, but it has also caused it embarrassment; for, like the slain Egyptian fertility god Osiris's dismembered body, these *disjecta membra* of Hellenism have retained within themselves a latent spark of life which has repeatedly burst into flame after lying dormant for centuries. Thus, unintentionally, the Christian Church has served as a carrier for un-Christian and even anti-Christian Hellenic ideas and ideals which have sometimes re-asserted themselves to their Christian purveyor's consternation.

The vitality of these Hellenic elements embedded in Christianity is illustrated by the history of the second risorgimento of the Oriental peoples who had revolted against Macedonian rule in the third and second centuries B.C. and had been re-subdued in the last century B.C. by Roman arms. The resumption of the Oriental counter-attack in the fifth century of the Christian Era did not take the form of armed insurrection against an Hellenic secular power. This time the battle was fought within the bosom of the Christian Church, and the weapons employed were theological and linguistic. Syriac, Egyptian, and Armenian-speaking Christians now asserted themselves against Greek and Latin-speaking Christians by embracing different doctrines about the nature of the Second Person of the Christian Trinity and by adopting their own national languages, in place of Greek, as their vehicles for the Christian liturgy and literature. In this second battle, fought with cultural weapons, the Oriental peoples were successful. South-east of the Taurus mountains, the Greek language and the Greek 'orthodox' version of Christological doctrine had been driven out of the countryside and confined within the walls of a few cities — Antioch, Aelia Capitolina (Jerusalem), and Alexandria — before the military conquest of the Roman Empire's trans-Tauran provinces by the Muslim Arabs in the seventh century of the Christian Era. But, while rebelling against the Greek language and the Greek-speaking hierarchy of the 'imperial' ('Melchite') church, the Oriental peoples were not closing their minds to Hellenic thought. They translated into their own languages out of the original Greek not only the works of the Christian Fathers but also the works of the Hellenic philosophers and men of science who had supplied the Christian theologians with their mental tools. In this way, Hellenic thought was propagated among the Oriental subjects of the Roman Empire by the Monophysite churches, and among the subjects of the Persian Empire by the Nestorian church. And, when both empires had been conquered by the Muslim Arabs, Oriental Christian converts to the conquerors' new Judaic religion supplied Islam with a theology of its own which was derived from the same Hellenic source as the theology of Christianity. The Hellenic philosophical and scientific works that had previously been translated out of Greek into Syriac were now translated into Arabic, and the Islamic World continued to accept the authority of Plato and Aristotle and Hippocrates and Galen after the Western Christian World had broken loose from the spell of Hellenic thought and had started to think for itself.

Thus, when three new civilizations — the Byzantine Christian, the Western Christian, and the Islamic — arose in what had once been the Hellenic civilization's domain, all three gave evidence of the Hellenic inspiration that they had received through Christian and Islamic channels. In fact, all three of them might be classified as being 'Hellenistic' as well as 'Judaic'.

A 'Hellenistic' civilization may be overtaken by an eruption of the explosive Hellenic spirit that lies buried, but not extinct, beneath its Christian or Islamic surface. And, at the present day, Western Christendom is still feeling the effects of one unusually violent eruption — popularly known as *the* renaissance — which started in Italy about six hundred years ago and spread from there, first to the rest of Western Christendom, and then to other parts of the world as a result of the recent worldwide process of 'Westernization'. In the field of the arts and sciences, the influence of the re-discovered Hellenic culture was digested and transcended by Western minds before the end of the seventeenth century. In the field of politics, a revival of the Hellenic worship of idolized local states is, today, the dominant religion of the West and of a rapidly Westernizing world. It is only thinly disguised by a veneer of Christianity, Islam, and other higher religions. The tragic history of the Hellenic World shows that this Hellenic form of idolatry is a ghost of Hellenism that we harbour at our peril. The Modern World must exorcise this demon resolutely if it is to save itself from meeting with its Hellenic predecessor's fate.

BIBLIOGRAPHY

A

Original Works in English Translations

HOMER: *The Iliad* and *The Odyssey:* E. V. Rieu. (London, 1956 & 1945, Penguin.)

HESIOD: *Hesiod (Theogony, Works and Days* &c.): H. G. Evelyn White. (This also includes the *Homeric Hymns.*) (London, 1914, Heinemann, Loeb Library.)

GREEK ELEGIAC POETS: *Elegy and Iambus:* J. M. Edmonds. (London, 1931, Heinemann, Loeb Library, 2 vols.)

GREEK LYRIC POETS: *Lyra Graeca:* J. M. Edmonds. (London, 1922–7, Heinemann, Loeb Library, 3 vols.)

Also *The Oxford Book of Greek Verse in Translation:* T. F. Higham, C. M. Bowra. (Oxford, 1938, Clarendon Press.)

PRE-SOCRATIC GREEK PHILOSOPHERS: *Ancilla to the Pre-Socratic Philosophers:* A Complete Translation of the Fragments in Diels, *Fragmente der Vorsokratiker:* K. Freeman. (Oxford, 1949, Blackwell.)

PINDAR: *The Odes of Pindar (Odes in Honour of Victors at the Panhellenic Festivals)*: Sir John Sandys. (London, 1915, Heinemann, Loeb Library.)

AESCHYLUS: *The Complete Plays (Tragedies)*: Gilbert Murray. (London, 1952, Allen & Unwin.)

SOPHOCLES: *Sophocles (Tragedies* — complete works): F. Storr. (London, 1912–13, Heinemann, Loeb Library, 2 vols.)

Individual plays translated by Gilbert Murray and published by Allen & Unwin are: *Antigone* (1941); *Oedipus at Colonus* (1948); *Oedipus King of Thebes* (1911); *The Trachinean Women* (1947); *The Wife of Heracles* (1947).

HIPPOCRATEAN SCHOOL OF MEDICINE: *Hippocrates (Collected Works) and the Fragments of Heracleitus:* W. H. S. Jones & E. T. Withington. (London, 1923–31, Heinemann, Loeb Library, 4 vols.)

HERODOTUS: *The History of Herodotus (A History of the Conflicts between Asia and Europe)*: George Rawlinson. (London, 1910, Dent, Everyman's Library.)

THUCYDIDES: *History of the Peloponnesian War (A History of the Great Atheno-Peloponnesian War)* 2nd ed.: B. Jowett. (Oxford, 1900, Clarendon Press, 2 vols.)

EURIPIDES: *Euripides* (*Tragedies,* complete works): A. S. Way. (London, 1912, Heinemann, Loeb Library, 4 vols.)

Gilbert Murray's translations of individual plays (published by Allen & Unwin) are: *Alcestis* (1915); *The Baachae* (1902); *Electra* (1905); *Hippolytus* (1902); *Iphigenia in Tauris* (1910); *Medea* (1906); *Rhesus* (1915); *The Trojan Women* (1906)—now obtainable in one vol., *The Collected Plays of Euripides* (1954). *Ion* (1954) is issued separately.

ARISTOPHANES: *Aristophanes* (*Comedies*—complete works): B. B. Rogers. (London, 1924, Heinemann, Loeb Library, 3 vols.)

Gilbert Murray's translations of individual plays (published by Allen & Unwin) are: *The Birds* (1950); *The Frogs* (1908); *The Knights* (1956).

PLATO: *The Dialogues of Plato,* 4th ed.: B. Jowett. (Oxford, 1953, Clarendon Press, 4 vols.)

The Republic: A. D. Lindsay. (London, 1954, Dent, Everyman's Library.)

XENOPHON: *The Hellenica* (*Hellenic Affairs,* a continuation of Thucydides' *History* down to the year 361 B.C.): C. L. Brownson & O. J. Todd. (This also includes *The Apology* (*Socrates' Defence*) and *The Symposium.*) (London, 1921–3, Heinemann, Loeb Library, 3 vols.)

The Persian Expedition (*The Return March of Cyrus the Younger's Greek Mercenaries,* 401–399 B.C.): Rex Warner. (London, 1949, Penguin.)

Cyropaedia (*The Education of Cyrus the Elder*): Walter Miller. (London, 1914, Heinemann, Loeb Library, 2 vols.)

Memorabilia and Oeconomicus (*A Memoir of Socrates* and *A Treatise on Housekeeping*): E. G. Marchant. (London, 1923, Heinemann, Loeb Library.)

ISOCRATES: *Isocrates* (*Lectures and Addresses*): George Norlin & La Rue van Hook. (London, 1928–45, Heinemann, Loeb Library, 3 vols.)

DEMOSTHENES: *Public Orations:* A. W. Pickard-Cambridge. (Oxford, 1912, Clarendon Press.)

Private Orations: A. T. Murray. (London, 1936–9, Heinemann, Loeb Library, 3 vols.)

AESCHINES: *The Speeches of Aeschines:* Charles Darwin Adams. (London, 1919, Heinemann, Loeb Library.)

ARISTOTLE: *The Oxford Translation of Aristotle:* vol. 1 *Logic:* E. M. Edghill, A. J. Jenkinson, G. R. Mure, W. A. Pickard-Cambridge; 2 *Philosophy of Nature:* R. P. Hardie, R. K. Gaye, J. L. Stocks, H. H. Joachim; 3 *The Soul:* E. W. Webster, E. S. Forster, J. A. Smith, J. I. Beare, G. R. T. Ross, J. F. Dobson; 4 *History of Animals:* Sir D'Arcy W. Thompson; 5 *Parts of Animals:* W.

Ogle, A. S. L. Farquharson, A. Platt; 6 *Minor Biological Works:* T. Loveday, E. S. Forster, L. D. Dowdall, H. H. Joachim; 7 *Problems:* E. S. Forster; 8 *Metaphysics:* Sir W. D. Ross; 9 *Ethics:* Sir W. D. Ross, St. G. Stock, J. Solomon; 10 *Politics and Economics:* B. Jowett, E. S. Forster, Sir F. G. Kenyon; 11 *Rhetoric & Poetics:* W. Rhys Roberts, E. S. Forster, I. Bywater; 12 *Select Fragments:* Sir W. D. Ross. (Oxford, 1912–52, Clarendon Press.)

Also *The Politics of Aristotle,* translated with notes: Sir Ernest Barker. (Oxford, 1948, Clarendon Press.)

The Nichomachean Ethics of Aristotle (from vol. 9, *Oxford Translation*): Sir W. D. Ross. (London, 1954, Oxford University Press, World's Classics.)

ARRIAN: *The Life of Alexander the Great:* Aubrey de Selincourt. (London, 1958, Penguin.)

THEOPHRASTUS: *Characters:* A. D. Knox. (London, 1929, Heinemann, Loeb Library.)

Enquiry into Plants: Sir Arthur Hort. (London, 1916, Heinemann, Loeb Library, 2 vols.)

MENANDER: *Menander (Comedies of Manners):* F. G. Allinson. (London, 1921, Heinemann, Loeb Library.)

Also *The Arbitration, The Rape of the Locks:* Gilbert Murray. (London, 1945 & 1942, Allen & Unwin.)

EPICURUS: *Epicurus: The Extant Remains:* with critical apparatus, translation, and notes: Cyril Bailey. (Oxford, 1926, Clarendon Press.)

POLYBIUS: *The Histories (A History of the Roman Conquest of the Hellenic World):* W. R. Paton. (London, 1922–7, Heinemann, Loeb Library, 6 vols.)

LIVY (TITUS LIVIUS): *Livy (A History of Rome,* volumes covering the years 218–167 B.C.): B. O. Foster, F. G. Moore, Evan T. Sturge, A. C. Schlesinger. (London, 1922–7, Heinemann, Loeb Library, vols. 5–13.)

Epitomes: *The History of Rome:* W. A. M'Devitte. (London, 1862, Bohn's Classical Library.)

CATO, MARCUS PORCIUS: *Marcus Porcius Cato on Agriculture:* W. D. Hooper. (London, 1934, Heinemann, Loeb Library.)

THE BOOK OF DANIEL: *The Bible: An American Translation:* Edgar J. Goodspeed. (Chicago, 1935, University of Chicago Press.)

THE BOOKS OF MACCABEES: *The Apocrypha:* Edgar J. Goodspeed. (Chicago, 1938, University of Chicago Press.)

DIODORUS OF AGYRIUM: *Diodorus Siculus (A Library of Universal History):* C. H. Oldfather, C. L. Sherman, Russel M. Geer, F. R. Walton. (London, 1933–57, Heinemann, Loeb Library, 12 vols.)

STRABO: *The Geography of Strabo (Geographica):* H. L. Jones. (London, 1917–32, Heinemann, Loeb Library, 8 vols.)

THE NEW TESTAMENT: *The Four Gospels:* E. V. Rieu. (London, 1952, Penguin.)

The Acts of the Apostles: C. H. Rieu. (London, 1957, Penguin.)

The Epistles and Book of Revelation: *The Bible: An American Translation:* Edgar J. Goodspeed. (Chicago, 1935, University of Chicago Press.)

EPICTETUS: *Epictetus* (*His Lectures from Arrian's Notebooks*): W. A. Oldfather. (London, 1926–8, Heinemann, Loeb Library, 2 vols.)

PLUTARCH: *Plutarch's Lives:* Bernadotte Perrin. (London, 1914–26, Heinemann, Loeb Library, 11 vols.)

Plutarch's Moralia: F. C. Babbit, W. C. Helmbold, P. H. de Lacy, B. Einarson, H. N. Fowler, H. Cherniss. (London, 1927–31, Heinemann, Loeb Library, 14 vols.)

MARCUS AURELIUS: *The Meditations of Marcus Aurelius* (*Private Journal*): J. Jackson. (Oxford, 1906, Clarendon Press.)

LUCIAN: *Lucian* (*Essays*): A. M. Harmon. (London, 1913–36, Heinemann, Loeb Library, 8 vols.)

PAUSANIAS: *Description of Greece:* W. H. S. Jones. (London, 1918–35, Heinemann, Loeb Library, 5 vols.)

CHRISTIAN MARTYRS' RECORDS: *Some Authentic Acts of the Early Martyrs: A Selection:* E. C. C. Owen. (London, 1933, S.P.C.K.)

MINUCIUS FELIX: *See under* Tertullian *below.*

TERTULLIAN: *Tertullian* (*Apology* with the *Octavius* of Minucius Felix): T. R. Glover & G. H. Rendall. (London, 1931, Heinemann, Loeb Library.)

Also *The Early Christian Fathers: A Selection,* edited and translated by Henry Bettenson. (London, 1956, Oxford University Press.)

ORIGEN (ORIGENES): *Origen Contra Celsum* (*A Reply to Celsus*): Henry Chadwick. (Cambridge, 1953, University Press.)

PLOTINUS: *The Enneads* (*Philosophical Papers*): Stephen MacKenna. (London, 1957, Faber.)

JULIAN, THE EMPEROR: *Julian* (*Works*): W. C. Wright. (London, 1913–23, Heinemann, Loeb Library, 3 vols.)

SALLUSTIUS: *Concerning the Gods and the Universe,* edited with Prolegomena and Translation: A. D. Nock. (Cambridge, 1926, University Press.)

EUNAPIUS: *Lives of the Sophists:* W. C. Wright. (London, 1922, Heinemann, Loeb Library.)

AUGUSTINE, ST.: *The City of God:* John Healy (ed. Tasker). (London, 1957, Dent, Everyman's Library.)

PROCOPIUS: *Procopius* (*The Emperor Justinian's Wars*): (London, 1914–40, Heinemann, Loeb Library, 7 vols.)

THE GREEK ANTHOLOGY: *Select Epigrams from the Greek Anthology,* 3rd ed.: J. W. Mackail. (London, 1911, Longmans.)

The Greek Anthology: W. P. Paton. (London, 1916–18, Heinemann, Loeb Library, 5 vols.)

B

Modern Works in English

1. General

Andrewes, A.: *The Greek Tyrants.* (London, 1956, Hutchinson.)

Bowra, C. M.: *The Greek Experience.* (London, 1957, Weidenfeld & Nicolson.)

The Cambridge Ancient History: 12 vols. of text and 5 vols. of plates, 1924–39; vols. i and ii of the text are being rewritten.

Ferguson, W. S.: *Greek Imperialism.* (London, 1913, Constable.)

Gibbon, E.: *The History of the Decline and Fall of the Roman Empire,* ed. by J. B. Bury, smaller edition. (London, 1900–2, Methuen, 7 vols.)

Glover, T. R.: *The Ancient World.* (London, 1953, Pelican.)

Griffith, G. T.: *The Mercenaries of the Hellenistic World.* (Cambridge, 1935, University Press.)

Hogarth, D. G.: *Philip and Alexander of Macedon.* (London, 1897, John Murray.)

Jaeger, W.: *Paideia,* translated by Gilbert Highet. (Oxford, 1939, Blackwell.)

Jones, A. H. M.: *The Cities of the Eastern Roman Provinces.* (Oxford, 1937, Clarendon Press.)

Jones, A. H. M.: *The Greek City from Alexander to Justinian.* (Oxford, 1940, Clarendon Press.)

Lot, F.: *The End of the Ancient World.* (London, 1931, Kegan Paul, Trench, Trubner.)

Marrou, H. I.: *History of Education in Antiquity,* translated by George Lamb. (London, 1956, Sheed & Ward.)

Myres, J. L.: *Who Were the Greeks?* (Berkeley, 1930, University of California Press.)

Parke, H. W.: *Greek Mercenary Soldiers from the Earliest Times to the Battle of Ipsus.* (Oxford, 1933, Clarendon Press.)

Rostovtzeff, M.: *The Social and Economic History of the Hellenistic World.* (Oxford, 1941, Clarendon Press, 3 vols.)

Rostovtzeff, M.: *The Social and Economic History of the Roman Empire,* revised edition. (Oxford, 1957, Clarendon Press, 2 vols.)

Tarn, W. W.: *Alexander the Great.* (Cambridge, 1948, University Press, 2 vols.)

Tarn, W. W.: *Hellenistic Civilisation,* revised edition. (London, 1952, Edward Arnold.)

Ure, P. N.: *The Origin of Tyranny.* (Cambridge, 1922, University Press.)

Webster, T. B. L.: *From Mycenae to Homer: A Study in Early Greek Literature and Art.* (London, 1958, Methuen.)

Zimmern, A. E.: *The Greek Commonwealth,* 5th ed. (Oxford, 1931, Clarendon Press.)

2. THE EXPANSION OF THE HELLENIC WORLD

Bell, H. I.: *Egypt from Alexander the Great to the Arab Conquest.* (Oxford, 1948, Clarendon Press.)

Carpenter, Rhys: *The Greeks in Spain.* (London, 1925, Longmans.)

Dunbabin, T. J.: *The Western Greeks.* (Oxford, 1948, Clarendon Press.)

Dunbabin, T. J.: *The Greeks and their Eastern Neighbours.* (London, 1957, The Society for the Promotion of Hellenic Studies.)

Narain, A. K.: *The Indo-Greeks.* (Oxford, 1957, Clarendon Press.)

Rostovtzeff, M.: *Dura-Europus and its Art.* (Oxford, 1938, Clarendon Press.)

Rostovtzeff, M.: *Iranians and Greeks in South Russia.* (Oxford, 1922, Clarendon Press.)

Tarn, W. W.: *The Greeks in Bactria and India.* (Cambridge, 1938, University Press.)

3. RELIGION AND PHILOSOPHY

Alföldi, A.: *The Conversion of Constantine and Pagan Rome.* (Oxford, 1948, Clarendon Press.)

Bailey, C.: *The Greek Atomists and Epicurus.* (Oxford, 1928, Clarendon Press.)

Baynes, N. H.: *Constantine the Great and the Christian Church.* (London, 1929, Milford.)

Bell, H. I.: *Cults and Creeds in Graeco-Roman Egypt.* (Liverpool, 1953, University Press.)

Bevan, E. R.: *Stoics and Sceptics.* (Oxford, 1913, Clarendon Press.)

Burnet, J.: *Greek Philosophy, Part I: Thales to Plato.* (London, 1914, Macmillan.)

Cochrane, C. N.: *Christianity and Classical Culture.* (London, 1940, Oxford University Press.)

Cornford, F. M.: *From Religion to Philosophy.* (London, 1912, Arnold; New York, 1957, Harper Torchbooks.)

Cornford, F. M.: *Principium Sapientiae: The Origins of Greek Philosophical Thought.* (Cambridge, 1952, University Press.)

Dodds, E. R.: *The Greeks and the Irrational.* (Berkeley, 1951, University of California Press.)

Festugière, O. P., A. J.: *Personal Religion among the Greeks.* (Berkeley, 1954, University of California Press.)

FREEMAN, K.: *The Pre-Socratic Philosophers.* (Oxford, 1946, Blackwell.)

GLOVER, T. R.: *The Conflict of Religions in the Early Roman Empire,* 10th ed. (London, 1923, Methuen.)

HARRISON, J. E.: *Prolegomena to Greek Religion.* (Cambridge, 1922, University Press.)

HARRISON, J. E.: *Themis: A Study of the Social Origins of Greek Religion,* 2nd ed. (Cambridge, 1927, University Press.)

JAEGER, W.: *The Theology of the Early Greek Philosophers.* (Oxford, 1947, Clarendon Press.)

JONES, A. H. M.: *Constantine and the Conversion of Europe.* (London, 1948, Hodder & Stoughton.)

KIRK, G. S. & RAVEN, J. E.: *The Presocratic Philosophers.* (Cambridge, 1957, University Press.)

LINFORTH, I. M.: *The Arts of Orpheus.* (Berkeley, 1941, University of California Press.)

MURRAY, GILBERT: *Five Stages of Greek Religion.* (London, 1935, Watts: The Thinker's Library, No. 52.)

MURRAY, GILBERT: *The Stoic Philosophy.* (London, 1915, Watts.)

NILSSON, M. P.: *A History of Greek Religion,* 2nd ed. (Oxford, 1949, Clarendon Press.)

NILSSON, M. P.: *Greek Piety.* (Oxford, 1948, Clarendon Press.)

NILSSON, M. P.: *Greek Popular Religion,* second printing. (New York, 1947, Columbia University Press.)

NOCK, A. D.: *Conversion: The Old and the New Religion from Alexander the Great to Augustine of Hippo.* (Oxford, 1933, Clarendon Press.)

PARKE, H. W.: *A History of the Delphic Oracle,* revised edition, (Oxford, 1939, Blackwell, 2 vols.)

SNELL, BRUNO: *The Discovery of the Mind.* (Oxford, 1953, Blackwell.)

4. ART AND ARCHITECTURE

(i) *Greek and Graeco-Roman Sculpture*

ANON.: *A Short Guide to the Sculptures of the Parthenon.* (London, 1950, British Museum.)

BIEBER, M.: *The Sculpture of the Hellenistic Age.* (New York, 1955, Columbia University Press.)

RICHTER, G. M. A.: *Archaic Greek Art.* (New York, 1949, Oxford University Press.)

RICHTER, G. M. A.: *Sculpture and Sculptors of the Greeks.* (London, 1950, Oxford University Press.)

RICHTER, G. M. A.: *Three Critical Periods in Greek Sculpture.* (Oxford, 1951, Clarendon Press.)

STRONG, E.: *Art in Ancient Rome.* (London, 1929, Heinemann.)

STRONG, E.: *Roman Sculpture.* (London, 1907, Duckworth.)

(ii) *Greek and Graeco-Roman Painting*

HINKS, R.: Catalogue of Greek, Etruscan, and Roman Paintings and Mosaics in the British Museum. (London, 1933, British Museum.)

MAIURI, F.: *Roman Painting.* (Geneva, 1953, Skira.)

RUMPF, A.: 'Classical and Post-Classical Greek Painting' (*Journal of Hellenic Studies,* vol. LXVII, 1947, pp. 10–21).

(iii) *Greek and Graeco-Roman Pottery*

BEAZLEY, J. D.: *The Development of Attic Black Figure.* (London, 1951, Cambridge University Press.)

CHARLESTON, R. J.: *Roman Pottery.* (London, 1955, Faber.)

LANE, E. A.: *Greek Pottery.* (London, 1948, Faber.)

RICHTER, G. M. A.: *Attic Red-Figured Vases.* (New Haven, 1946, Yale University Press.)

(iv) *Greek and Roman Architecture*

DINSMOOR, W. B.: *The Architecture of Ancient Greece,* 3rd ed. (London, 1950, Batsford.)

LAWRENCE, A. W.: *Greek Architecture.* (Harmondsworth, 1957, Penguin.)

PLOMMER, H.: *Ancient and Classical Architecture* (vol. 1 of F. M. Simpson's *History of Architectural Development,* new edition). (London, 1956, Longmans.)

ROBERTSON, D. S.: *A Handbook of Greek and Roman Architecture,* 2nd ed. (Cambridge, 1943, University Press.)

5. LITERATURE

MURRAY, GILBERT: *Aeschylus.* (Oxford, 1940, Clarendon Press.)

MURRAY, GILBERT: *Aristophanes.* (Oxford, 1933, Clarendon Press.)

MURRAY, GILBERT: *Euripides and His Age,* 2nd ed. (London, 1945, Oxford University Press; Home University Library.)

MURRAY, GILBERT: *A History of Ancient Greek Literature,* 2nd ed. (Chicago, 1956, University of Chicago Press; Cambridge, University Press.)

MURRAY, GILBERT: *The Rise of the Greek Epic,* 4th ed. (Oxford, 1934, Clarendon Press.)

MYRES, J. L.: *Herodotus, Father of History.* (Oxford, 1953, Clarendon Press.)

6. LOCAL STATES

BEVAN, E. R.: *A History of Egypt under the Ptolemaic Dynasty.* (London, 1927, Methuen.)

BEVAN, E. R.: *The House of Seleucus.* (London, 1902, Edward Arnold, 2 vols.)

FERGUSON, W. S.: *Hellenistic Athens.* (London, 1911, Macmillan.)

HANSEN, E. V.: *The Attalids of Pergamum.* (Ithaca, N.Y., 1947, Cornell University Press.)

LINFORTH, I. M.: *Solon the Athenian.* (Berkeley, 1919, University of California Press.)

MICHELL, H.: *Sparta.* (Cambridge, 1952, University Press.)

SHERWIN-WHITE, A. N.: *The Roman Citizenship.* (Oxford, 1939, Clarendon Press.)

WOODHOUSE, W. J.: *Solon the Liberator.* (Oxford, 1938, University Press.)

INDEX